D1084948

THE NEW MIDDLE AGES

BONNIE WHEELER, *Series Editor*

The New Middle Ages is a series dedicated to transdisciplinary studies of medieval cultures, with particular emphasis on recuperating women's history and on feminist and gender analyses. This peer-reviewed series includes both scholarly monographs and essay collections.

PUBLISHED BY PALGRAVE:

Women in the Medieval Islamic World: Power, Patronage, and Piety
edited by Gavin R. G. Hambly

The Ethics of Nature in the Middle Ages: On Boccaccio's Poetaphysics
by Gregory B. Stone

Presence and Presentation: Women in the Chinese Literati Tradition
by Sherry J. Mou

The Lost Love Letters of Heloise and Abelard: Perceptions of Dialogue in Twelfth-Century France
by Constant J. Mews

Understanding Scholastic Thought with Foucault
by Philipp W. Rosemann

For Her Good Estate: The Life of Elizabeth de Burgh
by Frances A. Underhill

Constructions of Widowhood and Virginity in the Middle Ages
edited by Cindy L. Carlson and Angela Jane Weisl

Motherhood and Mothering in Anglo-Saxon England
by Mary Dockray-Miller

Listening to Heloise: The Voice of a Twelfth-Century Woman
edited by Bonnie Wheeler

The Postcolonial Middle Ages
edited by Jeffrey Jerome Cohen

Chaucer's Pardoner and Gender Theory: Bodies of Discourse
by Robert S. Sturges

Crossing the Bridge: Comparative Essays on Medieval European and Heian Japanese Women Writers
edited by Barbara Stevenson and Cynthia Ho

Engaging Words: The Culture of Reading in the Later Middle Ages
by Laurel Amtower

Robes and Honor: The Medieval World of Investiture
edited by Stewart Gordon

Representing Rape in Medieval and Early Modern Literature
edited by Elizabeth Robertson and Christine M. Rose

Same Sex Love and Desire Among Women in the Middle Ages
edited by Francesca Canadé Sautman and Pamela Sheingorn

Sight and Embodiment in the Middle Ages: Ocular Desires
by Suzannah Biernoff

Listen, Daughter: The Speculum Virginum and the Formation of Religious Women in the Middle Ages
edited by Constant J. Mews

Science, the Singular, and the Question of Theology
by Richard A. Lee, Jr.

MEDIEVALISM AND ORIENTALISM: THREE ESSAYS ON LITERATURE, ARCHITECTURE AND CULTURAL IDENTITY

John M. Ganim

MEDIEVALISM AND ORIENTALISM
© John M. Ganim, 2005.

All rights reserved. No part of this book may be used or reproduced in any manner whatsoever without written permission except in the case of brief quotations embodied in critical articles or reviews.

First published in 2005 by
PALGRAVE MACMILLAN™
175 Fifth Avenue, New York, N.Y. 10010 and
Houndmills, Basingstoke, Hampshire, England RG21 6XS
Companies and representatives throughout the world.

PALGRAVE MACMILLAN is the global academic imprint of the Palgrave Macmillan division of St. Martin's Press, LLC and of Palgrave Macmillan Ltd. Macmillan® is a registered trademark in the United States, United Kingdom and other countries. Palgrave is a registered trademark in the European Union and other countries.

ISBN 1–4039–6320–7

Library of Congress Cataloging-in-Publication Data

Ganim, John M., 1945–
    Medievalism and Orientalism : three essays on literature, architecture, and cultural identity / John M. Ganim.
        p. cm. — (The new Middle Ages series)
    Includes bibliographical references.
    ISBN 1–4039–6320–7
        1. Medievalism. 2. Orientalism. I. Title. II. New Middle Ages (Palgrave Macmillan (Firm))

CB353.G29 2005
940—dc22   2004049589

A catalogue record for this book is available from the British Library.

Design by Newgen Imaging Systems (P) Ltd., Chennai, India.

First edition: January 2005

10 9 8 7 6 5 4 3 2 1

Printed in the United States of America.

For Beatrice
Ne li occhi porta la mia donna Amore

CONTENTS

ACKNOWLEDGMENTS

The completion of this book was supported by a fellowship from the John Simon Guggenheim, Jr. Memorial Foundation, and like all Guggenheim fellows, I owe the foundation a debt of profound gratitude. The College of Humanities, Arts and Social Sciences at the University of California, Riverside provided additional sabbatical and research leave for which I am grateful. A number of grants from the Committee on Research of the Academic Senate allowed research travel to libraries and archives. No one could be happier with the friends and colleagues whom I have thanked in previous books, but rather than list their names again here, I will simply reiterate that I work in one of the most remarkable university departments that one can imagine, and I hope that I have lived up to the encouragement my colleagues have provided over the years.

The various arguments of this book have been presented at a number of conferences and lectures, and I wish to thank the following for arranging these events: Andy Kelly of the Center for Medieval and Renaissance Studies at UCLA; Seth Gumbrecht, Howard Bloch, and Stephen Nichols for inviting me to the Symposium on Medieval Theatricality at Yale and David Wallace for his comments at those meetings; The Medieval Club of New York, and especially then officers Dan Rubey and Pam Sheingorn for inviting me to give the Rossell Hope Robbins Annual Lecture; Nancy Van Deusen of the Claremont Graduate University and the Society for Antiquity and Christianity for at least two of her many stimulating gatherings where some of these ideas were first circulated; Linda Georgianna at the University of California, Irvine; Aranye Fradenburgh and the Medieval Studies Research Group at the University of California, Santa Barbara; the University of California Dickens Project and the University of California, Santa Cruz and especially Joseph Childers; and Professors Jacek Fisiak and Sheila Delany for inviting me to address the Symposium on Medieval Literature, Language and Culture in Memory of Margaret Schlauch at Adam Mickiewicz University in Poznan, Poland.

The dedication of this book is an indirect way of saying that I am married to the most beautiful woman in the world, who, like the Beatrice whom the poet speaks of, is also luminous in her intellect and her presence. It is no surprise that Laura, Lisa and Eli, and Jon, Bill and Vivian have been as gracious and understanding as they have. I would also like to mention Juliet, Rosa and Jack, and Brandon and Michael and Andrea and Ellie and little Ray, because someday they will be thrilled to find their names in a book on a very high shelf.

INTRODUCTION

Is the Pacifique Sea my home? Or are
The Easterne riches? Is Jerusalem?
Anyan, and Magellan, and Gibraltare?
All streights, and none but streights, are wayes to them,
Whether where Japhet dwelt, or Cham, or Sem.

John Donne, Holy Sonnets, 87

In the Old World the east the Suez canal,
The New by its mighty railroad spann'd,
The seas inlaid with eloquent gentle wires;
Yet first to sound, and ever sound, the cry with thee O soul,
The Past! the Past! the Past!
The Past—the dark unfathom'd retrospect!

Walt Whitman, Passage to India

In the climactic scene of *The Book of Saladin*, the liberator of Jerusalem accepts the surrender of the city from its Christian garrison:

> "Tell your people," Salah al-Din told him, "that we shall not treat them as your forebears treated us when they first took this city. As a child I was told of what Godfrey and Tancredi did to our people. Remind these frightened Christians of what Believers and Jews suffered ninety years ago. The heads of our children were displayed on pikes. Old men and women of all ages were tortured and burnt. These streets were washed in blood, Balian. Some of the emirs would like to wash them again, but this time in your blood. They remind me that we all believe in an eye for an eye and a tooth for a tooth."

Saladin appears here simultaneously as an opposite figure of the fanatical Crusaders, as the enlightened exception found in Western accounts themselves, and as the legendary military hero of Islam. In passage after passage, the projections of Western Christianity are revealed as projections: it is the West that is intolerant, fanatical, millenialist and vengeful. The West is represented by traitors, anti-Semitic fanatics, sociopaths, and a few enlightened individuals who dimly perceive the more powerful truths of Islam. The East is represented by subtle and complex thinkers, profoundly human military and political leaders and enormously complex national and ethnic identities. It is the East that reminds the West what its highest ideals should be, it is the East that defines the West. *The Book of Saladin*, that is, reverses the structures of Orientalism at their point of origin.[1]

The Book of Saladin is of course, not a medieval narrative at all, but a late-twentieth-century novel published in 1998 and written by the British Pakistani author, producer, and activist Tariq Ali. As such, it is not only an account of Salah-ud-Din's life fully aware of medieval Arabic and other chronicles as well as Western sources, but also a meditation on politics, both of the Western and international Left, and probably also something of a roman a clef. Written in a Britain transformed by both the 1960s postimperial immigration and Thatcherism, it is replete with modern and postmodern subplots. Salah-ud-Din was a Kurdish warrior, and his minority status is an important part of the story (as indeed it was historically) and his self-consciousness. The fiction of the novel is that the story of the Kurdish hero is being narrated to a Jewish scribe. The chief romantic relationship in the novel is a lesbian affair between the principal Sultana and another member of the harem. Homosexual relationships are smilingly accepted in the Moslem camp, secretly and furtively destructive in the Christian camps. Eunuchs (mostly enslaved choirboys) turn out to be only partly incapacitated. Even heroic leadership itself is represented ironically, since Salah-ud-Din is often ill, uncertain and politic in his exercise of military and political power through caution and calculation rather than charisma and dynamism. Although Jerusalem is recaptured, the "Franj" are not entirely expelled, and the campaign ends with a negotiated settlement (as indeed it did).

Indeed, at times the novel reads like an allegory of negotiation, cultural, political, and personal. *The Book of Saladin* and its author are intensely aware of the postcolonial condition. The Crusaders have occupied the Eastern Mediterranean coast for centuries. Their presence divides rather than unifies the forces of Islam, torn apart by their own conflicting political goals. At the same time, the confluence of Christian, Islamic, and Jewish ideas and practices results in a crossfertilization and alliances often confusing even to its participants. The form *The Book of Saladin* takes, as much of the historical romance as of the historical novel, is a form with a hybridized origin. Like the novel itself, it is a form that is most Western when it seems most Eastern, most Eastern when it seems most Western, most historicized when it seems most modern and most modern when it seems to be recreating the past.

Its tone is as much elegiac as heroic, and it imagines an orientalized "Middle Ages" as both origin and point of decline.

If *The Book of Saladin* reverses the categories of Otherness as they articulated themselves in the later Middle Ages, it should remind us that some crucially dominant ideas about the Middle Ages in the West, especially as the West discovers its own modernity (which involved the very nomenclature of the "Middle Ages"), depended on a geographic as well as a historical distinction. The past is another country. The famous opening of L.P. Hartley's *The Go-Between* has taken its place as one of the truisms of popular writing.[2] The argument of the following chapters is that this aphorism turns out to be literally true of attitudes toward one specific component of the European past, the Middle Ages. Usually imagined as the point of origin of national identities (and just as often as a model of a pan-European unity), the medieval past is also, often simultaneously, described as a result of foreign incursion, of alien influence, of disruption in what should be the natural movement of history. The following chapters trace the most explicit expression of this hybrid identity, the twinned association of medievalism and Orientalism. As with space, so with time. We no longer conceive of the present moment as the knife-edge of futurity. We concede, in our discussions of style and of civil society, that the past haunts our present endeavors and that not forgetting the past does not free us from the condemnation of repetition, so much as it makes us keenly aware of our recursions. On the one hand, the historical past has come not to stand for an archaeologically reconstructed otherness, but as a dialogic intervention in the present, which no longer can be thought of as essentially "modern." On the other hand, we freely admit that the past, like many aspects of cultural identification, is "imagined," constructed, a fiction by which we allow ourselves to proceed, or not.

The purpose of the following chapters is to point out that the idea of the Middle Ages as it developed from its earliest formulations in the historical self-consciousness of Western Europe is part of what we used to call an identity crisis, a deeply uncertain sense of what the West is and should be. The idea of the Middle Ages as a pure Europe (or England or France or Germany) both rests on and reacts to an uncomfortable sense of instability about origins, about what the West is and where it came from.[3] The definition of medieval culture, especially literature and architecture, from its earliest formulation in the Renaissance through to the twentieth century has been a site of a contest over the idea of the West, and by definition, that which is non-Western. As my argument implies, to say that the past is another country no longer is to say that it is cut off from us in some essential way. Some of the intellectual developments of the past few decades, loosely categorized under the rubrics of postcolonial and postmodern studies, have complicated what we mean by the past, and by "another country." "Another country" may be a construct of otherness, somewhere where we are not at home, which is to us, as it were, *unheimlich*. But it also may be, as Edward Said's *Orientalism* suggests, an imagined emptiness on to which we may project our desires and fears. In the hierarchies so often constructed by nationalisms, another country is by definition inferior, and hence, deserving of conquest or subordination. As postcolonial studies have alerted us, such a strict division between one country and another is in practice more fluid and dynamic, the conquered often transforming the conqueror, as much as the discourses of dominance inevitably transform the identity and culture of the dominated.

The Middle Ages is an especially challenging test case for such an investigation, partly because it consists of so many layers of interpretation and is the site of so many competing claims, though in these respects it is simply more striated rather than different from other arbitrary categorizations of the past. But "the Medieval," as I shall call it to emphasize its status as category as much as temporality, is also challenging because of its recent decline as a critical component of modern self-definition. To the late-twentieth-century lay reader, medievalism, in both its scholarly and popular varieties, is almost synonymous with escapism. Filtered through the lenses of Tolkien, Disney, various theme restaurants, commercially produced "fairs," and even Las Vegas (where one of the slightly faded casinos is called "Excalibur," having been superseded by the Renaissance and Mediterranean themes of Venice and Bellagio), popular medievalism has acquired the function of licensing innocence. Alongside the enormous sophistication of present scholarship on the Middle Ages or its continuing power as a source of imagery for popular culture, from films to computer games, the Medieval has lost its status as a critical discourse in relation to the present. It is no longer an Utopian ideal to be recovered, while its negative rhetorical implications, from "medieval justice" to the "medieval" social conditions and practices in, most typically and revealingly, Islamic states, remain almost unquestioned. This situation was by no means always the case. In the nineteenth century, medievalism was constructed as a fierce reproach as well as a utopian escape from the present and that reproach was framed in explicitly political terms. The most famous exemplars of nineteenth century medievalism in its position as social critique are such authors as Sir Walter Scott, Thomas Carlyle, John Ruskin, and William Morris. That is, literary medievalism in the nineteenth century seems to chart a political trajectory from conservative paternalism to socialist utopianism, from right to left, in however halting a manner. Beneath this apparent pattern, I shall argue, medievalism is a more continually contested terrain, often problematizing the political implications its proponents wish to draw.

The political ambiguity of the appeal to the past, on a literary as well as on a political level, is also reflected in the methodologies we use to pursue that past. As in the late twentieth century quite literal fantasy of the Middle Ages, modern scholarship has sought a certain purity in the Middle Ages, in method as well as in content. The Middle Ages, and the study of it, is perceived as mercifully free of the conflictual issues that haunt the study of contemporary culture. But the materials that the following chapters explore reveals that some concerns of current critical discourse—race, gender, nationality, modernity—have a prehistory in the earliest reception and construction of the Medieval, a Medieval which is often fantasized as resistant to and prior to such concerns. I am less concerned in "applying," say, gender theory or postcolonial analysis to medieval texts than in uncovering a pattern woven as much by the scholarly and popular veneration—and execration—of the Middle Ages as by the Middle Ages itself. For the Medieval, almost by the very root of its terminology, has always been imagined by the West as both ourselves and something other than ourselves, as unified and as anarchic, as origin and as disruption, as the hyperfeminine and the hypermasculine.

The following chapters investigate a number of topics—architectural, literary, and historiographical—in which this doubled Middle Ages is revealed. In the sixteenth and seventeenth centuries, the condemnation of the Gothic and the defense of neoclassical models and the anxiety over the formlessness of medieval narrative was expressed in a rhetoric of foreignness, citing their sources in "Saracen" and Eastern cultures. This is especially true of genres and forms that later medievalisms interpret as metonymically medieval, such as Gothic architecture and medieval romance. Gothic architecture was interpreted at times as deeply native, as when the interior roof vaulting of Gothic was thought to imitate the trees of the northern forests inhabited by the "Goths," but even that emphasis was unflattering, meant to suggest a certain crudeness and barbarism. At other times, however, the pointed Gothic arch was ascribed to Eastern, usually "Saracen" influence, "overrunning the Civiliz'd World" and "debauching" the forms of classical architecture.[4] Christopher Wren (1632–1723), the architect of St. Paul's Cathedral, in defending his own classicism, denigrates "The Saracen mode of building, seen in the East, soon spread over Europe, and particularly in France."[5]

Medieval literature, or at least medieval romance, was also regarded, even by its earliest defenders, as a record of a national past, but also as foreign, and particularly Eastern, in conception. The eighteenth century, which defends and even invents medieval romance, is obsessed with its non-Western origins. To defend Romance, for its eighteenth century champions, was to defend fiction itself, to defend the validity of imagination.[6] Such potentially uncontrollable wildness is ascribed to an otherness both within and without, to the West's barbaric past on the one hand, and the model of Eastern literatures on the other. The metaphor of the earliest studies of medieval romance is one of miscegenation. In contrast to the condemnation of the uncertain parentage of medieval cultural forms as expressed by Renaissance writers, eighteenth-century scholars were in fact attracted to the possibility of cultural mixture. Thomas Warton (1728–90) opens his *History of English Poetry* with an argument that medieval romance, and fiction in general, is virtually created by the meeting of Saracen and Crusader. At roughly the same time, Pierre-Daniel Huet's essay on romance was translated into English, repeating the speculation that romance has its origins in Moorish influence upon Spain. Huet describes fiction itself, with its layers of allegory and rhetoric, as originating in the East, insinuating into the West through various routes.[7] Arguments were mounted on both sides of the question of origins, most pointedly by the generally dismissive Joseph Ritson, but throughout the long period of relatively amateur and pre-academic reconstruction of medieval literary history, the triad of Romance, Fiction and the East is a constant theme.[8] In the eighteenth century, the recovery of these forms resulted in a celebration of the very exoticism that the Renaissance had condemned. The antiquarianism of the eighteenth century was inseparably linked in its sensibility with the fascination with oriental exoticism and the wonders of the primitive world. The champions of romance—Percy, Hurd, and Warton, constructed a medieval world that was both a native past and an exotic otherness.[9]

The connection between Romanticism, medievalism and Orientalism is so much a given that we accept it as a matter of literary or architectural taste. As Edward Said has pointed out, however, in his essay on Raymond Schwab, the connection was more dynamic and pervasive than the concept of motif allows. Said describes Schwab's study, *Le Renaissance Oriental*, which regards the Romantic movement as a second Renaissance, but one turned toward awareness of the East and appreciation of the complexity of medieval culture as much as the Renaissance of the fifteenth and sixteenth centuries turned to Western languages and classical antiquity and pointedly erased, or indeed, invented the "middle" ages.[10] The Romantic revolution, then, refigured many of the medievalist discourses in ways more profound than simple enthusiasms, though enthusiasm itself became a positive rather than suspicious motive. The monstrous, employed by anti-Gothic polemics to suggest the almost inhuman barbarism of medieval architecture and literature, is redeemed as an inescapable, even sublime, component of the human, and therefore by no means a negative quality. The primitive is no longer an indication of a fall from grace or a decline from a higher and more noble form, but a point of origin, even a source of vitality.

By the late eighteenth century, this dual understanding of the medieval as embodying the imaginative and creative abilities of an East imbued with the gift of fantasy as well as the primal record of historical origins is complicated by the reality of mercantile expansion and the beginnings of the imperial project, with its concomitant intellectual apparatus, an apparatus that begins with a positive and celebratory attitude toward its object of study. In the wake of Sir William Jones's establishment of the Asiatick Society of Bengal and his thesis that the classical languages of the west and Sanskrit were descended from a common source, a phase of celebration of all things Indian ran through German Romanticism.[11] Jones (1746–1794) thought that not only language, but religious myths were shared by these cultures, their common polytheism a degeneration from an original monotheism. It was this enthusiasm that ignited Friedrich von Schlegel's (1772–1829) original interest in Sanskrit. An Indian Golden Age was imagined as an earlier form of a spiritually unified Middle Ages. This idealism did not last too long into the early nineteenth century, when evidence began to weigh against some of Jones's assumptions, but a general notion that European civilizations shared with Indian and other civilizations a common source, that we, or some of us, were all branches from a common tree, remained the controlling explanation for the striking new evidence of a shared linguistic source.

If we follow Raymond Schwab in his *Renaissance Orientale*, the Renaissance of the fifteenth and sixteenth centuries was a rediscovery of Europe, which, as he puts it, flatters and assimilates Europe to itself.[12] Europe was the world as we knew it and its past was history as we knew it. This may explain why, in my terms, the Renaissance had to figure the Middle Ages as incursion as well as break, as foreign as well as native. To Schwab, Romanticism represents an "Oriental Renaissance," which recognizes the crucial importance of Asia and the Middle East, thereby multiplying the world. Schwab borrows his title from Edgar Quinet (1803–75) who coined the term in his 1841 *Génie des religions*. Quinet compared the role of Sanskrit for the nineteenth century to the importance of Greek and Roman manuscripts in the Renaissance. Being in place, in Europe, was the fundamental state of the humanist Renaissance and its most typical productions were the visual and plastic arts. Romanticism was above all a verbal enterprise, not only in poetry, but in its obsessive interest in linguistics, origins and multiple influences. Schwab sketches a rough taxonomy of what the "Orient" meant for the many varieties of Orientalism, including the Biblical Orient, the Assyrian or pre-Biblical Orient, the Islamic Orient, the Persian Orient, and China. India was, he says, an "antiquity of today," a sense of geography being transmuted into history that is repeated throughout the discourse of medievalism and orientalism.

BRIDWELL LIBRARY
SOUTHERN METHODIST UNIVERSITY
DALLAS, TEXAS 75275

After the inclusion of India into the Empire after the mid-nineteenth century, however, and the newly powerful influence of race as a defining factor in history and the dual linkage of civilization and progress as concepts, the egalitarianism and prelapsarianism of Romantic Orientalism was replaced by a historiography of conquest. How could the evidence of the great Indian past be reconciled with the colonial challenge of governing an inferior people and a decadent civilization? The high moment of Indian civilization was imagined as the result of conquest and control of a higher "Aryan" civilization over a lower and not coincidentally darker and more southerly "Dravidian" civilization. Again, the Middle Ages turned out to be a useful metaphor. The deep layers of Indian civilization and its hidden affinities with the West were again imagined as medieval, as in Sir Henry Maine's (1822–88) parallel of the Anglo-Saxon and Indian village. (Indeed, even the plural nomenclature of medievalism in English, partly historically responsible and partly a matter of national self-definition based on the conquest, turns out to be usefully employed, refining the singular Middle Age of German or French scholarly language.)[13] Maine attempted to justify the British modernization of India by claiming it was an inevitable indigenous development, and he did so, remarkably enough, by analogy to the Middle Ages. According to Friedrich Karl von Savigny (1779–1861), the imposition of Roman law on Germanic village organization transformed village custom into the basis of the modern nation-state. Maine appropriated from J.M. Kemble (1807–57), the great Anglo-Saxonist, an idealization of the Anglo-Saxon village, and pointed to similarities with the Indian village. Where the English were in the Middle Ages, so was India today.[14]

These ideas took material form. International exhibitions, mounted in most of the Western European capitals through the second half of the nineteenth century, simultaneously advertised their new industrial accomplishments and their new colonial acquisitions. The fairs justified themselves by comparison with medieval trade fairs, as did the Crystal Palace Great Exhibition of 1851. Indeed, at the Exhibition of Ancient and Medieval Art of 1850, a year before, medieval artifacts were shown as a Ruskinian inspiration to modern manufacturers to higher standards of design and craftsmanship.[15] At the Crystal Palace, one of the most popular exhibits was the India section. Still informed by the notion of Aryan origins, and before the absorption of India into the Empire, the India section emphasized luxury and undirected wealth. Interestingly, however, there was also a "medieval" section, which led from a display of metallurgy, particularly armor, to Pugin's controversial Medieval Court. The Crystal Palace famously sheltered all its exhibits under one roof, but by the 1867 International Exhibition in Paris, colonial and exotic pavilions created a park around the central and featured roofed area. This created a model in which scholarly anthropological displays, pavilions of exotic foreign cultures and circus-like entertainment were grouped together away from the exhibits of the technological and scientific achievements of the imperial powers.[16] At the 1886 Colonial and Indian Exhibition in London, the intent was to suggest an analogy between the temporal present in the colonies and the medieval past of the home country. Among the displays of Southeast-Asian artifacts, flora and fauna, England itself is represented by an "Old London" street, constructed of a pastiche of pre–Great Fire London. The Eiffel Tower, at the 1889 International Exhibition in Paris, was originally surrounded by such "villages." The central exhibition of modern technology was approached through exotic cultural displays, including Old Paris and Old Vienna, both of which lumped together medieval and Renaissance details to equate the "old" with pre-Enlightenment cultures, whether European or not. In International Exhibitions and World's Fairs, medieval "villages" are associated with colonial and imperial displays, in a complex representation of history as geography. While such structures could easily be dismissed as curiosities, in the context of the ideology of World's Fairs, they present the Middle Ages as both domestic and foreign.

This almost physical marginalization of the Middle Ages suggests the diminishment of the importance of medieval culture as an ideal model as the twentieth century begins. The image of the Middle Ages as foreign and marginal had to be countered by twentieth century medievalism as a result. Attempts to recover medieval imagery in Progressive America, for instance, from Henry Adams (who never mentions these historical theme villages in his famous description—and medieval retreat from—the Paris 1900 Exhibition) through Woodrow Wilson, are marked by an association of medieval ideals with lost civic virtues. Such an association, however, is not able to overcome an increasing sense of the Middle Ages as an irrelevant and dated avocation. Even the Renaissance of medieval studies in 1920s America and the founding of the Medieval Academy emphasized how the Middle Ages was really, well, the Renaissance, the real origin of modern society. Just as Progressivism was a political means of maintaining the ideals of a genteel Protestant America facing the challenge of immigration and rapid change, for much of the twentieth century scholarship on medieval literature has tended to emphasize its sophistication, its intellectual framework, and its structural and ideological coherence (notwithstanding the fact that the vehicle of that coherence was the Church). The positivist achievement of this perspective has been huge, but it is interesting to note how its mandarinism, until recently, has had to exclude or anathematize positions that might undermine respectability.

Two of the most controversially heterodox scholarly positions of the early- to mid-twentieth century, for instance, have been the theory of the

Celtic origins of Arthurian literature and the theory of the Arabic origin of courtly love. The scholarly literature surrounding these positions has been deeply contested, and is too vast to summarize here. French scholarship from the 1920s on, including such widely read scholars as the approving Denomy and the disapproving de Rougemont, have ascribed the major themes and sources of late medieval love literature to sources in Arabic and Mozarabic poetry.[17] The thesis is arguable on questions of historical evidence and direct transmission, but the circumstantial evidence is powerful. The possibility, even the likelihood, of cross-cultural influence and literary revisionism has disappeared from the scholarly radar screen, largely because Anglo-American scholarship has more or less made courtly love itself disappear, dismissing it as a neo-romantic historical fantasy, or explaining it as a transmutation of a European tradition of erotic poetry descending from Ovid.[18]

The relation of Arthurian romance to Celtic myth is widely known through the literature of high modernism, the most notorious example being T.S. Eliot's footnotes to *From Ritual to Romance* in *The Waste Land*, and, in fact, *The Waste Land* itself. This approach to Arthurian romance was born in the "Cambridge School" interpretation of Greek drama as displaced ritual, and fostered by the enormous influence of Frazer's *The Golden Bough*, central to Eliot's own reading. But the scholarly project is carried out in greatest detail by R.S. Loomis and his collaborators.[19] Loomis traced as many possible conceivable details of Arthurian romance back to Celtic myth. He moved the debate from the Frazerian association of previous scholars to a question of precedent. For Loomis, even Celtic myth is rendered as if it were a literary tradition, rendering it to some extent palatable to progressive (and positivist) medievalism. Loomis's ability to combine anthropology and literary history renders his enterprise still useful. But what is especially interesting is the withering barrage of his opponents, both of his Celticism and of his mythic priorities. By emphasizing the British origins of Arthurian legend, Loomis drew the wrath of a French Arthurian establishment. Of course, the Celtic thesis, once a strong position particularly in America, is now the province largely of popular medievalism and a somewhat worn Jungianism.[20] If the generally anthropological approach to Arthurian romance has its roots in the colonial projects of the nineteenth century as I have described them above, at the same time the lack of serious consideration of the subaltern sources of British culture is also problematic. In the English fairs I have mentioned above, Ireland and Scotland were typically depicted in terms of their romantic "medieval" past, complete with hand-weaving demonstrations and folk singing, while England was symbolized by manufacturing and science, representing the Celtic parts of Britain as if colonies within. In any case, this older Romantic thesis of the Celtic origin of many of the expressions of high medieval culture has been inverted and politicized by a postcolonial perspective. The position of Ireland, Wales, and Scotland (and less so Cornwall) in relation to English rule, and the relation between Celtic culture and English culture in general, has been studied in ways informed by, and even to some extent has predicted, the discourse of postcoloniality. The history of medieval geographic and national formations is a constant shifting of borders, political and familial allegiances, and a pattern of conquest, absorption, and resistance. The multiple languages of most medieval societies reveal a complex striation of imperial and subjugated peoples on the one hand, and an equally complex layering of resistances, protests, and parodies of power and authority.[21]

It is unlikely that these fringe theses will be revived in anything resembling their earlier form, but more recently a new anthropology, although drastically redefined, has been revived as an approach to medieval and early modern texts through the New Historicism and the sporadic impact of the ideas of M.M. Bakhtin. This is also true of the nonliterary scholarship to which much current medieval literary study is indebted. Historians such as Natalie Davis in the United States, Carlo Ginzburg in Italy, Aron Gurevich in Russia, Peter Burke in Great Britain, and the turn toward the history of *mentalité* among the *Annales* school, infused what used to be the province of folklore and anthropology with renewed importance for other disciplines, albeit in a much more rationalized and less romantic mode.[22] Moreover, the internal critique of anthropology by Marshall Sahlins and Clifford Geertz, and the interest in medieval ritual by Victor Turner has also moved medieval studies as much toward anthropology as towards history. In so doing, we have moved toward an admission of the anthropological status of the Middle Ages from its earliest formulations as a category of knowledge.[23] Beneath its apparent stability as an idea, the Middle Ages has repeatedly been represented as both domestic and foreign, as both historical origin and historical rupture, as both native and "native."

Since its classic formulation in Edward Said's *Orientalism*, the subject of Orientalism has been subsumed into the larger question of postcolonialism. Given the broad influence of the questions raised by these approaches, it is not surprising that medieval studies, somewhat cautiously, has considered its relation to postcolonial studies. An early and influential formulation was Allen Frantzen's coinage of the term 'Anglo-Saxonism,' modelled on Said's 'Orientalism,' to describe the state of Old English studies as by definition archaic and prior to the primary questions of literary and cultural study. More recently, medievalists have made attempts to reinsert medieval cultural productions within a discourse of a modernity that threatened to erase or render irrelevant the entire period. Many of these efforts, such as

Jeffrey Jerome Cohen's influential collection of essays (where some pages of
the present book first appeared), have worried about the applicability of a
frankly modernizing paradigm to earlier literature and culture.[24] Most of
the contributors to Cohen's collection insisted that the ubiquitous definitions of constructed national and personal identities borrowed from such
thinkers as Michel Foucault and Benedict Anderson ignore the complex
parallels to these topics in medieval culture, which is often imagined as part
of a previous paradigm. In an important essay, Bruce Holsinger has advised
that we need not be limited by this anxiety, "medievalists working within
the discourses of postcolonialism have been too quick to assume that their
disciplines have not already exerted a shaping role in the intellectual and
political work of postcolonial studies."[25] Holsinger calls upon medievalists
to trace the genealogies of their own practices in conjunction with those of
theory to plot the intersections and divergences. Holsinger points to the
ways that the transformations of methods and disciplines over the past three
decades often subsumed under the label of "theory" acknowledge debts to
questions and practices that first articulated themselves in medieval studies.
"Among medievalists and early modernists, at least," writes Holsinger
(p. 1199), "serious work on perhaps the most complex and difficult
dimension of our relationship to theory—the tracing of its intellectual
genealogies and their entanglement with those of our own disciplinary
pasts—has hardly begun." Holsinger traces the debt of the Subaltern Studies group to earlier work on the Middle Ages, including *Annales* historians
such as Marc Bloch and Marxist historians such as Robert Brenner and his
thesis concerning the peasant economy. Rather than a belated and desper-
ate attempt to render medieval studies relevant, the relation between
medieval studies and postcolonial studies is in fact a two-way traffic.

Such a direction had in fact been proposed in rather different ways, as
Holsinger also points out, by several writers. Kathleen Biddick's arresting
book *The Shock of Medievalism* urged a dialectic of postcolonial and
poststructuralist theory with the subject of medieval studies to both expose
the complicity of a certain attitude toward the medieval past with imperial
ideology and to reveal the surprising legacy of that complicity in contemporary medievalisms. In a special issue of *The Journal of Medieval and Early
Modern Studies*, edited by John Dagenais and Margaret Greer, the editors
and contributors pointed to the ways in which early modern "nation based
Empires" saw the medieval past as a historical other akin to the apparently
vast and empty spaces they sought to colonize.[26] Dagenais and Greer
observe that the Renaissance invention of the medieval past as a dark and
savage void is related to its awareness of a new geography to be mapped
and conquered. The new Renaissance imaginary is marked by "the inter-
convertibility of space and time" (435) in which "newly colonized lands

and The Middle Ages inhabit the same time" (435). They cite Petrarch's *Africa* as both a geographic and a historical starting point. In so doing, Dagenais and Greer also uncover a doubleness that is always revealed when modernity attempts to overthrow its medieval past: "The making of the Middle Ages turns out to be a double act, at once colonization and decolonization" (437). "In the end," they write, "the Renaissance, as Petrarch defines it, is a *risurgimento*, a native upsrising" (437).

Mention of Petrarch raises the question of medieval proto-Orientalism itself, medieval knowledge of and attitudes toward its South and its East. Because we begin our histories with Early Modern events, at least to the degree that we trace institutional and political developments that we assume shape our own moment, the Middle Ages is increasingly seen as that which is premodern. A corollary to that is we tend to assume that it lacked a sense of history as we know it. It is modern historians who must provide the Middle Ages with the sense of history that it lacked. Some of the most interesting scholarship of recent years has been corrective to that assumption. Similarly we assume that because it preceded the great age of geographical expansion, medieval culture lacked an understanding of that which was beyond its own spatial realm, and did not entirely comprehend that which was within its borders. Early Modern discoveries would test, and thereby overturn medieval imagined lands and peoples. Here too recent scholarship has attempted to correct this assumption and recent research has returned to the rich documentation and literature of travel and topography that was highly popular in the late Middle Ages itself.

As a way of emphasizing continuities and traditions in European thought, twentieth-century intellectual histories portray a Middle Ages almost exclusively of occidental precedents, resulting in the impression that an intellectual inwardness paralleled the xenophobia that apparently ran from *Chanson de Roland* to the Christian reconquest of Spain. The connecting link in that apparently insular thread is paradoxically the Crusades, whose militancy is an externalization of the explosive violence of the *Chanson* and whose unsuccessful energies are redirected into the finally successful reconquest. If nineteenth-century scholarship saw the Crusades as an opening to the wider and more sophisticated world of Islamic culture that the crusaders had set themselves originally against, much twentieth-century technical scholarship has emphasized how in fact remarkably little cultural transformation occurs as a result of the Crusades and the establishment of the Frankish kingdoms of the Levant.

But over the past quarter century, a more nuanced account of medieval orientalism itself has emerged. As it gained political superiority over its Moorish and Saracen adversaries, Western European culture could acknowledge and absorb its cultural contributions. As the great Moorish courts of Ammayid Spain fell to local control and subsequent Christian conquest, a period, however fragile, of interaction and translation among and between languages and religions resulted in a flood of new knowledge into Christian Europe. Venetian culture and commerce had always been open to influence and connection to the East, but with the establishment of the Norman kingdom in Sicily, an unusual amalgam of European and North African, Christian and Moslem and Eastern and Western Mediterranean cultures resulted. This amalgamation in turn was to influence the court of Henry II and Eleanor of Acquitaine, perhaps reflected in an orientalized tone to medieval romance and lyric. Whether or not courtly love as a cultural construct resulted from contact with Moslem philosophical, literary and cultural forms remains debated, as is the question of whether courtly love existed in any form at all outside some literary texts.[27] To simplify, the period from the tenth to the twelfth century witnessed a dualism toward the East, and the West's debt to the East, that would take different forms through the succeeding centuries. On the one hand, however much we may seek to understand their idealizing motivations, the Crusades remain a record largely of intolerance and aggression, a record broken by a few negotiations and interactions with their enemies. On the other hand, the increasingly weakening unity of Muslim Spain at the same time released what sometimes seems to be a flood of ideas, texts and dialogues to a Europe beginning to open up to a wider world in other ways than, though difficult to separate from, expansion and aggression. If Orientalism as a discourse develops as a condition of a dynamic west intellectually surveying once grand but now decadent (or even abandoned) lands and realms, medieval orientalism was enmeshed in a somewhat different matrix. Equally anxious and ambivalent about its other, medieval orientalism, if it can be called that, proceeded from an awareness of the East's intellectual grandeur and material ingenuity. Western Europe strained to distill what it could use from a complex and contaminated culture that was simultaneously alluring and threatening. Europe begins to understand and define itself through these newly purified texts and ideas and technologies. It defined, as it were, its own inferiority as a form of superiority.[28]

The following chapters treat the changing relation of medievalism and orientalism as outlined above through a series of overlapping and interwoven perspectives. In chapter one, I analyze the association of medieval romance and Gothic architecture with Eastern origins, first as an attempt by Early Modern neoclassicism to bracket off the Middle Ages in order to establish Greek and Roman architecture and culture as the main lineage of Western civilization, then by pre-Romantic and Romantic champions of the Middle Ages as a way of presenting an alternative and utopian view of both history and geography. The chapter concludes with a consideration of how some quite recent attitudes toward literature and culture subliminally reinsert the pairing of the Medieval and the Oriental. In chapter two, I trace the erasure of the Middle Ages as the formative period of Western identity in sixteenth- and seventeenth-century theories of national, ethnic, and racial origin, especially those that argue for the prehistoric settlement of Britain, and even the New World, by Phoenician or Hebrew visitors. In chapter three, I seek to describe the effort to write the Middle Ages as a phenomenon related to national and even personal identity, at the same time that representations of the Middle Ages, especially at World's Fairs, imagine the medieval in material forms that are inescapably orientalized. In all these chapters, my primary evidence is from British sources, but with somewhat different emphases, my conclusions could be seen to have implications for other Western European national cultures.

CHAPTER ONE

THE MIDDLE AGES AS GENRE

The story of the study of romance is in many ways the master narrative of the study of medieval literature and of medieval culture in general. Within the study of medieval romance, from its earliest inception, is a peculiar political dialectic, involving fantasies of race, gender, and power. The definition of romance in England (and elsewhere) starts with an obsession with origins, as one would expect of a genre of doubtful legitimacy. Inscribed in the description of romance from the earliest days of its study is a deep suspicion of its parentage. On one side, romance is imagined as indigenous, national, and local, as a form of history before historical consciousness takes shape. On the other side, the origin of romance is imagined as identical with the origins of fiction itself, and these origins are described with the imagery of otherness, which in the eighteenth century at least, meant a version of Orientalism. As with the literature of courtly love in the late nineteenth century, something so socially problematic is described as having originated elsewhere, probably from Arabic poetry through Moorish Spain. Warton's *History of English Poetry* in fact begins with the assumption that medieval literature, and Western fiction in general, is energized by the contact of Saracen and Crusader. Pierre-Daniel Huet's (1630–1721) influential treatise on romance was translated into English in the eighteenth century, and repeats the speculation that romance has its origins in Moorish influence upon Spain, but generally regards fiction itself, with its layers of allegory and rhetoric, as born in the East, infiltrating the West through various routes.[1] Although this speculative debate grows understandably baroque, and although there were skeptics, the connection among Romance, Fiction, and the East, remains a constant trope.

Where many objects of modern literary study were institutionalized (in however contested a manner) in the modern university during the nineteenth century and early twentieth century, the study of medieval English literature had a prior history. It was fostered, even invented, by several generations of amateur scholars, and by generations of antiquarians before them. This was also the case with some other literary subjects, but the peculiar conditions of pre-academic medievalism, and the prestige of its connoisseurs, meant that their attitudes toward medieval literature, and the cultural value they accorded it, had an extremely powerful influence on academic study. The study of medieval literature in general is born in a nostalgic love for the age and its imputed values, rather than in a veneration of authors (such as Shakespeare) or of particular texts. This sentimental romance of the period precedes any response to any particular work. Implicit in these early studies are conceptions of society, history, and the uses of literary language that still complicate our own responses to these works. This chapter seeks to trace some of these complications, particularly the peculiar circularity in which the study of medieval romance takes the form of its object of study. From its earliest formulations in the eighteenth century to the brief centrality of romance criticism in the mid-twentieth century, critical discourse surrounding the romances first imagines the Middle Ages as a romance, and then gradually becomes a species of romance itself.

This identification of the past as, or with, a dominant genre is complicated by the nature of that genre. For from the beginning of its identification as a form with a special relationship to the Middle Ages, romance has also been associated with a certain foreignness, a certain placelessness, indeed, a certain timelessness. If cosmopolitan pan-European cultural histories date their point of origin, or renewal, to the Renaissance, national histories often traced their more specific histories to the Middle Ages and to medieval culture in general, especially in the deeply interconnected historiographic imaginings of Romanticism and nationalism. Hence, the doubleness of the Middle Ages, its status as both interruption and point of origin, as both national archive and imported enchantment, is equated with, and sometimes identified as, the genre of romance.

I begin with a passage from Hippolyte Taine's (1828–93) once influential *History of English Literature*:

> It is impossible to translate these incongruous ideas which quite disconcert our modern style. At times they are unintelligible. Articles, particles, everything capable of illuminating thought, of marking the connection of terms, of producing regularity of ideas, all rational and logical artifices, are neglected. Passion bellows forth like a great shapeless beast; and that is all. It rises and starts in little abrupt lines; it is the acme of barbarism.[2]

Taine here is discussing Old English poetry, but his language, I believe, is paradigmatic. He invokes the trope of the medieval itself as barbarous, a trope that goes back as far as the vexed etymology of the Gothic as synonymous with the barbaric. The lack of decorum, the disruption of narrative logic, the expression of "passion" without some containing or compensatory dramatic development, all these constitute for Taine "barbarism," quite in the same way the visual and spatial distortions of Gothic art and architecture disturbed the apologists for neoclassicism.

Behind the language of Taine's stricture—and Taine is by no means unsympathetic to medieval literature—lies another category, one embodied in Horace's *Ars Poetica*, which also compares visual and literary representation. This category is that of the grotesque:

> Humano capiti cervicem pictor equinam
> iungere si velit, et varias inducere plumas
> undique collatis membris, ut turpiter atrum
> desinat in piscem mulier formosa superne,
> spectatum admissi risum teneatis, amici?
> credite, Pisones, isti tabulae fore librum
> persimilem, cuius, velut aegri somnia, vanae
> fingentur species, ut nec pes nec caput uni
> reddatur formae.

> (If a painter chose to join a human head to the neck of a horse, and to spread feathers of many a hue over limbs picked up now here now there, so that what at the top is a lovely woman ends below in a black and ugly fish, could you, my friend, if favored with a private view, refrain from laughing? Believe me, dear Pisos, quite like such pictures would be a book, whose idle fancies shall be shaped like a sick man's dreams, so that neither head nor foot can be assigned to a single shape)[3]

Horace provides the other pole of the otherness of the grotesque. Where Taine criticizes the masculinized excess of medieval narrative, Horace represents indecorous art as by definition sexually repulsive, a repulsion metaphorized as female. Where the definition of the grotesque becomes obscured in later uses, Horace's analogy is literally to the paintings first called grotesque—first identified in caves and grottos—and described in the same negative fashion by Vitruvius.[4] This passage, with its satirically articulated argument for decorum, becomes a precursor of neoclassical aesthetic argument.

These two passages are examples of tropes that one finds throughout the description of the medieval, both architectural and literary—the monstrous and the barbarous. So powerful are these concepts and so closely linked, that one finds them often used together in the same phrase. The negative connotations of the Gothic—and almost at the same time its metonymic association with the Medieval—occurs first in architectural theory and its most influential formulation is in Giorgio Vasari (1511–74):

> Eccì un'altra specie di lavori che si chiamano tedeschi, i quali sono di orna-
> menti e di proporzione molto differenti dagli antichi e da' moderni; né oggi
> s'usano per gli eccelenti, ma son fuggiti da loro come monstruosi e barbari,
> dimenticando ogni lore cosa di ordine.[5]

> [There are other kinds of works that are called German, which are very dif-
> ferent in ornament and proportion from the antique and the modern. They
> are no longer used by serious architects but are shunned by them as mon-
> strous and barbarous, since they disregard every recognizable idea or order.]

Vasari elsewhere (p. 128) refers to all medieval culture as "Gothic." This
broad sweep of the brush was to remain a more or less constant assumption until the clarification by Warton and other eighteenth century
commentators.[6] Vasari is making here one of the first, although not the
first, distinctions between the Gothic and the Classic. Significantly, his distinction is made in terms of architecture—the passage here is a commentary on yet another passage from Vitruvius—but specifically in terms of the
category of the grotesque. Vitruvius in fact was discussing decoration—
the grotesque line, literally the curlicue designs of organic forms found
on the walls of grottos, but Vasari combines it with Vitruvius' interest in
architectural proportion and form.

Behind and following Vasari's formal contempt is a set of assumptions,
which are not formal at all, but deeply connected with those aspects of race
and gender that we group together under the category of "otherness," but
that Freud's concept of the uncanny renders much closer to home. For what
we find behind the terms of the monstrous and the barbaric are a set of
hidden codes signifying the Occident and the Orient, and linked with them
the Masculine and the Feminine. The Barbaric is gendered as Masculine and
the Monstrous is gendered as the Feminine; the Occident is gendered as
Masculine and the Orient is gendered as the Feminine. And yet the Gothic
and the Medieval turn out to be enormously disturbing precisely because
they refuse the separation of these categories.[7] Nor do these categories work
in only one direction. As Partha Mitter has amply demonstrated, Indian and
Asian art in general were regarded by Western observers as monstrous.[8]

This collapsed polarity is not a modern fantasy, but a fantasy of the earliest inventors of the Medieval as a concept. The pointed arch was
interpreted as Eastern in origin and the general form of vaulting was
understood to imitate the canopy of the northern forests, which
the "Goths" inhabited. The racialism of the concept of the Gothic and the
Medieval runs through some of the most influential statements in architectural and literary history. Throughout the history of this association of

the Medieval with the monstrous and the barbaric, writers sometimes are referring to bad proportions and structures, sometimes about the monstrous decorations, and sometimes about the entire style. Sir John Evelyn (1620–1706) in his *Account of Architects and Architecture* explains the Gothic explicitly in terms of racial invasions: "It was after the Irruption, and Swarmes of those Truculent Peoples from the North; the Moors and Arabs from the South and East, over-running the Civiliz'd World; that wherever they fixed themselves, they soon began to debauch this Noble and Useful Art."[9] In the introduction, I cited Christopher Wren's reference to "The Saracen mode of building, seen in the East, soon spread over Europe, and particularly in France."[10] Wren's phrasing repeats an English trope of French capitulation, even France as a source of foreign ideas. The Orient, as it was later said, begins at Calais.

The Gothic could also be infantilized through metaphor. John Aubrey's (1626–97) unpublished *Chronologia Architectonica* surveyed English architectural styles through the seventeenth century, dating and categorizing buildings through the evidence of architectural details. He noted the shift from Romanesque to Gothic and was able to describe the varieties of Gothic style, including the development of decorated Gothic. Throughout, however, is a sense of the Gothic as decline in all areas of design, including lettering: "As the Roman Architecture did degenerate into Gothick in like manner did the Roman Character."[11] Gothic architecture is described by Aubrey as "the Barbarous Fashion." Aubrey also describes medieval romance in terms of the category of the grotesque: "As to this Gothique way of Romans, and attempting to write above Nature, we see what fulsome stuffe they give us; like Grotesco, with Dogs and Fishes terminating in Flowers"[12] [T.G. c. 24 257 v.]. For Aubrey, despite a few high points and despite his nostalgia for medieval principles of charity and his regret at the destruction of so many medieval monuments, the Middle Ages was a period of superstition, equated in his terms with folklore and the supernatural, largely passed down by women: "When I was a Child (& so before the Civill warres) the fashion was for old woman & maydes to tell fabulous stories nightimes and of Sprights, and walking of Ghosts & c.: this was derived downe from Mother to Daughter & c." [MS A 21, 13] Here Aubrey equates Gothic design with the germs of what will later be called Gothic fiction.

A similar set of tropes informs the debate about medieval literature in the seventeenth and eighteenth century, but there, slowly, we see the categories begin to change their relative valence. For James Beattie (1735–1803), in *Dissertations Moral and Critical*, the neglect of the classics in the Middle Ages is only an obvious result, or cause, of this monstrous aesthetic: "While the taste continued for everything that was incredible and monstrous, we may suppose that true learning and the natural simplicity of the classics would not be held in general estimation."[13] For someone like Beattie, the paradigmatic critique of romances is the response of Cervantes's *Don Quixote*: "And thus the extravagance of those books being placed, as it were, in the same group with the appearances of nature and the real business of life, the hideous disproportion of the former becomes so glaring by contrast that the most inattentive observer cannot fail to be struck with it" (562–63). Beattie's effort is in fact to defend the position of what he calls the "romance," but what we would call the eighteenth-century novel, and he is obliged to bracket off these earlier fantastical romances. The monstrous is a category that its earliest defenders imputed to medieval literature. Thomas Warton is typical: "for however monstrous and unnatural these compositions may appear to this age of reason and refinement, they merit more attention than the world is willing to bestow."[14] Richard Hurd (1720–1808) even in defense of the Gothic uses the language of opprobrium. "When an architect examines a gothic structure by Grecian rules he finds nothing but deformity."[15]

In the paradigmatic *Letters on Chivalry and Romance*, Richard Hurd attempts to revise the neoclassical contempt for the Gothic, but he does so on a theoretical level by invoking Horace, and at the same time dismissing his positions as a encumbrance on the imagination.[16] If we cannot have centaurs and harpies and cyclopses (all, interestingly, classical monsters) we cannot have poetry. Of course, Hurd is discussing the content of romance rather than its form, but it is interesting for our purposes what he does with that content. On one page he defends the imaginative freedom that would allow such creatures to appear in one's narrative, while on another, he seems to virtually allegorize them. The "Giant" and the "savages," which appear in so many romances, are in fact representations of overbearing overlords and wild local barons.[17] The knight fights against injustice rather than against the unnatural, except in so far as the unjust is unnatural. So, too, we learn shortly after, the other monsters we find in medieval romance. Oddly enough, this process of symbolic replacement is precisely the method Hurd imputes to the earlier defenders of Romance, who, imitating the moralized interpretations of Homeric fantasy, "palliate the no less monstrous stories of *magic and enchantments*."[18]

"We have lost," wrote Hurd, "a world of fine fabling."[19] His statement is heavily freighted with a set of characteristic assumptions. The world of the Middle Ages is a lost Golden Age, perhaps even a childhood, to which we can never return. Imagination holds the place in the Middle Ages that reason holds in the eighteenth-century present—a way of defining and creating culture. Romance itself is valued as a therapeutic and subjective means of recovering that imaginative coherence. If, rather than unpacking these assumptions, we rewrite them, the message is even clearer: the Middle Ages is imagined as a romance. "Romance," defined as escapist and utopian, is emplaced as the stereotypical genre of the Middle Ages. History is read as a literary genre. The Gothic revival of the late eighteenth century propounded a conception of the Middle Ages that apparently bore no political relevance to the present save nostalgia and inspiration. The utopian possibilities inherent in romance remain implicit in their construction of the genre, but both nostalgia and renewal are imagined by them in terms that require as little contingency with the present or the future as possible.

Here the Gothic is to be valued because of its almost pre-civilized status, a status that seems peculiarly timeless and devoid of actual social or political contexts. The Gothic (and by extension the romance) are not just aesthetic forms, they are ancestral traditions that Warton's and Hurd's modern world can reinvoke through imagination. A steady-state conception of history conceives of change only by constructing an opposite and prior world, in its own way as timeless as the present. Romance is nostalgically celebrated for its preservation of our wilder past, which is constructed as both a lost world and an other world. But it also offers an avenue toward utopian renewal of our underdeveloped imaginative capacities.

This aestheticized view of the Middle Ages and of romance was by no means inevitable or itself without a context. Interpretations of English medieval history had been deeply fought over in the seventeenth and early eighteenth century. The parliamentary and legal debates that surrounded both the Puritan Revolution and the Restoration depended heavily on historical precedent. It mattered profoundly in political terms whether the Norman conquest was a conquest or a legitimate assumption of power. Equally important was the question of whether anything like parliamentary representation existed among the "Saxons," a position favored by supporters of Parliament and whether there was any political inheritance from the pre-"Gothic" world of the Celtic Britons, a position favored by supporters of the monarchy. Efforts to legitimize monarchical or parliamentary authority found themselves constructing highly elaborate arguments as to the nature of the Conquest, the Magna Carta or the "Gothic" freedoms of pre-Conquest Saxon England.

By the early eighteenth century, the most sophisticated of these arguments had developed into an interpretation of the English medieval past as a series of historical stages. Partisan debates about this historiography had dwindled down, and historians imagined the Medieval period as one of a series of phases through which history passed before arriving at a far preferable present. The various conflicts that the partisan ideologues of the previous century had seen in the Middle Ages were now envisioned as separate streams flowing into the institutions of the present.[20] The political utility of the Middle Ages was reduced and the Middle Ages represented as a step through which civilization moved to the present, enlightened, quite other, stage. This Whig interpretation of history—the vision of the best of the past informing the institutions of the present—replaced conflict and struggle with concord and stability. The odd result was a minimization of the importance, cultural or political, of the Middle Ages. By the time of the Gothic revival rediscovery of romance in the late eighteenth century, the political and social dimensions of romance, and of its now metonymic period, the Middle Ages, were reduced.

The result of this minimalization of the historical and political centrality of the Middle Ages is a conception of medieval romance as mythic invention. In keeping with this, romance is imagined both as strange and faraway on the one hand, its origins typically described as oriental, and as indigenous, national and local, as a form of history before historical consciousness takes shape. It is both familiar and strange. For part of the appeal of medieval romance for its earliest champions was that it represented a wilder, freer past, one that gave free reign to an imaginative freedom that contemporary aesthetics and mores had repressed. For the early romance scholars, romance is a model of aesthetic liberation.

From its earliest formulation in English, the notion of the Gothic was a vexed term. Its use as a synonym for the barbarous and the primitive in matters of aesthetics and manners, was already widespread by the early eighteenth century. But in the seventeenth century the "Gothic" had a peculiar history. The Jutes were given pride of place among the Germanic invaders, and identified, on relatively slight evidence, with the "goths"— even Bede was called upon for confirmation.[21] It is easy to find anti-Gothic observations in the early eighteenth century, though curiously, laments against the interruption of classical learning and art by the "Gothic" centuries shade into criticism of any interest in things medieval. Alexander Gordon (ca. 1692–ca. 1754), an antiquary who relished Greek and Roman antiquities, appealed to the newly reformed Society of Antiquaries "that by them Antiquity and Learning may flourish in this Island, to the total extirpation of *Gothicism*, ignorance and a bad Taste."[22] Gordon was also a member of the "Society of Roman Knights," which took on Celtic and Roman names and pledged to preserve the classical antiquities of Britain. William Stukeley (1687–1765), later to be involved in the Gothic revival himself, contributed a statement to the Society of Roman Knights bemoaning "the delusion and abonimable superstition of cloysterid nuns and fryers. What the fury of the wars could not demolish their inglorious hands have destroyed. . . .Whilst others therefore are busying themselves to restore their Gothic Remanants, the glory is reserved for you to adorn and preserve the truly noble monuments of the Romans in Britain."[23] Stukeley here echoes complaints by others, such as Roger Gale, that the Society of Antiquaries was overrun with "Goths" who, like the Barbarians themselves, have no appreciation of the beauty of classical antiquity.

As Samuel Kliger observes in *The Goths in England: A study in Seventeenth and Eighteenth Century Thought*, the Gothic in the seventeenth century was predominantly a political rather than an aesthetic category.[24] The Germanic tribes, celebrated in Tacitus as a reproach to Roman decadence, were metonymically baptized as "Goths." Relying on Tacitus, seventeenth-century parliamentary reformers identified the institutions of democratic liberty with the "Goths," including parliament, democratic elections and judicial process, and identified royal authority with an enervated Roman empire. The Gothic countryside and forest was contrasted with the Imperial Roman capitol.

Even in this first revival of the Gothic as an idea, however, its bases were potentially unstable. The Barbarians at the Gates are represented as more civilized than the indolent beneficiaries of Empire. While Tacitus notes the relative respect for females among the Germanic tribes, seventeenth-century political rhetoric imagines the Goths as masculine, honorable and pure, and the Romans as decadent, effeminate, and corrupt. The empire is imagined as enervating culture, the Goths as energizing nature. As the Gothic develops as an aesthetic in the eighteenth century, these polarities are deconstructed. Nevertheless, the political implication of Gothic versus Roman models are not always as clear as political propaganda would have it, even in the seventeenth century. Gothic enthusiasts on an aesthetic level could be Tory or Whig, and could change either their taste or their party. Symbolically, however, the Gothic building (or garden or landscape), with its apparent wildness and chaos, was associated with the limitless freedom of Whig reforms; the classical temple was associated with Tory values of stability, hierarchy, and order. Either association could be reversed, the Gothic leading to anarchy and rebellion, the classical orders stifling individual freedoms.[25] Association with the Roman or the Gothic could be used to attack or defend one's self or one's opponents.

One of the writers who provides an Asiatic link with the "Goths" is the sixth-century historian named Jordanes.[26] It is Jordanes who groups the Germanic tribes together as "Goths," a term that will remain in place through the eighteenth century. He locates the original homeland of the Goths in an arctic island named "Scandza." From here they spread over Europe and Asia. In returning to Western Europe, the "Goths" bring with them something of the Orient. While Jordanes' account of the dispersal of the "Scandza" was one source for the notion of an "Eastern" origin of medieval culture, the myth of Odin, spread through a number of medieval sources, also places the Goths in an Asiatic setting. The *Heimskringla* located Odin's kingdom in Asia, from where he leads the Goths to Scythia.[27] In the *Prose Edda*, a complicated genealogy has the Goths descended through many generations from the tower of Babel (Jupiter, Neptune, Pluto, and

Zoroaster all play a part in their history), until Odin's forces face Pompey's army, at which point they retreat to Europe.[28] Widukind's Saxon account traces the Saxons back to the remnants of the Macedonian forces under Alexander the Great.[29] The Macedonians, according to some medieval accounts, were considered Trojans. The Trojan origin of Britain which follows on this version is a common variant, and is widely distributed through Geoffrey of Monmouth. Throughout the eighteenth century, the Odin myth, with its location of the ancestors of the Germanic people in the East, is repeated by one authority after another, with only a few skeptical voices. Aylett Sammes' (ca. 1636–ca. 79) *Britannia antiqua illustrata: or the Antiquities of Ancient Britain derived from the Phoenicians* employs the myth of Odin as evidence of his theory that British culture is in fact Phoenician in origin, citing classical and medieval authorities to "learn the Procession of our Ancestors from Asia under Woden."[30]

Huet asserted that the invention of romance "is due to the Orientals, I mean to the Egyptians, Persians and Syrians."[31] Even the supporters of a Northern "Gothic" origin of Romance, however, admitted the possibility of earlier cultural contact with the East, perhaps through the mythical conquest of Odin or the diffusion of "Scandza" Goths throughout the world. In these scenarios, an original Western culture is transported to the East, and then returns to its ancestral home, perhaps having absorbed Oriental influences. William Warburton (1698–1779) admits the importance of the crusades for the rise of romance, but argues that the idealism generated by the crusades transformed "barbarous" Northern customs into the motifs of romance.[32] Thomas Percy (1729–1811) and others, however, insist that the Arabic connection is unnecessary to postulate, since "Odin and his followers are said to have come precisely from those parts of Asia, we can readily account for the prevalance of fictions of this sort among the Gothic nations of the North, without fetching them from the Moors in Spain."[33] Warton's "Of the Origin of Romance Fiction in Europe," offers a synthesis of these theories:

> That peculiar and arbitrary species of fiction which we commonly call Romantic, was entirely unknown to the writers of Greece and Rome. It appears to have been imported to Europe by a people, whose modes of thinking, and habits of invention, are not natural to that country. It is generally supposed to have been borrowed from the Arabians.[34]

Warton then goes on to propose his thesis that contact between Europe and the Orient occurred much earlier, dating from the Muslim conquest of Spain.

In general, writers such as Huet emphasized the Saracen origin of Romance. Percy tended to stress the origin of the constituents of romance, including duelling and jousting, the elevation of women and the idealization of the individual knight, with the north. Warton accomodated both the Eastern and Northern theses, in a solution that resembles similar interpretations of Gothic architecture as combining Eastern and Northern motifs and qualities. John Husbands, collecting *A Miscellany of Poems By Several Hands* in 1731 favorably compares the oriental to the classical imagination, "the genius of the East soars upon stronger wings and takes a loftier flight, than the muse of Greece or Rome."[35] William Collins's (1721–59) *Oriental Eclogues* contrasts the "strong and nervous stile" of northerners with the "rich and figurative" quality of "an Arabian or Persian."[36]

The Gothic novel was also informed by implicit and explicit Orientalisms, in terms of treatment, theme and source. This was recognized by eighteenth-century contemporaries. Nathan Drake's (1766–1836) *Literary Hours* defines a "vulgar Gothic," by which he means the machinery of romance as opposed to a racially and culturally defined Northern culture, as being influenced by "the fictions of the East, as imported into Europe during the Crusades."[37] The Gothic novel combines these qualities, and in some examples, "the transition is immediately from the deep Gothic to the Arabic or Saracenic superstition."[38]

Thus, the "Gothic" became the site of another polarity. It seemed to partake of what eighteenth-century ethnology assumed was the relative lack of imagination of the northern races, even if the stubborn primitivism of the "Goths" had beneficial political effects. Yet this dimness was not enough to explain the bad taste of Gothic design, for this sprang from an excess of imagination. As anyone who knew anything about such things knew, this excess of the imagination could come from only one place—the East. Hence, the fanciful migrations of the Gothic people became, however redundantly, an explanation of Gothic style: rough, primitive, and stolid on the one hand; wildly profusive, exuberant and fantastical on the other.[39] Medieval literature, that is, has been understood as simultaneously historical record and historical escape. The record has been thematized as largely heroic, the escape largely as the province of romance and lyric. The record may be allegorized as the knight-subject, the escape as the female-other Lamia, the descendant of Horace's picture of literature gone wild, gone grotesque. The Barbaric North and the Monstrous East become symbolic origins of the Gothic. By the middle eighteenth century the fantasy of Eastern origin was already called into question by responsible scholars, but even the famous debates about architectural style in nineteenth-century Germany found it necessary to refute the fantasy.[40]

The debate about romance is in fact a debate about fiction itself, and the relation of romance to reality, to morality and to social use, replicates, even initiates, similar concerns about the uses of fiction. This alternation of fascination and repulsion, celebration and dismissal, can be found in definitions of romance, particularly in English studies, down to the present day. Romance as metaphor eclipses romance as genre. Latent in this view of fiction as romance is a simultaneously luxuriant, eroticized fantasy on the one hand, romance as a harem, and a suspicious, distancing rejection on the other. In a familiar paradigm, foreignness and sexuality both attract and repel. The polarities of romance take on the dichotomies of gender itself. Romance is a document of (European or English) history, and directly reveals the inscription of that history, both its actual social existence and its imaginative reality. Romance embodies an idealism, a nobler and simpler time, and in its representation of chivalry and heroic combat, comes close to the quality of epic. These generally masculine virtues, however, are counterpoised to a set of more disquieting qualities. Romance is fantastic and overgrown, the literature of unbridled passion and wild, untrammeled form. Its origins lie elsewhere than at home, and as such it has about it always the quality of the uncanny, the "unheimlich." This uncertainty translates itself into an ambivalence about the uses of romance. As a result, one can find romance celebrated as a model of chivalric and aristocratic behavior by conservative celebrants of medieval virtues early in the nineteenth century, but treated with some suspicion by the more self-consciously virile conservatism of the later part of the nineteenth century, partly as a result of the impact of "muscular Christianity" and the return of a nationalizing identification with nordic traditions as opposed to gallic and continental traditions.

The therapeutic and regenerative strain in eighteenth-century medievalism, however conservative its proponents might have been, led to one of the chief inspirations for high Romantic poetry.[41] The alterity represented by the "gothic" was one of the ideological sources for the Romantic poetic program, however askew its understanding of the "gothic." Coleridge and Keats were directly inspired by medieval sources. The Romantic poets in general especially found in the quest romance a form congenial to the exploration of the poetic Self, even if, as in Shelley's case, the romantics knew little of medieval romance and found medievalism, as did Byron, acutely distasteful and reactionary. The conception of nature essential to Romanticism's self-definition grew out of a conception of nature linked to Gothic wildness, even if such a conception of nature was not held by the actual inhabitants of the Middle Ages. The challenge to the canons of poetic form and poetic language represented by medieval poetry inspired the revolution in poetic form and poetic language that was Romanticism. Through the misty haze of the "gothic," medieval literature seemed to embody the organic coherence romanticism sought in its own aesthetic. Despite this connection with the revolutionary politics and aesthetics of romanticism, the curation of medieval romances was to remain a largely conservative enterprise during the early nineteenth century.

While the scholars of medieval romance in the late eighteenth century insistently denied the political relevance of their scholarship, this denial masked the conservatism of their enterprise.[42] This politics becomes overt in the reception of the fruits of their labors in the early nineteenth century. The tremendous surge in enthusiasm for, and a considerable number of collections of, romances, which appeared in England during the wars against France, almost certainly appealed to an anti-republican bias, and the main popularizers of the genre, including Sir Walter Scott (1771–1832), adapted strongly conservative and hierarchical political views. (In this light, Scott's multivolume biography of Napoleon is an ironic testament, reading Napoleon as a romantic antihero, and shifting blame to the Republic.) The Middle Ages was presented as a critique of modernity, a critique of industrialization, urbanization and democratization. The social world imagined in this scheme idealized both aristocracy and folk. The aristocracy was imagined almost entirely in terms of chivalry, to the exclusion of other traits, and "romance" was valued chiefly to the degree it reflected chivalric models. The rest of society was honored with the capacity for cultural production, but imagined as fully itself when accepting, even demanding, hierarchical paternalism.

By the early nineteenth century, romance had become a "popular" genre and the medieval revival had become a widespread style. Not only were medieval romance and medievalism fashionable, they defined social ideals. Medievalism was propounded as an ideology, with a specific religious, political, and cultural agenda. Medievalism was associated with a return to high Anglican ritual. Antirevolutionary at base, conservative reform groups like the "Young England" movement sought to transform noblesse oblige into a political platform. The idiosyncratic antiquarianism of the eighteenth century was magnified into a symbolic cultural masquerade, the inspiration for which was the medieval romance. By and large, the nineteenth century, especially in England, received romance as a profoundly Western and often specifically national genre, in contrast to the orientalized pan-European model of most eighteenth-century commentators. This westernization, even nationalization, of romance, was often accompanied by an emphasis on the masculine attributes of romance and its heroes. Moreover, while the British and Celtic origin of romance, particularly Arthurian romance, is never entirely eliminated, an emphasis on the English, even Anglo-Saxon, qualities of romance can be detected. Nevertheless, medieval romance was a profoundly unstable center for such an enterprise. The study of popular culture has alerted us to the ways in which forms such as romance embody private desires as well as shared public values. These uneasy negotiations result in a ceaselessly contested form. Such contestation marks the unofficial history of medieval romance in the nineteenth century. In *Idylls of the King*, his retelling of Malory, Alfred Lord Tennyson is unable to reconcile the subversive eroticism of romance with the public vision of medievalism, but the effort to do so accounted for the work's enormous and continuing popularity. Similarly, later in the century, William Morris and others appropriated medieval romance for revolutionary politics, precisely the position the romance revival of the early nineteenth century defined itself against. In works such as *News from Nowhere*, William Morris' utopian tale of a future in medieval dress, romance becomes the formal vehicle of apocalypse and utopia, an association it briefly held in high Romantic poetry.

As Stephanie Barczewski has abundantly demonstrated, the medieval legends of the peculiarly contradictory national heroes, Robin Hood and King Arthur, were by no means immune to changing attitudes toward race in the nineteenth century. By drawing a crude paradigm of Norman usurpers and Saxon natives, Sir Walter Scott's *Ivanhoe* provided a template for nineteenth-century racializations of these myths. Scott's hope for a union of races and temperaments, and his generally positive assessment of the role of the Jews, was not, however, to survive the rise of scientific racism in the mid- to later-nineteenth century. The response to the Indian Mutiny is often regarded as the turning point in British Imperial policy and racial and ethnic policies, signalling an end to whatever valorization had been accorded Eastern civilizations as inheritors of their past glory. But by the 1850s, racial attitudes in Britain, Germany, and elsewhere in Northern Europe begin to reify previous ethnic and linguistic differences and subsume them under the category of race.[43] Robin Hood is increasingly portrayed as a displaced Saxon hero, as Teutonic qualities become valorized as closest to Aryan origin. If accounts of the origin of British civilization in the biblical Middle East, including the thesis that the original language of the islands was Hebrew, were common in the sixteenth and seventeenth centuries, by the late nineteenth century, Jews were repositioned as absolute other, now on racial as well as religous grounds. King Arthur's racial status was even more troubling, since the hierarchy of racial superiority required the promotion of Anglo-Saxon over Celtic identities, despite the considerable eighteenth-century achievement in forging a larger British identity based on a union, however forced, among different, and perhaps indistinguishable, racial groups.

One particularly interesting case is that of the scholar Joseph Ritson (1752–1803), not because he reflects the early nineteenth-century pattern of conservative medievalism, but because he defies it, and in defying it exemplifies some of the difficulties implicit in the entire enterprise for both left and right positions. Ritson was early on a radical republican (as well as a vegetarian, traits that Sidney Lee in the *Dictionary of National Biography* associates with his eventual madness) and fearsomely irascible. Ritson died a month after barricading himself in his library and setting his manuscripts on fire. Yet despite Ritson's radicalism, which did not prevent a respectful association with Sir Walter Scott, his version of romance is consistent with the idealizing patterns of late-eighteenth-century antiquarianism, even as he rejects its most egregious misconceptions. The introduction to Ritson's edition of *Ancient Engleish Metrical Romanceës* gores many oxen necessary to drive the eighteenth-century conception of romance. He ridicules the notion of romance, expounded by Warton, emerging as a result of contact with the Arab invaders of Spain. More importantly, Ritson attacks the idea of an infinitely receding origin for romance:

> That they may likewise, "have a multitude of sagas or histories on romantick subjects, some of them writen SINCE the times of the crusades" wil be read-ily admited; but there is not the slightest proof or pretext for asserting that "others" were so "LONG BEFORE."[44]

Ritson is here concerned with the possibility of Scandinavian origins of romance, but his rejoinder expresses his skepticism in the lack of manu-script evidence or reliable witnesses. Ritson's skepticism about the racial origins of romance is not confined to Scandinavian or Arab. He is only partly persuaded by theories of primitive Celtic origins. "The Welsh," he writes, "have no 'tales' or 'chronicles' to produces of 'the elder Welsh bards,' nor any other writeër mor early than by Geoffrey of Monmouth."[45] Much firmer is his vitriolic dismissal of any Anglo-Saxon origins of romance. Speaking of the Saxons, he writes:

> Though these treacherous strangers are not known to have brought over with them books or letters, or, in short, any kind of literary stock, while they continue'd pagans, they were unquestionablely a brave and warlike nation, but, upon their conversion to Christianity, their kings became monks, their people cowards and slaves, unable to defend themselves, and a prey to every invadeër.[46]

The politics of Ritson's analysis here is interesting. Alfred, normally the hero of progressive political imagining in the seventeenth and eighteenth century, is dismissed by Ritson as a "wretched bigot." At the same time, Ritson echoes the trope of the "Norman Yoke": William "would make them draw the plough like oxen."[47] In an earlier formulation, the theory of the Norman Yoke celebrated Anglo-Saxon political institutions. Democratic change, such as that imagined by the radicals of the seventeenth century, meant a return to a birthright of free English yeomen. Ritson, while contemptuous of Blackstone's legalist view of the Conquest as a form of contract, nevertheless does not romanticize the Anglo-Saxons. His radical republicanism explodes in anger at the already corrupting influence of the Church over the Anglo-Saxons, even before the invasion, and in the earlier acceptance of royal dominion.

Where does this radical skepticism leave romance in Ritson's scheme? Eighteenth-century definitions of romance were concerned both with the romances' origins and with their ambiguous national status. Ritson dismisses both of these as obsessions rather than realities. Moreover, the appeal of romance as history, the other side of otherness, is equally brushed aside by Ritson:

> Bevis and Guy were no more "English heroes" than Amadis de Gaule or Perceforest; they are mere creatures of the imagaination, and only obtain an establishment in history because (like mister Wartons) it was usually written upon the authority of romance.[48]

The claims to a particular national excellence in English romance is also rejected by Ritson. He accepts French romances not only as obviously earlier, but as obviously better.

Ritson's criticism of the idea of uniqueness of Middle English romance as compared to French romance is the first expression of a disenchantment with the former. His motivation may have been partially a reaction against a certain provincial nationalism that he critiques elsewhere, and partly an allegiance to the France of the Revolution, but it was almost certainly driven by Warton's elevation of minstrelcy and romance as part of the splendor of Norman aristocracy, against which Ritson can barely contain himself. Ritson finds himself slashing out at overgeneralizing schemes on the one hand, but at specific historical placement on the other. For all his quarrels with other scholars, Ritson ends up by ratifying the urge toward romance as a universal human trait, sometimes more successfully expressed than at other times. By so doing, Ritson enacts precisely the quandary that scholars of romance find themselves in to the present day. The scholarly study of romance ends up by disenchanting the very idea of romance that draws us to it.

His contemporaries, such as Sir Walter Scott, could admire Ritson's accuracy at the same time that they felt free to ignore some of his positions as the products of a deranged mind. Yet Ritson's skepticism and the chivalric fantasies of the early nineteenth century left a problematic dual legacy. For by mid-century, the study of Middle English romance had partly joined the academic institutionalization of literature.[49] In so doing, it was subject to a number of forces that threatened to minimize its place in the canon, and to retard its study except for the editions of texts. The Germanic model of scientific philology had no particular allegiance to romance as a privileged form. The Arnoldian stress on high culture threatened to marginalize all but major medieval authors, and, given Arnold's famous observation on Chaucer lacking high seriousness, even some of them. The institutionalization of literary study in the nineteenth-century academy was led by medieval studies, but the ironic result was the relegation of the study of medieval romance in England, which had been at the center of the medieval revival of the eighteenth century, to the periphery.

The most important of the Victorian publishing series was the Early English Text Society, inextricably intertwined with its chief founder, F.J. Furnivall (1825–1910).[50] Earlier literary societies were gentlemanly, even exclusive affairs, in keeping with the social values of medievalism. A lawyer and amateur editor, committed to Christian Socialism, Furnivall's energy and enthusiasm is reflected in the original series, both in its indiscriminate attempts at comprehensiveness and in its varying quality of scholarship. Where earlier antiquarians defined the Middle Ages through the privileged genres of romance and ballad, Furnivall's projects suggest a broader sense of a medieval social world, one consistent with his own politics. Such a broader sense was not one necessarily limited to left politics, but was rooted in the social consciousness of high Victorianism. While impelled by a sense of mission, Furnivall's medievalism is nevertheless relatively secularized, and the literary past imagined in the Early English Text Society, taken as a single project, is pluralist and multifaceted. The odd collection that make up the EETS series, while it may reflect the range of medieval discourse, hardly even fits the literary idea of the Middle Ages constructed by the antiquarians of the previous generation, let alone a contemporary public. Furnivall's agenda combined an educational populism with the scientific model of Germanic philology, and it is through the publishing societies, as much as through the universities, that this scientific model was institutionalized. It was an agenda that opposed itself to the amateur aristocratic antiquarianism of the previous generation as much as it was to be in opposition to the gentlemanly belletristic impressionism of the next. As a result, the romances that did not fit the romantic conception of romance inherited from the previous generation were rendered safe from commentary. At the same time, Furnivall's celebration of Middle English literature as an expression of Englishness, one with a direct connection to the experience of common men and women, reoriented the entire canon of Middle English literature. If romance was of any special interest, it would be in its inadvertent revelation of national character.

Furnivall's protofeminism and socialism meant that the rubric of that character could include multitudes. But slightly later, in W.P. Ker's

(1855–1923) *Epic and Romance*, which crystallized its positions for several generations of scholars, Middle English metrical romances are excluded from the outset, "whole tracts of literature," he writes, "have been barely touched on—the English metrical romances."[51] For Ker, the mythic Middle Ages is embodied in epic, and romance is a mechanistic, secondary simulation of the primal power of epic. "Epic" is the literature of an earlier epoch, it is heroic rather than chivalric; even the Battle of Hastings is allegorized as the battle of epic against romance. For Ker, romance is medieval modernity, epic is medieval traditionalism. Romance is "hot and dusty and fatigued. It has come through the mills of a thousand literary men, who know their business, and have an eye to their profits. . . . [It] is almost as factitious and professional as modern Gothic architecture . . . A 'romantic school' is a company for the profitable working of Broceliande, an organized attempt to 'open up' the Enchanted Ground."[52]

The language of Ker's description, moreover, introduces metaphors whose implications he would seem to be aware of. Romance is "brilliant and frequently vainglorious.[53] "Whatever epic may mean, it implies some weight and solidity; Romance means nothing, if it does not convey some notion of mystery and fantasy."[54] Ker is aware enough to retreat from too hard polarization, but he does so in caricature rather than description: "The Crusader may indeed be natural and brutal enough in most of his ways, but he has lost the sobriety and simplicity of the earlier type of rover."[55] Ker significantly, and apparently naturally enough, equates military strategy with literary form: "If nothing else, his way of fighting—the undisciplined cavalry charge—would convict him of extravagance as compared with men of business, like the settlers of Iceland for instance."[56] But there is a heavy and perhaps ironically late Victorian freight behind these images, for romance is described as crusading warfare, which is described as the military style typical of the romantic native. Romance is described again as Foreign, becoming so in its conquest of the Foreign, an associational move more akin to Conrad than to Kipling. Ker's opposition of epic and romance inverts the duality of eighteenth-century medievalism, which privileged romance over epic. Implicit in Ker's move is the difficult place of "civilization" in late-nineteenth-century imperialism. Ker's celebration of epic over romance, while on the surface dismissable as a militarizing and imperial fantasy, on a deeper level reveals an anxiety about the possibilities of, combined with a nostalgia for, the heroic virtues.

Ker redefines the relatively romantic medievalism of Morris into a historical continuum. Despite its aristocratic base, heroic society is represented as more egalitarian, without the "contempt of the lord for the villein."[57] The later Chivalric age is complex, specialized, and striated. Moreover, for Ker, romance is the cultivation beyond proportion of one of the "fairy interludes" of Epic. But in romance, this "mystery and the spell of everything remote and unattainable" is taken out of context. Romance is not only effete and foreign, it is also monstrous. Ker's Provence is Ruskin's Venice. One suspects that for Ker, romance takes on the qualities of Wilde and Swinburne, to which the study of medieval epic seems almost an antidote. Another association, again metaphoric, also expressed in a revised Ruskinianism, is between romance and production, as if romance were manufactured, professional, reproducible (as opposed to the "natural" growth of epic). Romance, oddly enough, is projected by Ker as unfettered and amoral capitalism. Ker is obviously extending the politics of romantic medievalism to its contradictory conclusion, but the association of capitalism and romance is bizarre and striking at best. For Ker, the *frisson* of romantic poetry is what he means by romance, and he reads medieval romance as an unnatural attempt to manufacture it.

Ker published *Epic and Romance* in 1897, when he was forty-two. The Scotland that Ker had born into was still indebted to Sir Walter Scott's cultural program, and Ker's division is an inverse homage to Scott's chivalric heroism, despite Ker's devaluation of romance. Ker also adhered to the political tradition of romantic medievalism; a lifelong conservative, his celebration of heroic poetry appropriates some of the virtues the socialist Morris also ascribed to it. As what we would call a comparatist, Ker could also explicitly pay homage to Gaston Paris. Yet in rejecting precisely the idea of romance that Paris was helping to construct and in celebrating an image of an earlier Middle Ages, Ker was in fact constructing a paradigm of medieval literature that was English, nordic, and primitive rather than French and cosmopolitan. Perhaps because it was a convenient cultural strategy, perhaps because this marginalization of romance carries forth into twentieth-century scholarship, the almost pre-academic attitudes toward romance form the basis for romance scholarship in English literature in the twentieth century. The great exception to this marginalization, the study of Malory's Arthurian work, finds its most powerful expression in a content-obsessed, anthropological ahistoricization of Malory, in which myth becomes romance.

We might also note that in parallel with the Occidentalization of Romance, Gothic architecture acquires nationalizing, or at least westernizing qualities by the end of the first quarter of the nineteenth century. In the eighteenth century, both medieval revival architecture and the architecture of the Orient (which could mean anything from Islamic to Far Eastern architecture) became part of the lexicon of the picturesque. Period styles were conceived of as a vocabulary, and the appropriate style could be chosen to suit the atmosphere of a particular project. Yet to some extent the picturesque aesthetic conceived of the Gothic and the Oriental as opposite values, the Gothic associated with seriousness, melancholy, and indigenous history the Oriental with pleasure, sensuousness, and distant exoticism (even when the source model happened to be a mosque or a shrine). Horace Walpole (1717–97) and others could comfortably call upon medieval and oriental motifs as alternatives to other more mundane options, but by the time of A.W.N. Pugin's (1812–52) celebrity, beginning in the 1820s, the Gothic is associated with purity rather than hybridity, discipline rather than riot and authenticity rather than cultural masquerade.

The "Gothick" was not necessarily an apolitical or conservative movement. Horace Walpole, one of the great popularizers of the Gothic revival, was the son of Sir Robert Walpole, one of the eighteenth century's most powerful prime ministers. The elder Walpole was still heir to debates about the relation between medieval history and the origins of British liberty. Although Sir Robert's mansion was a suitably Palladian building, the architect, William Kent, was one of the first architects to pay serious attention to medieval style as a possible alternative to Palladianism. Kent's associate and contemporary, James Gibbs, builds a significant "Temple to Liberty" (1741) in the Gothic style at Stowe House, Buckinghamshire.[58] Whatever the picturesque and apparently recreational agenda of the "Gothick" of the early nineteenth century, it shared with the Gothic novel a difficult and recursive sense of history simultaneously ludic and haunted. Part of Pugin's contribution was to clarify and brighten Gothic architecture. In so doing, he also articulated a dialectic between an orientalized and a westernized Gothic that runs through nineteenth-century debates. And, of course, Pugin's own position emphasizes its purity and occidental origin, even though a suspicious strain of theatricality seems at times to undermine this purity. Pugin's early training and career were in the theaters of the Regency period, and his sense of theatricality, appropriate for the church building that comprised most of his output, marks much of his work. Even the sense of visual apprehension in his churches, with much revealed but much hidden, is not unrelated to set design. For Pugin, fidelity to religion meant fidelity to traditions of ritual, and to the architecture that supported and incorporated that ritual. But Pugin's reactionary liturgical purism and his devotion to chancel screens as essential to church design would be increasingly idiosyncratic as the Oxford Movement peaked and as Newman's conversion to Roman Catholicism loomed. Pugin's own hostility to Irish Catholicism and its potentially radical politics rendered his influence there minimal, despite a few commissions. By the 1840s, devotional practices that filtered in from Italy were increasingly popular, with dramatic processions, singing of hymns and a formal benediction. Pugin's own scholarly knowledge of liturgical history, reflected in his screened altars, was lost on most parish priests.

For Pugin, the apparent superiority of Gothic architecture lay in its truth to materials. The design of the marble Greek or Roman temple, argues Pugin, is based on an earlier technique of wooden and log building. The move to stone did not result in any significant change in design principle, "the finest temple of the Greeks is constructed on the *same principle* as a large wooden cabin."[59] But the actual affront is that classical architecture is a result of "the blind admiration of modern times for everything Pagan, to the prejudice and overthrow of Christ in art and propriety." What is interesting about Pugin's defense of Gothic is how specific his definition of "pointed" architecture is, referring to late-fourteenth- and fifteenth-cetury Gothic. What is significant about this design choice is, first, the decorative complexity of the model style, one that dovetailed with the love of rich detail in Victorian England, and second, the historical moment of the last complete hegemony of Catholicism, on the eve of the Reformation. Returning to "pointed Gothic," that is, symbolically returns to a broken authentic religious and architectural tradition.

Pugin's advocacy of decorated Gothic also provided a strategic link between his own desire for a pure medieval liturgical Catholicism and the Anglican reforms along similar lines sought by the Cambridge Camden Society. Here the historical rupture represented by the Henrician Church allowed the late Gothic to symbolize the point of origin of the Anglican institution, at the same time that it allowed the Camden Society (and the Anglican Church) to consider itself as the heir to the true Church. As with uneasy alliances between relatively doctrinaire theological groups throughout history, the radical opposition between them seemed less threatening than the homogenizing and diluting effects of modernization.

By the time Pugin was called in by Charles Barry and James Gillespie Graham to work on the Houses of Parliament, he had grown critical of late Gothic perpendicular, but proceeded to join them anyway. It is conceivable that his objection was aesthetic, but it was also likely to be doctrinal. Late Gothic perpendicular is stereotypically an "English" permutation of Gothic, noted by Rickman and since repeated in architectural histories to the present day, but it is also closely associated with Henry VIII's projects, and therefore with both apostasy and persecution of Catholics, though Pugin never makes this rationale explicit. In any case, Pugin had already decided that sixteenth century-Tudor was already a "debased" architecture. Since his Camden allies agreed, it is unlikely that the ideological motivation I have imputed ever needed to surface. Barry (a Protestant) and Graham (a Catholic) had decided on the perpendicular to fit into the context created by St. Stephen's Cloister and the Henry VI Chapel at Westminster Abbey.

Simultaneous with his rejection of perpendicular Gothic, however, was an opening to his Camden Society (now the Ecclesiasticum Society) allies.

In the second edition of *Contrasts*, which earlier celebrated the Perpendicular or Tudor as preferable to later abominations, he specifically retracts his blame on Protestantism ("the so-called Reformation") for cultural decline. Instead, the problem, he suggests, was the Renaissance, with its admiration for "the luxurious styles of ancient Paganism" which is at fault. Such Paganism is contrasted with the "self-denying Catholic principle," a particularly Puritan and English inflection of Catholicism.[60]

What is interesting about the anti-Renaissance rhetoric of the Second Edition of *Contrasts* is that it correlates with a new enthusiasm for Italian Renaissance church planning on the part of Newman and his followers, once allies of and champions of Pugin. In the office politics of Victorian Gothic, Pugin stands with his Camden allies, at once almost victorious and increasingly marginalized by their intransigence. Pugin was also as contemptuous of evangelical protestantism as he was of the masses of Irish Catholics who threatened to overwhelm his own Church. Pugin's rhetoric is dramatized by his praise of Savanarola, "that great champion and martyr for the truth" and his remarkable linkage of the "gardens of the Medici, filled with Pagan luxury, and the independent preaching houses that now deface the land," as if evangelical dissenters were an excess resulting from the internal corruption of Renaissance Catholicism.[61] For Pugin, Gothic architecture succeeds because of its ability to communicate the mystery of faith, through its height, its decoration and its use of light, and because of its appropriateness to a liturgy in which the congregation stands, as well as because of its indigenous creation: "They borrowed no ideas from no heathen rites; nor sought for decorations from the idolatrous emblems of a strange people."[62]

While Pugin focuses on architecture, or more, properly, the relation between architecture and religion, he does briefly mention the visual arts. He complains of students who go to Italy to study classical or Renaissance art, and instead directs them to the "Italian art of the 13th, 14th and 15th centuries. . .the beau ideal of Christian purity, and its imitation cannot be too strongly inculcated; but when it forsook its pure, mystical, and ancient types. . .it sunk to a fearful state of degradation."[63] Although Raphael is mentioned as an example of a great "Catholic artist," Pugin comes very close to predicting the Pre-Raphaelite aesthetic.

Whatever his polemics and politics, Pugin's idea of the Gothic was profoundly architectural, in that he understood the importance of spatial sequences and the relationship between human action and built setting, in addition to the decorations, ambience and patterns beloved of eighteenth-century picturesque "Gothick" and produced superbly by himself. His eventual defense of thirteenth-century Gothic, because of its purity, integrity, and structural logic, has earned him a place of grudging respect in modernist architectural theory, where, from the Bauhaus through the early development of postmodern historicism, Gothic revival has a peculiarly protected place because of its apparent structural clarity. Moreover, despite his own intemperate polemics, his sophisticated understanding of the importance of a coherent building program and his taxonomy of building types within Gothic was responsible partly for his enormous practical impact.

Pugin had defined the Gothic as the expression of a traditional society and culture and religion. In most respects, he shared the autocratic values of the previous generation of Gothic revival architects. It would be much later when Morris would claim the medieval style as appropriate to a radically egalitarian social vision, teasing out the left assumptions of Carlyle's and Ruskin's simultaneously radical and conservative positions. In France, the picture was somewhat different. If Pugin in the 1830s could rely on and reprint tracts by Montalbert (who, a supporter of Pugin, was nevertheless more liberal in his social views) on the decay of French Gothic monuments, and the importance of a renewed Catholicism, by the 1850s, Eugène-Emmanuel Viollet-le-Duc and Jean-Baptiste Lassus could justify their renovations of Gothic monuments by identifying the mid-thirteenth century with the glory both of cathedrals and the free cities they were built in, loosening French society from the tyranny of feudalism.

Lassus and Viollet-le-Duc offered a Gothic marked by sophisticated structural and mathematical logic. It is an interpretation of Gothic that has had a strong hold even to the present day, and reaches its intellectual conclusion in Panofsky's *Gothic Architecture and Scholasticism*. But it should be noted that the emphasis on intentionality and intellectual sophistication is at least partly a result of a reaction to the famous dismissal of the Gothic in Quatremère de Quincy's *Dictionnaire Méthodique d'Architecture* (1832), which considered Gothic architecture as the prduct of a decaying social order, akin to structures produced by animals acting through instincts, such as "the architecture of certain animals, notably beavers."[64]

The French Gothic revival therefore had a substantially different social context from the religiously based English Gothic revival. Instead of regarding the Middle Ages as an alternative to scientism, industrial process and untrammeled capitalism, Viollet-le-Duc and his circle pointed to the Middle Ages and its supposed building techniques and respect for the workman as the source of the liberal, scientific French spirit. Viollet-le-Duc took the enlightenment critique of the Gothic and stood it on its head. If in France, the debates were framed around the question of Gothic as an indigenous French style and classicism as an import, German architecture after the 1830s took yet another turn toward revival styles. Under Schinkel, German architecture aimed at a synthesis (quite different from the eclecticism urged by some French opponents of Gothic purism) of neoclassical and Gothic motifs and techniques.[65]

For the mid-nineteenth century, however, it was John Ruskin's (1819–1900) interpretation that became the perspective through which the Gothic was seen. Paradoxically, Ruskin's understanding of Gothic was no more fully articulated than in *The Stones of Venice*. But Venice was by no means a "pure" example, to Ruskin's frequent frustration and even horror. Historically open to the East, Venetian Gothic incorporated aspects of Islamic design, partly through conquest, partly through imitation and borrowing, and partly through the requirements of site, which encouraged the employment of screened walls and planes. For Ruskin (as often in other histories of medieval culture, as in Chambers' *Mediaeval Stage*) geologic rather than biological (and therefore ethnographic) metaphors are employed to describe architectural synthesis:

> The lava stream of the Arab, even after it ceased to flow, warmed the whole of the Northern air, and the history of Gothic architecture is the history of the refinement and spiritualization of Northern work under its influence.[66]

If Ruskin had shown some sympathy for Islamic influence in *The Stones of Venice*, by the 1850s his attitude had changed, and Islamic design is lumped together with other abstracting tendencies. Where Islamic designs could be accorded some value and influence when incorporated into Gothic by the early Ruskin, the later Ruskin begins to polarize Gothic and Islamic design.[67] This is especially true in his discussion of ornament:

> All ornamentation of that lower kind is pre-eminently the gift of cruel persons, of Indians, Saracens, Byzantines, and it is the delight of the worst and cruellist nations, Moorish, Indian, Chinese, South Sea Islanders and so on.[68]

Here the geographical determinism of the early Ruskin, with his allowance for the powers of syncretism, is refigured as a polarized racism.

It is now axiomatic to read Ruskin's interpretation of a virtuous medieval Venice transforming into a fallen Renaissance as autobiographical. Ruskin moved to Venice shortly after his marriage and famously delayed consummation until he could finish his book, since children would presumably have been a hindrance to its completion. Perhaps the most elegant account of Ruskin's projection of his personal horror onto Venice itself is in Richard Ellman's *Golden Codgers: Biographical Speculations*, which suggests further that Ruskin and his marriage serve as a source for John the Baptist in Wilde's *Salome*.[69] Ellman even suggests that Ruskin apparently arbitrarily dated the fall of a virtuous Republic, against most historical authority, to exactly 400 years before his own conception. Ruskin's letters defend Effie's chastity even while describing her late-night partying, her flirtatiousness and her general love of pleasure. It is Renaissance Venice that bears the brunt of Ruskin's anger, portrayed as the Whore of Babylon, corrupting the medieval purity and honesty of her own former self. What is of interest for our purposes is the place of oriental influence in Ruskin's scheme, whatever his projection onto them. For the Oriental becomes part of a pattern of betrayal, decadence and treachery, explicitly so in his newly racialized writings of the 1850s and 1860s, whereas in his earlier writings the relationship between medieval architecture and its Eastern interlocutors is represented as productive and creative.

Byzantine architecture represented a special problem for Victorian interpreters, partly because it was a Christian architecture with a claim to great antiquity. This antiquity, often used to celebrate other styles, was used against it. "Byzantine" was hypostatized into its current connotations— complex, vaguely incomprehensible, timeless and unchanging. It was, that is, "Oriental" in the terms employed by nineteenth-century conceptions of civilizations (even employed by Marx and Engels in their vexed definition of "Oriental despotism.") Through the mid-nineteenth century, Byzantine architecture was described as a gradual and changeless decline from the high water mark of the Hagia Sophia. The Gothic, in contrast, was found to be capable of infinite variety, development, and change.[70]

Ruskin's interpretation of Byzantine architecture, famous for his description of St. Mark's, still read by visitors today, is so well known as to hardly require extended summary. His interest in its syncretic sources, resulting in solutions to material, site, and design, is free of the racialism of his later writings from the 1850s and 1860s and is marked by his attention to formal and structural details. Byzantine architecture was inseparable from a certain development of Gothic, according to Ruskin, reflecting the latter's ability to adapt to circumstance and place. By the later part of the century, Ruskin's reading of the Byzantine, particularly its use of materials and recycling of them into highly encrusted surfaces, would be influential, especially on the Arts and Crafts architects and designers.

Partly as a result of ceaseless lobbying by the Camden Society, but also as a result of the identification of the Gothic with Englishness by both colonizer and colonized, the Gothic spread in various permutations, many of them anathema to *The Ecclesiologist* and its successors, throughout the Empire. According to Biddick (36), the crisis in "originality" that followed can be traced to repercussions such as William Morris' refusal to sell his work to ecclesiastical Gothic revival projects, because of the consequent lack of originality. Biddick reads Morris' reaction as a sort of "panic" in the face of the "queerness" of Gothic ornament, or at least Gothic revival ornament. For Morris, according to Biddick, authenticity requires the hand of

the medieval workman. Interestingly, for our purposes, she cites Morris'
1881 Lecture to the Workingman's College, almost subliminally repeating
the analogy of the medieval to the contemporary Eastern peasant: "I am
most sure that all the heaped up knowledge of modern science, all the
energy of modern commerce, all the depth and spirituality of modern
thought, cannot reproduce so much the handiwork of an ignorant, super-
stitious, Berkshire peasant of the fourteenth century, nay of a wandering
Kurdish shepherd, of a skin-and-bone Indian ryot."

Ruskin is not only influential in his conception of the medieval past, but
revealing in the tropes and analogies he uses to defend that past. His essay,
The Opening of the Crystal Palace is occasioned not by the Great Exhibition
of 1851, but by the move of the Crystal Palace to Sydenham, where it
remained until its destruction by fire in 1936.[71] The Crystal Palace is only
an excuse, however, for Ruskin to segue from his distress at its many
imitations of works of art to the state of Gothic monuments in general,
especially in France, where massive reconstructions were underway. Ruskin
objects to the detailed reconstruction of churches and other buildings.
Although admiring the craftsmanship and enterprise put into such projects
as Chartres and Rouen and other sites, he criticizes their urge towards
completeness and a misguided sense of accuracy. Ruskin expresses a preference for the earlier ruined state of these structures. Ruskin's reaction is
not a call for the picturesque. Rather, consistent with his overall aesthetic,
he prefers the honesty of half-ruined structures, which at least suggest the
experience of their builders and earlier inhabitants rather than a more
modern idea of what the Gothic was. For Ruskin, authenticity remains an
essential category, and he prefers partial and fragmentary evidence of the
authentic over the most careful reconstructive surgery that seeks to "scien-
tifically" replicate the past. There are passages in the essay that read like
reverse writings of Benjamin and Baudrillard, who accept as inescapable
what Ruskin perceives as a morally dangerous slippery slope of simulacra.

Ruskin contrasts the few monuments of Gothic that are being restored
with other ancient remains. In so doing, he recalls the language of visceral
repulsion that we discovered earlier in the discourse of Gothic monstrosity: "Despised! and more than despised—even hated! It is a sad truth that
there is something in the solemn aspect of ancient architecture which, in
rebuking frivolity and chastening gaiety, has become at this time literally
repulsive to a large majority of the population of Europe" (*Opening*, 10).
Perhaps unintentionally, by facing off sobriety against pleasure, Ruskin
figures Gothic as Puritan witness, against the excessive pleasure of
"Restoration." It is one step in the Protestantization of Gothic over the
course of the nineteenth century, very different from Pugin's understanding
of the Gothic as Catholic revelation. The almost visceral sense of repulsion

suggests a somatic power to the Gothic, a nakedness that overrestoration is attempting to disguise.

Interestingly, Ruskin goes on to critique urban development, with its emphasis on recreation, consumerism and ostentation in ways that mirror our own anxieties about gentrification and "Disneyfication":

> the real, earnest effort of the upper classes of European society is to make every place in the world as much like the Champs Elysées of Paris as possible. . .vast hotels, like barracks, and rows of high, square-windowed dwelling-houses, thrust themselves forward to conceal the hated antiquities of the great cities of France and Italy. Gay promenades, with fountains and statues, prolong themselves along the quays once dedicated to the commerce. . .And when the formal street, in all its pride of perfumery and confectionery, has successfully consumed its way through the wrecks of historical monuments. . .the whitened city is praised for its splendour.[72]

Ruskin can hardly resist sexualizing his imagery, so that the honest and naked Gothic is contrasted to a fallen painted, perfumed, and sweetened present.

The incomplete Gothic monument is described not only as naked and honest and vulnerable, but also as hidden from view as the poor. If it were rendered more visible, it would shame us into rescue:

> If, suddenly, in the midst of the enjoyments of the palate and the lightnesses of the heart of a London dinner-party, the walls of the chamber were parted, and through their gap, the nearest human beings who were famishing, and in misery, were borne into the midst of the company—feasting and fancy free—if, pale with sickness, horrible in destitution, broken by despair, body by body, they were laid upon the soft carpet, one beside the chair of every guest, would only the crumbs of the dainties be cast to them—would only a passing glance, a passing thought be vouchsafed to them?[73]

Yet again the Gothic is represented as the suppressed and repressed, but also as akin to "bodies," starving and sick. Here Ruskin's sympathy is with the wasting body of the Gothic, so that the terms of repulsion are reversed from earlier representations of the Gothic as inhuman. The consistency of Ruskin's aesthetics and politics allows him this arresting image, and, again, predicts, or rather, establishes the lineage of some modern urbanist critiques.

The relationship between nineteenth-century male subjectivity and romance, and the consequences of this relationship was not limited to Ruskin's private life or aesthetics. The White Man's Burden, the responsibilities and travails of Empire, as well as the frequent military setbacks in maintaining that Empire, found a natural narrative in the pure, suffering

Grail knight, and from mid-century on, the Grail, purged of its Catholic associations, becomes increasingly popular as a model for military and civil behavior in the colonies. Where the Grail quest may originally have been promulgated (as some of its nineteenth-century commentators noted, as an anti-chivalric and clerical response to Arthurian legend, and where its adventures pointedly take place in Western Europe, internalizing the failure of the Crusades, Grail and Crusade are now conjoined in a powerful model for the isolated Englishman (and frequently Frenchman) in the East. As Barczewski argues, "The grail quest thus was able to represent the dual nature of late-nineteenth-century British imperial culture, which combined a self-confident exterior with an extremely uncertain interior."[74] It is a model that will retain its ideological force, as well as its role in constituting subjectivity and memory, through World War I, as Allen Frantzen has shown.[75]

T.E. Lawrence's *Seven Pillars of Wisdom*, and, indeed, Lawrence's persona constructed by the publicity machine that invented him as a romantic cinema hero even before David Lean's authoritative motion picture, has until recently imprinted itself on the modern Anglo-American imagination as an epic attempt of the West to lead the East to its own destiny.[76] Once represented as a tragic failure by Lawrence himself, in a narrative that tells of his own sacrifices and that of the legions he organizes as co-opted and betrayed by French and British imperial grand plans (a narrative that is repeated in Lean's cinematic biography), Lawrence has been reduced to the almost anonymous human scale he himself seems to have sought in his later years as a private airman with a changed name. Irving Howe's important essay read him as part and parcel of a typically twentieth-century failed heroism, which can only achieve something close to heroism in failure.[77] John Mack's extraordinary biography attempted to demonstrate that Lawrence's sexual secret life and his illegitimate family, facts often employed to denigrate his political ideals, rendered him both agent and subject of larger political forces and inner motivations.[78] Arab responses to Lawrence's account have emphasized the relative independence of the Arab legions and the relatively minor role Lawrence himself played in the cause of pan-Arab unity; other critiques, both Arab and Western, have argued that he was little more than a Conradian double agent, almost entirely subservient to his role as a British agent. Said's *Orientalism*, for instance, contrasts Lawrence's apparent sympathy for the Arab cause with Sir Richard Burton's more profound immersion in Islam, and regards Lawrence as typical of the agent in the field serving the interests of British foreign policy while indulging in a fantasy of private exploration. Only recently has it been acknowledged how fully late Victorian medievalism shaped Lawrence's perspective and ideals, though his expertise as an archaeologist of Crusader castles, the basis for his intimate knowledge of the landscape and language of the greater Arab lands, was always well known. In *The Medievalism of Lawrence of Arabia*, M.D. Allen traces the echoes of Lawrence's medieval reading, from epic and romances through ascetic hagiography, in his public and private writings.[79] In a postscript, Allen aligns his conclusions with Said's paradigm of an imagined East, constructed as much through previously read texts as through observation. There is, I would add, a performative dimension to late Victorian medievalism, one that impelled its practitioners to live in a recreated Middle Ages, from the staged tournaments of the Young Englanders movement to the utopian retreats of Morris. Combining Muscular Christianity with an imitation of the ascetic Grail knight, especially in the wake of pre-Raphaelitism, the homoeroticized mysticism of a certain model of masculinity could still inform intellectual combatants in the Great War, as it did Lawrence. From this perspective, the East was always already the Middle Ages, or at least the site of the great medieval clash of East and West in the crusades, which hopefully could now be rewritten as a chivalric synthesis rather than ambiguous disaster, a hope which was to be disappointed yet again.

Almost as if in emulation of the form of its subject, the history of the study of medieval literature takes the shape of a grand struggle between myth and history. This struggle is quite literal. The most powerful agendas of the past quarter century have claimed to a more specific historical location, as opposed to sentimental illusions about the Middle Ages. But from the very beginnings of the systematic study of medieval literature, it has been justified as either historical artifact or generative myth, and in the earliest scholarship seems to have been both. Indeed, the earliest claims to the study of medieval literature as literature celebrated precisely what we would now identify as mythic status. As we have seen, the discovery, indeed, the invention of the idea of romance was one with the invention of the idea of medieval literature, even the idea of the medieval, and perhaps with an idea of literature itself that now shows signs of strain.

The understanding of romance as myth in the twentieth century is firmly rooted in some of the canonical texts of high modernism, the most notorious being T.S. Eliot's footnotes to *From Ritual to Romance* in *The Waste Land*, and, in fact, *The Waste Land* itself. The association between Orientalism and medievalism that was forged in Romanticism would carry on through the modernist revolution. In Eliot, Pound, and Yeats, oriental and medieval themes continue to run parallel, and in the *Cantos* and especially *The Waste Land*, they merge as a reproach to the present. Eliot's poem is famously based on anthropological interpretations of the Grail legends, but its last words are in Sanskrit, and, like many nineteenth-century intellectuals, Eliot and Pound both took the study of Sanskrit to be as much as part of education as the study of Greek and Latin. In Pound, Chinese and Provencal form part of the lost languages of poetry he seeks to reintroduce into English. The theory of spatial form in modern literature may be related to this fascination with the Middle Ages and the Orient in modernism. Joseph Frank long ago coined the concept of "Spatial Form in Modern Literature" to describe the retreat into myth as an escape from history on the part of the modernists.[80] Their formal inversion of spatial and temporal limits, emphasizing the spatial rather than the "naturally" temporal dimension of language, created a timeless retreat from the complexity and turmoil of a present they found socially and aesthetically intolerable. One aspect of this spatialization might be seen to be the invocation of past ages and places, the Middle Ages and the Orient (though actually medievalism and Orientalism) to critique and perhaps even to rejuvenate and order an enervated and chaotic modern world.

This approach to romance was born in the "Cambridge School" interpretation of Greek drama, which flourished in the early twentieth century, as displaced ritual, and fostered by the enormous influence of Frazer's *The Golden Bough*.[81] Partly anthropological, partly ritualizing, the project is carried out in greatest detail by R.S. Loomis and his collaborators, working chiefly on Arthurian materials. Loomis's importance for our schema here is that he manages to express the romantic and neo-romantic reverie about the genre with the scholarly apparatus of professional medievalism. "To think of Medieval Romance is to gaze through magic casements opening on the foam of perilous seas in faery lands forlorn," his first book, a source study, opens.[82]

Loomis's importance partly derived from his energy and unprecedented thoroughness in tracing as many possible conceivable details of Arthurian romance back to Celtic myth.[83] Where the pursuit was carried out by previous scholars, most of them were much more heavily indebted to ritualistic and seasonal explanations. Loomis rendered the possible chain of associations a matter of precedent and source rather than forgotten associations. In so doing, he subsumed the sometimes free associations of previous scholars to the rigors of philology and literary history. Indeed, in Loomis' schemes, Celtic myth itself took on the trappings of a literary tradition. Interestingly, Loomis's rigor did not exclude a certain concern for the nonspecialist public's appreciation of medieval literature, and he edited translations of medieval texts, many non-Arthurian. Presumably, for Loomis the power of the literary work, romance or other, did not necessarily reside in the unique language of the text. Loomis's combination of anthropology and literary history rendered his enterprise still useful despite the withering barrages of the opponents, both of his Celticism and of his mythic priorities. Stressing the ultimately British roots of Arthuriana pitted Loomis and his followers against a French Arthurian establishment, which strove to minimize Anglo-American Arthurian studies. Loomis's obsession with sources and origins (one of the prime categories, as we have seen, of eighteenth-century romance scholarship) was itself minimized by the New Critical concern with individual texts and with the ways in which the language of literary forms such as romances is chiefly responsible for its effects.

For our purposes, in fact, the most interesting opposition develops not between Celtic and continental theories of Arthurian origins, but between one of the later formulations of myth criticism, a book by John Speirs entitled *Medieval English Poetry: The Non-Chaucerian Tradition* and C.S. Lewis (himself the author of fictional works frequently classified as "myths" or "romances.")[84] Speirs resurrected a Frazerian anthropology and rationalized it through a Leavisite concern with identifying an Englishness and a tradition. Hence, while Chaucer was associated with continental and self-consciously literary creation, other Middle English works, argued Speirs, continued a folk tradition of pre-Christian myth. Works like *Sir Gawain and the Green Knight* are powerful because they embody such vegetative myths as the struggle of Winter and Spring. Speirs argued that such mythic images lay behind the language of the text, and the power we feel is the power of the myth. The work of Loomis and others was important, said Speirs, but it was not "literary criticism." C.S. Lewis could hardly have cared to defend Loomis; indeed, he begins his essay with a critique of Loomis. He was probably more concerned with Speirs's allegiance to F.R. Leavis and to his paganization of medieval literature. Lewis attacks Speirs' substitution of ritual origins for specific literary effects. Yet, interestingly, Lewis' attack was not based on the importance of literary language in the New Critical mode (for this was Speirs' rather ill-fitting armor), but on the generic nature of romance as a specific type of literary work created by authors and read by readers who responded directly, rather than indirectly, to the power of the narrative:

> The romancers create a world where everything may, and most things do, have a deeper meaning and a longer history than the errant knight would have expected; a world of endless forest, quest, hint, prophecy. Almost every male stranger wears armor; not only that there may be jousts but because visors hide faces. Any lady may prove a fay or devil; every castle may conceal a holy or unholy mystery. . .Until our own age readers accepted this world as the romancers' "noble and joyous" invention. . .It was invented by and for men who felt the real world, in its rather different way, to be also cryptic, significant, full of voices and "the mystery of all life." There has now arisen a type of reader who cannot thus accept it.[85]

Lewis' description is quite lovely, but it disguises a complex circularity. Ostensibly defending the literariness of romance, Lewis in fact implies that the modern reader (with Speirs as his exemplar) cannot respond to a lost belief system, and therefore must invent an extreme referent to explain what is already there and obvious. But what Lewis sees as there is precisely the highly mythologized world of romance. What Lewis objects to is that Speirs must remythologize the already magical. In the case of the study of medieval romance, the debate engages not history against myth, but myth against myth.

Such debates were nevertheless overshadowed by the politicization of mythic, ritual, and folkloric approaches in the 1920s and 1930s. Folklore studies always had close ties to both left and right populism, and sometimes Frazerian anthropology found itself allied with Social Darwinist and racialist impulses in the early part of the twentieth century. Nazi rhetoric and official scholarship then appropriated ritual and mythic discourse to the extent that its liberal adherents were forced into defensive moves. For the editorial circle around the French journal *Annales*, for instance, the question arose as to how or whether to continue the publication of its research into popular culture, which might then be seen to be an act of collaboration.[86] More generally, the resurgence of interest in myth and anthropological interpretation in the post–World War II period was tied to a sanitization of the entire enterprise, freeing myth and ritual criticism from its heavily politicized context.

The single most influential statement on the nature of romance in the twentieth century has undoubtedly been Northrop Frye's *Anatomy of Criticism*, which allowed romance to overcome its status as secondary to the novel and to realism:

> The romance is nearest of all literary forms to the wish-fulfillment dream, and for that reason it has socially a curiously paradoxical role. In every age the ruling social or intellectual class tends to projects its ideals in some form of romance, where the virtuous heroes and beautiful heroines represent the ideals and the villains the threats to their ascendancy. This is the general character of chivalric romance in the Middle Ages, aristocratic romance in the Renaissance, bourgeois romance since the eighteenth century, and revolutionary romance in contemporary Russia. Yet there is a genuinely "proletarian" element in romance too which is never satisfied with its various incarnations, and in fact the incarnations themselves indicate that no matter how great a change may take place in society, romance will turn up again, as hungry as ever, looking for new hopes and desires to feed on. The perennially childlike quality of romance is marked by its extraordinarily persistent nostalgia, its search for some kind of imaginative golden age in time or space. There has never to my knowledge been any period of Gothic English literature, but the list of Gothic revivalists stretches completely across its entire history, from the Beowulf to the writers of our own day.[87]

No one could accuse Frye of either lack of sophistication or of naivete. Yet the picture of romance he paints here reinforces a certain sense of the Middle Ages as naive. Frye's brilliant essay, which might have promised a freedom to regard Middle English romance on its own terms, ends up by establishing as self-conscious method the celebration of mode over any particular exemplar of that mode. While it may be argued that genre criticism always assumes such prioritization, Frye seems as much concerned with defining an ur-romance, or super-romance, of which all expressions are copies. In his later, more biblically oriented work, this agenda is made explicit. While aware of and critical of the fallacy of Gothic revivalism, with its nostalgia for an ur-form that existed only in the work recalling it, Frye finally constructs a formal parallel to precisely such a fallacy. He recognizes at the outset the social component of romance (in terms almost certainly influenced by William Empson), but almost immediately, within a sentence or two, shifts to the perennial idealism of romance.[88] Frye's own work mimics the form of romance, moving from adventure to adventure without worrying about the precise relations of these adventures.

In one sense at least, Northrop Frye's celebration of myth in *Anatomy of Criticism* involves liberating ritual and mythic criticism from its political and historical associations. And he succeeds in doing so partly by relying on the traditional affiliation of myth and romance. Frye's defense of romance as a significant mode (a move reflected in the influential work on the novel during these years by such scholars as Richard Chase and Leslie Fiedler) makes myth criticism free for liberal humanism. Romance (along with myth) becomes one of the dominant critical categories of the 1950s and early 1960s, precisely at the moment when North American political and social thought, with awkward timing, announces the end of ideology.

The effort of the past few years has been to remedievalize medieval romances. In so doing, its agenda is also to replace a static and romanticized conception of the medieval past with one more complex and striated. Such an effort involves the demythologization, even the deromanticization of romance. A demythologized, radically historicized version of medieval romance is clearly outlined in some influential recent books. This common agenda connects, for example, the extreme historicization of Susan Crane's *Insular Romance* and the high structuralism of Susan Wittig's *Stylistic and Narrative Structures in Middle English Romances*.[89] Crane places the Middle English romances securely within a very specific English cultural and political setting. Wittig similarly treats the apparently conventional patterns of the Middle English romances as part of a particular cultural code. Neither seeks to defend the romances as transcendent literary forms. Rather than seeking to make a case for romances as high literature, or to claim a hegemonic role for romance (as C.S. Lewis and Northrop Frye respectively might be said to have attempted), the newly historicized versions of medieval romance are, perhaps more implicitly than explicitly, part of a larger deconstructive agenda.

"Even if," writes Crane in *Insular Romance*, "the ways in which literature and history overlap and interact are elusive, even if the past is only imperfectly accessible to us, the effort to reconnect literature to history is vital for those who believe that literary texts are social communications that played a part in the lives of their first audiences."[90] In *Negotiating the Past*, which devotes three of four chapters on single texts to romances, Lee Patterson articulates a sophisticated critique of "why the historicism of the medievalist should so sharply differ from that of critics working in later periods," and asks for an awareness to the historicity of our interpretative modes as well as to the historicity of texts.[91]

Literary scholars specializing in areas outside the medieval period might be puzzled by this self-criticism, since medieval studies seem impregnably, even militantly, historical in nature. Indeed, this is precisely Patterson's point. At the same time, however, the historical defensiveness of both avant-garde and traditional medievalists is in reaction to another underlying assumption, one that the lay reader, the student, even the above-mentioned literary scholar from another field, might hold, which is that what is most powerfully attractive about medieval literature is something that escapes, even precedes, history. The historicizing anxiety of the modern medievalist derives from a sometimes unspoken concern about the reductive dangers of a naive response or an assumption of naivete, a reductiveness that would render medieval literature below and beyond the apparatus of systematic study.

It becomes increasingly difficult to speak of a unified "Middle Ages," or even a "later Middle Ages," with its Hegelian, and largely Burckhardtian echoes. The historiographic innovations of the study of early Modern Europe have suggested as many continuities as discontinuities between what we have thought of as medieval and Renaissance centuries. The influence of Annales historiography has emphasized gradual rather than abrupt change, and abrupt change itself is now understood as the result of long-standing cultural and social undercurrents. However, these conceptual transformations are common to many forms of cultural and social history. In literary history, however, even in the history of literary criticism, medieval romance has a special place. The canonization of medieval romance, coincidental with the earliest stirrings of romanticism, is inseparable from the critical agenda of romanticism: the establishment of national literary histories, the self-representation of the romantic poet as the hero of the quest-romance, the valorization of "primitive" epochs over classical and neoclassical periods. The late romantic aesthetic itself, with its celebration of the fragmentary, the supernatural and the transcendental, declared its version of medieval romance as one of its chief sources. To the arguable degree that modernism itself is an extension of romanticism, our very idea of literariness grows out of the appreciation of romance.[92] The conception of the literary work as possessing an irreducible aura, as being a fundamentally different kind of discourse than other writing, is one central to the romantic-modernist tradition, and it has evolved in no small part from the sense of medieval romance as enchanted other. There are, of course, other strains in modernism than its romantic origins, and there are other traditions for the inspired nature of the poetic, but the vehicle for the formulation of these into a coherent aesthetic was medieval romance.

The disenchantment of romance current in modern criticism of medieval romance, then, has wider repercussions than a more comprehensive understanding of its historical context and its relation to other medieval writings. It may be seen as part of a larger questioning of the idea of the literary, a skepticism as to whether literary discourse does differ in important fundamental ways from other sorts of discourse. The evidence of the preponderance of medieval writings, frequently found together with romances, would seem to suggest that in the Middle Ages, such a distinction was either not made or had not yet been fully formulated. In one sense, we find ourselves returning to the idea of the preliterary. In another sense, of course, recent cultural studies in fact valorize literary discourse, insisting on the textuality, hidden narrativity and allusive connotation of all discourse, perhaps even of all events. Such an imperial claim for the literary, even if in the name of historicity, resembles the impulse, however inversely expressed, that initially defined medieval romance as myth.

At the same time, the retheorization of the grotesque in medieval literature, enabled by the work of and the reception of M.M. Bakhtin since his translation into English in the late 1960s, has almost literally moved certain aspects of medieval literature and culture from the margins to the center of the canon and the theoretical debates about that canon.[93] The powerful metaphor of the medieval grotesque in scholarship, which understands medieval literature as the monstrous and barbaric, itself has as a result acquired a new and even reminted currency. What the revision of the grotesque in Bakhtin allows is the celebration of that monstrosity as essential, in a literary-historical analogy to what Tolkien accomplished for *Beowulf* in his famous essay. At the same time, this celebration has not been without its problems, and among these problems is the reification of assumptions that have haunted, and perhaps limited, the study of medieval literature since its liberation, even its invention, by Romantic scholarship. These contradictions are revealed, I believe, in the intertwined histories of the reception of medieval literature on the one hand, and medieval architecture on the other that I have outlined above, but they resurface in a somewhat different way in Bakhtin.

The parallelism I have traced is different from the dichotomy usually associated with the grotesque as a category. In Kayser's standard study, for instance, the grotesque is paired with and opposed to the sublime.[94] The grotesque becomes the opposite number, the defining negative, of the transcendentally exalted. Such a polarity is the traditional polarity of Romanticism crudely defined, and of the Romantic interpretation of the medieval, the fascination, for instance, with the gargoyle as the necessary complement to the aspiration of the cathedral. Kayser provides us with a mildly helpful etymology of the term grotesque, from its technical use as a painted border and architectural decoration embellishing, disguising, or imitating structural members, but marked by a confusion of animate and non-animate images, to its application as a literary term, a transfer he first locates in Montaigne.

It is, of course, Kayser's conception of the Grotesque that Bakhtin takes aim at in *Rabelais and His World*, and Bakhtin's reformulation of the grotesque is so familiar to us now that we have all but forgotten Kayser's, which is why I could, for instance, trace the history of the "monstruosi e barbari" as I have. I have already said as much as I have to say about the usefulness of Bakhtin for interpreting medieval literature, and I want to focus here on another, related topic, that has sometimes confused this first topic.[95] This second topic is the Middle Ages in Bakhtin, and it will disturb those who ask for absolute consistency between intention and result that while I have argued that Bakhtin's ideas can be enormously useful for the understanding of medieval texts, I argue here that the image of the Middle Ages in Bakhtin is often paradoxical and even confused. That confusion is at once historical, cultural, and geographic. For one thing, the Middle Ages of Eastern Europe is a different Middle Ages from that of Western or even Central Europe, a point I shall return to shortly. For another, Bakhtin's grotesque, and his "Middle Ages," intervenes in the long history of spurious associations I have traced above. His own definition of the medieval was not meant to be historically accurate; instead, it was meant to be itself carnivalesque and dialogic, responding to and parodying definitions that had attempted to repress the anarchic energies he admired.

Bakhtin's Middle Ages is located not in time but in space. That space is defined by architectural, or more accurately, urban form, as the marketplace and the square, the space defined outside of built structures. The processes of Bakhtin's ideal space is much like his notion of language—it is created between fixed points of origin and intention, and is changed by what happens in that space between. The agent for that performance or enactment is not only language, it is language embodied. Gestures and embodiment become essential to his sense of language. The body, that is, becomes a kind of anti-architecture, disturbing and challenging what the buildings surrounding the square stand for. And Bakhtin's body, by definition, is the grotesque body, the body Horace warned us against. And this body, with its permeability and renewal on the one hand and its insistent bullying and outrageousness on the other, disturbs easy categories as to gender and desire, which are defined almost organically, on the level of the pre-social.

The feel of Bakhtin's towns and village squares, moreover, has a curiously unreal quality. His medieval town is like no medieval town one finds in historical records or in actual existence. Bakhtin's version of the Middle Ages is in many ways an imaginary carnivalization of cultural geography. This cultural geography, which Bakhtin describes in terms of class, has a quite different valence in the Bakhtin before *Rabelais and His World*.[96] In his earlier writings, Bakhtin had defined the metropolitan and the cosmopolitan in terms of the Alexandrian settings he mischievously celebrated as mixing East and West, language, race, and culture. While we may find this Bakhtinian multiculturalism appealling, I suspect that in terms of its original presentation it had a specifically political cast, opposed to the pan-Slavic xenophobia that was prevalent not only in noncultural circles, but even in sectors of the pre and post revolutionary avante-garde, where strains of a pure Slavic medievalism could be found lyricized. That is, although Bakhtin talks about the town and village market as his site for cultural performance, the fact of the matter is that that site is only created through the performance, and through the critical mass of periodic assembly, such as the festival or fair. And when that happens the town and village is transformed into something else, something resembling the Hellenistic city. In nineteenth century anthropological terms, terms even Marx and Engels used, what Bakhtin gives us is the Middle Ages as Asiatic capitol.

The end of the nineteenth century, which is to say the height of the great colonial empires of the Western European states, complicated the perspective on national folk customs. (Interestingly, in France, medieval studies was institutionalized almost immediately as a national defense program in the late nineteenth century, and when it did, the antiquarian and folkloric underpinnings of British medievalism were entirely absent, and a more formalist and historicising agenda was developed.) If an anthropological perspective was necessary to comprehend the exotic otherness of the fruits of empire, this perspective could not help but be turned on the strangeness of even local and indigenous customs of the colonizers themselves. In fact, such a process had informed, in a much less methodologically consistent way, the antiquarianism of the eighteenth century, which was inseparably linked in its sensibility with the fascination with oriental exoticism and the wonders of the primitive world—indeed, a case could be made that Percy, Hurd, and Warton invented a Middle Ages that was both a national past and a strangely exotic alterity.

But there is also a specifically East European and Russian context for Bakhtin's ideas. For in the late nineteenth century, while a certain stratum of the gentry could imitate the neo-Romantic medievalism found in the "Gothicizing" of German, French, and English fashion, the fact of the matter was that reviving medievalism was not a high priority for an intelligentsia who saw a feudal culture all around them, and for whom the very Enlightenment that Romantic medievalism reacted against was an incomplete and urgent agenda. In late nineteenth century Russia, aesthetic medievalism took the form of identity with the Orthodox Church (and sometimes its simultaneously mystical and progressive wings) on the one hand, and Slavic folklorism on the other, with its conservative populist urges.

The plague of Russian self-image has always been its sense of incomplete modernization, a sense that has driven its cultural and political programs from Peter the Great through Gorbachev. Yet in a sense incomplete modernization is the experience of modernity—the obvious contrast between the present and the past embodied in the physical landscape—telegraph poles and railroad lines running along the feudal countryside. Bakhtin's carnival in fact celebrates this paradox by deconstructing it: the order that modernization requires is constantly subverted by the once and future premodernity of carnival. As in Morris' *News from Nowhere*, the Middle Ages is the Future. But Bakhtin ironizes this utopian idealism by stressing the virtual impossibility of complete modernization. Carnival is from one point of view the repressed past and revolutionary future within the medieval, but from another point of view, when it is no longer situated within a discussion of the medieval, Carnival becomes the medieval in the modern. In its own way, the Bakhtinian grotesque continues the long tradition of constructing the medieval as a critique of modernization.

The most compelling description of "the experience of modernity" is Marshall Berman's *All That Is Solid Melts Into Air: The Experience of Modernity*.[97] For Berman (as for Marx from whom the title is borrowed) the constant transformation occasioned by urbanism, industrial society, and capitalist economy is the primary modality by which modernity is experienced or defined. Yet it is almost impossible to separate such a stance from a certain nostalgia for a communal life, an imagined *gemeinschaft* that is so often represented as medieval. C.S. Lewis could, after all, argue for a distinction between the medieval and modern worlds with the advent of the industrial revolution and its concomitant "assumption that everything is provisional and soon to be superseded."[98] In so many formulations, both radicalizing and traditionalizing, the apparent timelessness of the Middle Ages is opposed to the constant change of modernity.

Bakhtin's Middle Ages also might be regarded within the framework of Russian and specifically Soviet academic medieval studies. Official Soviet interpretations of what is called the "feudal" period, since the 1930s, had stressed economic to the exclusion of social history, with emphasis on the condition of the peasantry as its litmus test.[99] But as with constructivist architecture and supremacist art, formalist literary criticism and avant-garde performance and poetry, the period just before and just after the Revolution witnessed innovations in historical method that predicted later developments elsewhere. A number of scholars were working on approaches that anticipated the agenda of *Annales* and the attempt to define *mentalite* that followed as part of that agenda. From the 1930s to the 1960s it was virtually impossible to develop those approaches, but the Khrushchev thaw (Khrushchev's public persona is itself so Carnivalesque that one wonders whether the Rabelais book contains a portrait of sorts) allowed a number of latent approaches to flower. The Tartu school of semiotics also began to articulate itself. Although the Tartu semioticians have differences with Bakhtin and the apparent orthodoxy of some of his writings on linguistics—if all of these are in fact by Bakhtin—they nevertheless carried on this earlier, discontinuous exploration. The Russian medievalist best known in the West, the historian Aron Gurevich, shared some of their concerns, and some of Bakhtin's, though Gurevich's conception of medieval popular culture is significantly less oppositional than Bakhtin's.[100] In the original and in translation, Bakhtin's "unofficial" is in fact the same as a term used to describe this heterodox scholarship. It would take an entire separate essay to clarify these strands, but it reveals Bakhtin's roots in a very common discontinuity in Soviet intellectual and academic life.

It may be that the best uses of Bakhtin may come not from direct application to literary texts, but from the consideration of his theories as they are discussed and applied in historiography, anthropology, and colonial and postcolonial studies, precisely the fields—as they existed in earlier transformations—that he drew his inspirations from. But it may also be that the analysis I have offered here clarifies in some way the peculiar limitations and uses of Bakhtin's Middle Ages. It is, after all, a Middle Ages constructed from a reading of an early modern text, Rabelais' *Gargantua and Pantegruel*, and while Rabelais book is a dangerously unstable point of reference, it is also, like *Don Quixote*, engaged in the discourse of medievalism rather than reflecting the Middle Ages itself. So too with Bakhtin's theoretical position and the lessons of that position. At the same time that Bakhtin's work opens up unexpected new vistas, his heavy obligation to earlier philological assumptions also reinscribes some older and unexamined assumptions, such as the association of the non-Western with the multivalent, the excessive and the incongruent, with which this chapter began.

CHAPTER TWO

THE MIDDLE AGES AS GENEALOGY, OR,
THE WHITE ORIENT

What do I see? The Briton Saxon Roman Norman amalgamating
In my Furnaces into One Nation the English: & taking refuge
In the Loins of Albion. The Canaanite united with the fugitive
Hebrew, whom she divided into Twelve, & sold into Egypt
Then scatterd the Egyptian & Hebrew to the four Winds!

—William Blake, *Jerusalem*

This chapter describes a peculiar tributary in the stream of discourse
linking the Medieval with the Oriental. With the rise of humanism,
skepticism arises about the legend of the Trojan foundation of Britain, as
recounted in Geoffrey of Monmouth. With the rise of parliamentary
debates, uneasiness about the aristocratic apology implicit in the linking of
chivalry with Trojan origins, and with Geoffrey's account of royal lineage
also grows. The result is a displacement, and sometimes an overlay, of the
legend of the Brut with older Biblical schemes that the Brut legend was
itself originally designed to replace. Yet the association between the origin
of culture and an ultimately Eastern source remains strong even in this
alternate history, even as the trappings and institutions of medieval political
thought, religion, and aesthetics were up for debate. In this new, if equally
esoteric, Early Modern version of the British past, the importance of the
Middle Ages is reduced to a medium for primal institutions and beliefs that
had been imported from elsewhere.

Theories of Oriental origins could be found in medieval writings themselves. The most notorious theories of British origins in Arthurian

romance, such as Geoffrey of Monmouth's popularization of an ultimately Trojan origin for British culture and aristocracy, conceived of medieval civilization itself as a geographic translation or overlay. The Middle Ages orientalized its own past. Oriental and African influence play a role in Geoffrey of Monmouth (ca. 1100–ca. 55), the source of much Arthurian legend and the basis for many subsequent histories of Britain, if only as corrections to his apparent inventions. In Geoffrey of Monmouth's *Historia* (VIII: 10-2), for instance, Stonehenge is transported by giants from Africa, with a stop in Ireland.[1] Its magical powers and its final assemblage by Merlin is therefore prepared by an association with an always already magical South and East. Such assertions themselves help prepare the way for a later Early Modern occult association between ancient Britain and Egyptian mysteries. Frequently in Geoffrey of Monmouth, the magical, except insofar as it is domesticated by Merlin, has its source in the Moslem South and East, especially Spain and Africa. When King Arthur fights against Rome, his cause is implicitly justified by Geoffrey by the fact that the Roman emperors are allied with fourteen or more oriental and African nobles, from such lands as Spain, Africa, Libya, Egypt, Syria, and so forth. Troy itself had a liminal status between East and West, and acquired an Oriental coloring in post-Homeric retellings. And it was from Troy that Brutus comes to settle Britain and to introduce chivalry. Conversely, the end of British influence is described by Geoffrey as a result of the conquest of the British by the Saxons, but a Saxon army reinforced by African troops. With a semidivine origin from the East, Geoffrey's Britons are defeated by an alliance of the North and the South. It is an original and quite unique schema, though in other competing accounts the place and power of the East will be even more pronounced.

Another theory of the origins of Western, and particularly British culture, also ran like a conspiracy theory through early modern thought. This was the theory that Britain was originally settled by Phoenicians, and this theory itself was buttressed by a Biblically inspired anthropology. Nennius (8th c.), the source for many of Geoffrey's geographic assertions, had earlier claimed that ancient Egyptians had settled in Ireland. This alternate theory, then, also proposed an orientalized origin for British culture, one that underlay, rather than shaped, the Middle Ages. Moreover, rather than conceiving of an Eastern origin as a contamination or hybridization of Western identity, it imagined a true European identity as in fact tracing its descent from the point of origin of human creation. As with some of the other theories of origin that are traced in this study, these theories, once the province of humanists and antiquarians, have a disturbing afterlife in recent political history.

The result of these various legends were two quite different narratives of British (or other) origins, despite the acknowledgement of the primacy of the Biblical account in the Brut narrative. A largely monastic and pessimistic sense of history, described definitively in James Dean's *The World Grown Old in Medieval Literature*, understood present human society as a declining and weakening race, worn down by time and cursed by original sin.[2] Most of the societies of the civilized world could be understood in these terms (and with the discovery of the New World, aboriginal peoples were further categorized as the remnants of cursed tribes). But another sense of history developed simultaneously, and in a sense covertly, in competition with this pessimism. From this other perspective, the missing elements in Genesis (and competing narratives in apocrypha and in Rabbinical commentary) point toward a race that exists before Adam, and that settled the world independently of the entropic and diasporic history of the Jewish people. Here the myth of Phoenician origin, linking Christianity with older forms of divine knowledge, including Hermes, Zoroaster, and the Druids, played a key role.

As Robert Hanning pointed out in *The Vision of History in Early Britain*, a book that itself served as a point of origin for a new interest in medieval historiography, origin stories have considerable political valence.[3] There are, as Hanning notes, no origin stories in Gildas or Bede, who assume a more or less orthodox descent from ecclesiastical history. With the *Historia regum Britanniæ*, however, claims are made for a connection between British and Roman genealogies, staking claims for an imperial inheritance. Different manuscripts of the *Historia regum Britanniæ* include conflicting origin stories. In MS Harleian 3859, Brutus (who is cursed with a prophecy of patricide and matricide) is expelled from Rome, founds the city of Tours, and then comes to Britain. In this version, observes Hanning, "the Britons are a new order."[4] Hanning notes another genealogy which reasserts the traditional descent of Western Europeans from Japhet, the son of Noah, a version that makes no political claims toward either distinct nationhood nor imperial destiny. Interestingly, notes Hanning, yet another genealogy, missing in some manuscripts, combines the Biblical with the Trojan–Roman versions, suggesting "the response of a conservative Christian tradition to the challenge of a new vision of history."[5]

Another variant of the pre-Trojan state of Britain is the account of the adventures of Albina and her sisters in the *Anonymous Riming Chronicle*, contained in the Auchinleck manuscript.[6] Daughters of a Grecian king, Albina and her sisters plan to murder their oppressive and purportedly low-born husbands, but the plot is leaked by the youngest sister to her husband. The sisters are set out to sea and arrive on an island that Albina names after herself. They cohabit with a devil, the offspring of which is the race of giants who inhabit Britain until the coming of Brutus. In the *Prose Brut*, the sisters become the daughters of the king of Syria, shifting their origins from a classical descent that pits them against Brutus's lineage as a recursion of the Trojan war, to a more generalized and orientalized origin.[7] The alternate origin myth proposed by the Albina legend posits both a feminized and orientalized point of origin for British history, one that is defeated and written over in the larger narrative of the Brut.

One of the most intriguing variants on the received Brut legend was in the Scot tradition, which revised an earlier brief mention in Nennius concerning the settlement of Ireland and Scotland to offer an account of the settlement of Scotland that traced its origins to ancient Egypt. The Egyptian origin of Scotland parallels the well-known legend of the Milesian settlement of Ireland. Originally from Scythia, the Milesians (named for the eventual settler of Ireland) emigrate to Egypt, where their fate is intertwined with that of Moses and where the Scythian Nial marries Scota, who is a daughter of the Pharoah also, and eventually find their way to Spain and then to Ireland. According to Hector Boece (ca. 1465–ca. 1536), friend of Erasmus and one of the founders of the University of Aberdeen, a Greek named Gathelus serves the Pharaoh's armies under Moses, and succeeds Moses as commander.[8] He marries one of the Pharaoh's daughters, Scota. Scota and Gathelus are the source of the names of the Gaels and the Scots. Escaping from the plagues, they journey along the northern coast of Africa and settle in Spain. As their colony grows, their son Hiber (hence both Hibernia and Iberia) explores and settles what is now Scotland. Part of the legend involves the marble throne that one of their descendants, Symon Brek, brings from Galicia to Scotland, which becomes the Scottish throne and afterward the Stone of Scone. Here again an ancient and Eastern origin is called upon to legitimize a Scots identity and a tradition of independent rule. In establishing a priority to a separate foundation of Scotland, Boece's account, and some of the chronicles and poems he used as sources, renarrate the standard Arthurian history with rather more sympathy for Mordred, who becomes a son of Scotland resisting an imperial Arthur. Hector Boece's alternative history of British origin resulted in a torrent of scorn concerning his veracity, but the union of the royal houses of Scotland and England incorporated both traditions into a syncretic lineage, appropriating the potentially separatist implications of the separate origin. Holinshed incorporates Boece's account into his history, where Shakespeare famously finds the story of Macbeth. As with some other medieval and Early Modern accounts of the ultimately Phoenician, Egyptian or Greek settlement of Britain, the legend has been revived in recent times to argue for a Biblical origin of British (and Anglo-American) racial identity, tracing the stone itself back to Jacob's pillow and beyond.

In fact, arguments similar to that of Boece had been put forth in an earlier debate crucial to the political history of Scotland. In response to

Boniface VIII's attempts in 1301 to broker a peace between England and Scotland, Edward I had appealed to the legend of the Brut to justify his claims. The counterargument was mounted in crucial documents prepared by Baldred Bisset, the *Instructiones* and the *Processus*. Here the account of the settlement of Scotland by the descendants of Scota and Gathelus is meant to both supplement the notoriously leaky sequencing of Geoffrey of Monmouth's history and to appeal to the antiquity and Biblical status of Egypt over and above the descent from Troy so central to the legend of the Brut. By recognizing the symbolic status of the coronation stone and removing it to Westminster Abbey in 1296, Edward inadvertently imbues its history and its place with an aura that allows it to function as an absent presence, akin to the ark.

A second important medieval precursor of Boece's anti-Brut was John of Fordun's *Chronica Gentis Scotorum*, written from the 1360s on.[9] In synthesizing previous accounts of Scottish history (legend has him travelling all over Scotland piecing together its history after Edward supposedly removed all possible documentation of an independent Scottish nation), he provided a basis for many subsequent histories, and for a long time was known only as part of Walter Bower's early-fifteenth-century *Scotichronicon*. Fordun (late 14 c.) almost certainly modelled his somewhat topographic history in response to Higden's *Polychronicon*, expanding the legend of Scotland's Egyptian origin to outweigh Higden's claim that the Brut narrative justified English dominion over Scotland.[10] As with some of the other Scottish histories, Fordun's narrative emerges from an intertextual dialogue with a prior English account, and its frequent modulations and negotiations rest uneasily next to sweeping nationalist claims. In his important discussion of Fordun's use of sources, R. James Goldstein notes that Fordun inherits several possible personalities for Gathelus, one peace-loving and the other combative, and several reasons for his exile from both Greece and from Egypt, either by choice or because of conflict. It is as if the Scottish narrative from its legendary inception was beset with contradictions that continued to play themselves out through its history. Fordun emphasizes the long-suffering and exiled Gathelus and Scota, identifying them with the Hebrews as much as with the Egyptians, appropriating the mantle of destiny claimed by the Brut legend.[11]

Tudor histories begin by largely accepting the settling of Britain according to Geoffrey of Monmouth, at least partly out of a desire to assert a new sense of nationhood. Even as late as 1592, someone like John Stowe in his *Annales of England* could repeat the legends of Brutus and Arthur as if they were historical fact.[12] Holinshed's *Chronicles*, widely known as one of Shakespeare's historical sources, opens with the familiar recital of the habitation of Britain by the sons of Japhet after the Flood, followed by the giant

Albion, who is slain by Hercules, until Brutus, aided by Gogmagog, conquers the island.[13] Yet this history becomes subject to new questions. Newly demanding standards of documentary evidence, however nascent, raise serious questions about Geoffrey's veracity. The rigorous humanist Polydore Vergil's (ca. 1470–ca. 1555) *Anglica Historia* openly derides Geoffrey's account, though spirited defenses of the Trojan and Albion myths abound.[14] More complex forces were also at work revising these myths themselves. The older Biblical chronology, tracing the settlement of the known world to the children of Noah after the Flood, over which Geoffrey imposed his own more specifically national and racial history, start to loom larger as Biblical literacy, and literalism, start to grow. More crucially, the requirement that an independent English church establish its own history and lineage lent new force to certain aspects of these competing narratives. Joseph of Arimethea's appearance in Britain is offered as evidence of a separate genealogy for English Christianity on the one hand, while a newly emerging occult history of Britain begins to imagine an archaic past in which forms of Christian belief already exist, on the other.

   The Christianization of Britain now becomes not only an issue of pride of historical place, but of the sacramental lineage of the Church of England. One of the most influential of these accounts is Bishop Bale's (1495–1563) 1553 *Vocacyon*, which cites Joseph of Arimethea's mission to Christianize Britain as evidence that "from the schole of Christe hymsel haue we receyued the documentes of oure fayth, from Jerusalem & not from Rome" (12v–14).[15] Lucius, King of the Britons, is baptized by Timothy, the follower of St. Paul, establishing a parallel and competing history with that of the Roman Catholic Church.[16] The positive Orientalism that directly connects England with the Biblical center of the world has another side. The authors of Holinshed's *Chronicles*, for instance, repeat a widely circulated medieval legend, sometimes used to emphasize Becket's independence in ignoring his heritage, that Thomas á Becket was half Syrian on his mother's side, and that, moreover, she was a Saracen.[17]

   Reacting against Polydore Vergil's dismissal of Geoffrey of Monmouth's account of the founding of Britain, Bishop Bale developed one of the earliest elaborate alternative genealogies of the history of Britain, linking Britain to the Biblical account of the founding of the peoples of the world by the sons of Noah after the Flood.[18] The key figure in his scheme is one Samothes (not mentioned in the Bible and later to be identified as a "Phoenician" in similar scenarios by others) grandson of Noah and son of Japhet. Samothes becomes the leader of the Celts on the continent and the British Isles, and gives them a legal and civic foundation. Samothes's son Magus brings the science of building to the Britons and establishes the beginnings of several cities and towns. As his name suggests, he also taught the Britons the secrets of the magic arts. Magus' son Sarron supposedly introduces philosophy to the island. The genealogical onomatopoeia continues with Bardus, who teach the Britons music and poetry and whose name is reflected in the "Bards." Meanwhile, the other side of the family of Noah begins to exert its influence. The offspring of Ham includes Isis and Osiris, who introduce agriculture to the world. Osiris travels to Britain and teaches them how to make beer. A descendant of Isis and Osiris is the giant Albion, whose name is an alternative nomenclature for Britain. He teaches the Britons how to sail. But his rule ushers in the Age of Iron, and the Britons live in misery for 500 years until the enlightened Brutus arrives from Troy. Hence, according to Bale, the origin of the giants that Brutus defeats. Bale's history is based on a historical hoax perpetrated by one Annius of Viterbo in 1498, which claimed the authority of the historian Josephus and certain documents based on his account. These documents were supposedly the work of Berosus, the Chaldean chronicler of Alexander the Great and continued by the occult Egyptian historian, Manetho. Later historians modify Bale's account somewhat, especially claims concerning the historical existence of Albion.

Up through and even including William Camden's (1551–1623) *Britannia*, the most important fact about British history was that Britain had been a province of the Roman Empire. Because of the iconic status of Rome and Greece in the Renaissance imagination, the obviously signal contribution of the Germanic invaders was minimized. Geoffrey of Monmouth's fantastic association of English nobility with the descendants of exiles from Troy, and his Celtic agenda, was now positioned as an embarrassment, even as fraudulent. Even so, Geoffrey of Monmouth's account of the history of early Britain, from its founding by scions of Troy who displaced ancient Giants, continued its powerful hold on the English imagination through the seventeenth century. Polydore Vergil's counter-history, based on documentary sources, scornfully rejected Geoffrey's account, and was promptly met with dismissal in England as being itself foreign and Roman propaganda. Even Camden's *Britannia*, beholden to Polydore Vergil's methodology, sidesteps the controversy by simply bracketing Geoffrey's enormously popular myth as a question insoluble by his methods, which it admits, reveal no evidence to support Geoffrey's most flamboyant claims, or any of his points at all.[19] Camden suggested that the ancient Britons were an offshoot of the Gauls, of whom there was ample documentary evidence and who could plausibly have inhabited the British Isles. Linking this humanistically inspired assumption with the older Biblical chronology, he points out that the Gauls were the offspring of Gomer, son of Noah, and the settler of Europe in the emerging neo-Biblical histories. Post-Reformation archaeology and history would accord a new importance to Germanic and

Saxon, and therefore, medieval, history. The accounts of Camden and Leland only scratched the surface of a potentially infinite history and complexity, which would have to be catalogued and interpreted in ways consistent with a newly coherent British national identity. There was also a theological and institutional impetus to this new antiquarianism. Jacobean scholarship, most famously exemplified in Sir Robert Cotton's great library, sought to establish a relatively independent lineage for a newly established Church of England. Such a lineage would inevitably trace itself through the ecclesiastical history of Anglo-Saxon and Norman England. As often in the history of medievalism, the political agenda of one group or generation frequently resulted in discoveries that provided for a very different political interpretation of another generation or another group of scholars. The appeal to origin and tradition inevitably resulted in a conflicted genealogy or history.

In his review of the debates surrounding British antiquity in the sixteenth and seventeenth centuries, Arthur B. Ferguson, in *Utter Antiquity: Perceptions of Prehistory in Renaissance England*, argues that more was at stake in the criticism of Geoffrey's account than the existence of Arthur, it was the nature of historical evidence itself.[20] The opponents of the received Geoffrey of Monmouth British history were themselves aware not only of the fragmentary evidence in support of Geoffrey's version, but also the paucity of evidence in support of an alternative version of the settlement of ancient Britain. As a result, both sides found themselves in an ambiguous situation in which literary and fictional sources competed persuasively with documentable facts and material artifacts. Even among some of the supporters of the legend of the Brut, the new methodologies of antiquarianism and chorography initiated a tide of skepticism and empiricism that began to subvert the older Brut–Arthur scheme from within. It would have seemed that the rise of humanism would be antithetical to the maintenance of the legend of the Brut, and certainly Polydore Vergil's humanist history is a flash point of the controversy, but humanists could in fact array themselves on either side of the debate. Humanism, as Ferguson puts it, was a "precondition" to the dismantling of the British history, rather than its antidote.

If the Renaissance has typically represented the dawn of modernity for most lay people (and even reflected in the recent scholarly nomenclature of the Early Modern), if the rediscovery of Greek and Roman Antiquity provided for it a model and a source, Early Modern antiquarians were motivated by a powerfully traditional undertaking, for they were concerned with uncovering (we might now say "inventing") a lineage for British identity, the English Church, the British Crown (or conversely Parliament), and English law. What was special about the continuity, however interrupted, of English society, was not its newness and modernity, but its ancient origin and history. This history the antiquarians provided in the form of texts, objects, and the enumeration and description of places. And that history was profoundly and primarily of the Middle Ages.

This specifically English, and secondarily European, historical medievalism would serve the next few centuries as a unique articulation of a medieval past. Eastern societies are contrasted with the rich and organic connection of the present and the past in the West. They are pictured as static and undeserving of a glorious antiquity, which failed to pass its power and glory on to them. Indeed, in many respects it was Europe that was rewarded with the true inheritance of their antiquity in this view, which would emerge over several centuries, and provide yet another of the complex formulations of the chemistry of indigenous and foreign genealogies. For the antiquarians, however, their primary motivation was uncovering, sometimes literally, an English place and an English time that stretched out, illuminated in some places and obscured in others, back into as close to the starting point of the past as possible, as close to an infinite past as they would allow themselves to imagine.

Despite the intense Western and English bias towards a local microhistory in the work of the antiquarians, their most scholarly wing took a great interest in Oriental languages, above and beyond the loosely transmitted myths of the origins of the Celts (and of all nations and languages) at the Tower of Babel. Biblical scholarship in the atmosphere of the Reformation encouraged the knowledge of Hebrew, Syriac, and Aramaic, to establish as closely as possible the exact intent of scripture. The enormous enterprise of the translation of the New English Bible was obviously the engine of this new awareness. But there were also strategic ecclesiastical reasons for knowledge of the Greek Fathers in their Arabic translations, because they provided an alternative to the dominance of the Roman Church, and a sense of kinship developed, with a long and lasting history, between Anglican and Eastern Orthodox liturgies and learning. The key figure in this study of Oriental languages, especially Hebrew, was Lancelot Andrewes, and his student William Bedwell became the most accomplished Arabic language scholar of Renaissance England.[21]

There had been a tradition, dating back to Gildas, which deduced that Christianity had been brought to Britain by Joseph of Arimithea, and that Glastonbury was therefore an especially holy site. This legend of course informs Arthurian literature, especially its Grail sequences. It suggests a connection between the levantine origin of Christianity and Britain. The legend of St. Joseph of Arimithea, so central to the later fully developed Grail legend, was popular not least because it suggested a direct establishment of Christianity in Britain unmediated by Rome. The story of Joseph's founding of Glastonbury, then, was considered support for Anglican claims of a Christian lineage predating and independent of the Roman Catholic Church and the central role of St. Peter in its founding. Joseph's levantine origin, then, becomes a positive and central piece of this particular puzzle. But its implications were neither cultural nor racial. Rather, the story remained powerfully current in the seventeenth century because it suggests an even earlier date for the introduction of Christianity to the British isles, one unmediated by Rome entirely.

This larger motivation underlies some of the most serious research by sixteenth-century antiquarians. The documentary center of this research in the early seventeenth century was the famous library of Sir Robert Cotton (1571–1631). Its familiar form, with its shelves marked by busts of Roman emperors, probably only took shape when Cotton moved to Westminster, and before that the library had moved several times, so that its earliest atmosphere would have been archival and functional. From our vantage point, its glories were literary masterpieces, such as the *Pearl*-manuscript, stored on its shelves, but in fact literary texts, with the exception of *Piers Plowman*, played a relatively small part in early-seventeenth-century controversies. While Cotton had contacts with continental scholars, and while he shared the antiquarian agenda of establishing the genealogy of the Church of England, his primary interests were in the establishment of a national identity and national heritage, which for the antiquarians were one and the same. Cotton's political tracts, such as *The Danger Wherein the Kingdom Now Standeth* (1628) resulted in suspicion on the part of the Caroline court, since it attacked the influence of the Duke of Buckingham, himself assassinated in the same year.[22] The Cottonian Library was closed in 1629. Cotton was detained and interrogated, and never allowed back into the library, dying in 1631. Almost certainly, Cotton's close association with John Selden (1584–1664) whom he had trained and employed, and, whatever the explicit intent of the antiquarians, the apparent weight of the evidence they uncovered being in support of Parliament, was the cause of his downfall, rather than any hostility to the Crown on his part. Indeed, for all his modernity, Cotton's politics was expressed in a profoundly medieval complaint: if only the King received the right advice from the right courtiers, he would inevitably lead the state in the right direction.

Archbishop James Ussher (1581–1656), like Laud and Selden, developed an expertise in Semitic languages and collected oriental manuscripts. Ussher's *Chronology* was his most important contribution to his peers.[23] A synchronized dating system of world events was lacking for all but the relatively well-documented centuries of Greek and Roman antiquity. Like Selden, Ussher worked with William Bedwell (1563–1632), the premier 17th century Arabist. At the same time, Ussher's interest was directed largely toward Biblical chronology and toward the understanding of the literal language of scripture. He concluded, in the end, that only Hebrew paid off the effort to learn it. As Evelyn records his conversation, "how great the loss of time was to study much the eastern languages . . . excepting Hebrew . . . the Arabic itself had little considerable."[24] At the same time, Ussher did find not inconsiderable interest in British history and language. He could read Anglo-Saxon and collected Old English manuscripts. He also encouraged the teaching of Anglo-Saxon in the universities and championed Abraham Wheelock, who held the first Cambridge post in the language. Where Ussher had uncovered much of the ecclesiastical history of the Irish church in his effort to establish an independent lineage for Christianity in Britain, he was unalterably opposed to the translation of the Bible into Irish and insisted on preaching being conducted in English. The colonial rigidity of such a position was consistent with English policy since the fourteenth century, but a peculiar position to take in relation to Protestant evangelism. Ussher also wrote a history of the Irish Church. He tried to prove its independence from Rome, citing such customs as married clergy. Ussher argued against Pelagianism, to his embarrassment a heresy developed by a British Christian of the Fourth Century living in Rome, which emphasized the centrality of an individual's will in salvation. Augustine's withering attack emphasizing predestination, was also a foundation of Calvinist doctrine. The rise of a liberal Arminianism (championed by Bishop Laud and popular at Oxford and Cambridge) seemed to be a rebirth of Pelagianism and Ussher carefully (perhaps because King Charles was open to Arminianism) offered evidence against its dangers. He argued against Arminianism by detailing the dangers of Pelagianism.

John Selden's legal histories represented the most politically charged writings of early antiquarianism.[25] Most researches into the law, including Selden's, narrated a history of a long series of adaptations retaining a fundamentally consultative dimension, supporting a loosely Parliamentary position. The evidence, rather than the overt conclusions of Selden's works, ran counter to the claims of James I in regard to the primacy of the monarchy. Instead, Selden's evidence suggested a continuity of Saxon legal and political institutions, with an early historical emphasis on collective government. For Selden, it was critical to date the origin of English law to before the Conquest. While providing a fair account of previous mythological histories of Britain, including the origin of the Celts from the Tower of Babel and Geoffrey of Monmouth's narrative of Trojan origin, Selden nevertheless dismisses them as lacking in any sort of documentary evidence. Relying on Tacitus and Caesar, he draws a picture of pre-Roman British elites arriving at decisions and making common law through assemblies.

Such a narrative conflicted with the Jacobean history of Britain. King James, before his accession to the English throne, had drawn a picture of a barbarous Scotland tamed and governed by the Irish King Fergus, who imposed the rule of law. From its origin, argues James, British society had been both implicitly and explicitly absolutist. Indeed, Selden argues, in his commentary on Fortescue's influential dialogue, *De laudibus legum Anglicae*, for the antiquity and importance of the Common Law.[26] While he does not concur with Fortescue that the laws of England were the most ancient in Europe, he does argue that British civil law grew out of natural law and was modified to suit circumstances as they developed. He seems to be claiming (though Selden rarely makes direct political claims for obvious political reasons) that government by associations and consensuses of various sorts are the natural order of things.

These agendas, the constitutional history of the early Church and the variations on liturgy and ceremony, meant a relatively conservative cast to most early antiquarian politics, in the sense of a strong defense of both the Anglican Church and the Crown. Nevertheless, both Church and Crown were wary, associating nostalgia with Roman Catholic recidivism, and antiquarian research with parliamentary ideology. As one would expect, Puritans were suspicious of antiquarian activities, and antiquarians feared the Puritan reputation for iconoclasticism. As with most later medievalisms, however, loyalties were often divided, both within camps, in opposing camps and within individuals. Dugdale and Aubrey were committed Royalists, but Selden, predicting a late-seventeenth-century interest in the history of Parliament, had come to believe in a government by compact distinct from the Divine Right of Kings. Cotton's own politic sympathies leaned toward Parliament also. As with Selden, those antiquaries who were concerned with legal and constitutional history tended toward parliamenterianism and their research had the most political potency. It was no surprise, then, to find the Society of Antiquaries dissolving itself in the face of King James' displeasure and the King dissolving Sir Robert Cotton's library.

While Anglican sympathies ran deep among the antiquarians, the connection between medievalism and a persecuted and interrupted Catholicism, a common connection in later medieval circles, could be found in the influential work of Richard Verstegan (1548–ca. 1636). Nevertheless, Verstegan's chief work, was addressed to James (before the repression following the Gunpowder Plot) in an effort, apparently, to align Catholicism with patriotism. If the impetus among John Foxe, Matthew Parker and John Bale was to study Anglo-Saxon in order to uncover records establishing the continuity of an independent English Church, Verstegan's motivation must have been fundamentally different. He was the author of impassioned and detailed accounts of the persecution of Catholics by Protestants in England and the Continent, the publication of which had already resulted in his arrest. Verstegan's antiquarian researches are notable for their emphasis on the Anglo-Saxon origins of England. His *Restitutions* described a Germanic rather than Roman or Celtic foundation for England.[27] However modern that may sound, Verstegan was committed to the accepted notion that the Tower of Babel was the starting point of linguistic and national difference. For Verstegan, if the Goths were barbarians, it was only because barbarism could be expected at the formative phase of nationhood. Similarly, learning and culture were not unique to certain nations above others, but could be cultivated or could decline. And, he argues, the widespread Aristotelian association of climates with specific civilizations and cultural personalities was a myth.[28] One reason for Verstegan's currency, however, was his description of a Saxon government in which kings were elected and subject to recall. Such a position becomes crucial to later seventeenth-century debates about parliamentary governance, in which royal absolutism is regarded as a foreign imposition on native English liberties as "the Norman Yoke."

By the 1650s, however, marginalized Royalists occupied themselves with scholarship meant to bulwark their positions, and that scholarship was usually antiquarian in nature. Interestingly, the Restoration, concerned with stability, encouraged antiquarian research on material or physical remains, rather than ideas, institutions, or ecclesiology. Sir Henry Spelman (ca. 1564–ca. 1641), however, drew a more comfortably Royalist picture. From his point of view, English law lacked such an apparently great antiquity, and had been continually shaped by ruling forces and elites. While friendly to the Crown in its implications, Spelman's narrative also suggests a progressive evolution in governmental institutions. Parliament's origins were in the thirteenth century, not in the misty past of Saxon or Norman polities.

Thus, most antiquarians of the late sixteenth and early seventeenth centuries were primarily concerned with establishing the lineage of historical Britain. Motivated by certain political and ecclesiastical concerns (by no means consistent), such as discovering evidence of institutions that may have provided an ancestor for Parliament or discovering evidence of a Christianity independent of Rome even before the Reformation, they turned their attention to records, documents, and inscriptions. The practical result of such attention meant an increasing skepticism concerning such theories as the Trojan origin of Britain enshrined in Geoffrey of Monmouth, or the settlement of Britain after the fall of the tower of Babel by descendants of Noah. Attention was increasingly focussed on Anglo-Saxon evidence, and also on British civilization during the Roman Empire.

Yet exotic and quasi-Biblical accounts retained a strong imaginative appeal among certain antiquaries, and one result was the apparently bizarre theory of the Asiatic, especially Phoenician-Syrian, settlement of Britain. The authorization for such a thesis was the ancient geographer Strabo, who had received wide currency in a humanist edition by Isaac Causabon.[29] Strabo described the distribution of Phoenician colonies and the worldwide penetration of Phoenician traders and settlers. It did not take much for English scholars, who seized upon the image of Phoenicians scouring the world for tin deposits, to picture Phoenician settlements in the British Isles.

The Phoenician thesis had some obscure sixteenth- and seventeenth-century roots. John Twyne (d. 1581) had written a symposium-like dialogue in which it was deduced that Phoenicians may have settled in the British Isles sometime between the early founding of Britain by Giants and the later invasion by the Trojans.[30] A more widely distributed authority was the Frenchman Samuel Bochart (1599–1667), who proposed the identification of the Phoenicians as the Biblical Canaanites, displaced by the Israelites.[31] Bochart found evidence of Canaanite exploration of the entire known world, including the Pre-Columbian New World. Although relatively guarded in his acceptance of Bochart's diffusionist theory, Pierre-Daniel Huet, who wrote the influential tract on the origins of romance, *Traité de l'origine des romans*, discussed above, was close to Bochart, and accompanied him on his sojourn to Queen Christina's famous court in Sweden, before religious differences separated them. The Catholic (and eventually Bishop) Huet had studied with the Protestant Bochart, and the discovery of an Origen manuscript in Stockholm led to an edition by Huet that first established his reputation. Bochart later accused Huet of editing Origen in such a way as to support the Catholic position on the Eucharist. But even in his later treatises, Huet remains respectful, if critical of Bochart. Under the early and to some extent continuing influence of Bochart, Huet studied Arabic and Syriac as well as Hebrew, so that his account of romance has the authority of one who could have, in the seventeenth century, been considered an Orientalist. Huet's notion that romance, and fiction itself, is ultimately of Eastern inspiration cannot be separated from the general narrative of Eastern civilizations as culture bearers of a certain sort that is exemplified by Bochart and the other proponents of the Asiatic colonization of Western Europe.

A more scholarly basis for support was John Selden's *De Diis Syriis*.[32] *De diis syriis* was one of Selden's most arresting works, a study of the Levantine cults against which Jewish monotheism positioned itself. As a study of nonclassical and non-Greco-Roman anthropology, it represented something of a turn in Renaissance imagining of the past. Despite its entirely orthodox intention, and Milton's poetic use of it in *Paradise Lost* to describe the practices of the Fallen Angels, Selden's account, because of his painstakingly objective prose style, rendered his descriptions part of a developing Hermetic tradition he opposed, and still holds a place in occult mythologies. Selden's descriptions of various cults and mysteries, combining elements of Egyptian, Greek, Persian, and local deities and traditions, is an important predecessor of Frazer's *Golden Bough*, which rewrote Selden's theological account as Victorian anthropology.

What is particularly interesting to us, despite the breadth of his interest, is that Selden's research categories posit the Oriental as mythic, ritual, irrational, and pagan, even demonic, in contrast to a British history which is legal, documentary, rational, and practical (though Selden does point to some of the practical magical uses of certain cults in regard to agricultural fertility, predicting Frazerian anthropology), even through the medieval period. From this point of view, royal prerogative becomes a type of Oriental despotism, foreign to British social development. Selden's *De Diis Syriis* influenced other antiquaries as well. William Burton, in his *Commentary on Antoninus his Itenerary* (1658), his analysis of a third-century catalogue of the military routes of the Roman Empire, refers to Selden's description of pre-monotheistic cults as common across Europe, from Syria all the way to Britain.[33] Despite his use of *De Diis* and his orientalized portrayal of heathen rites and demonic conduct in *Paradise Lost*, Milton was dismissive of Phoenician origins of Britain in his *History of England*.[34]

The first generations of antiquaries with few exceptions accepted the Biblical and apocryphal account of the settling of Western Europe by the sons of Noah after the Flood.[35] Such an argument is not wholly fanciful. Diffusionist positions, even the materialist argument of Gordon Childe, have always assumed, in rough parallel to Indo-European linguistic dispersal, that aspects of Near Eastern civilization found their way to the prehistoric cultures of Europe.[36] The evidence of a Bronze Age in Britain encouraged the thesis of foreign settlement, owing to the assumption that copper work had been an ancient Eastern discovery. It was presumed, then, that Eastern peoples wandered far and wide in search for tin, the alloy material needed for brass. This assumption led to the thesis, first suggested by John Twyne's *De Rebus Albionicis* (1590), against Geoffrey of Monmouth's account of a settlement by Brutus and the Trojans, that Britain had been settled by the Phoenicians. The thesis was developed in a more elaborate form by Samuel Bochart in *Geographia Sacra*, and then located specifically in British history by Aylett Sammes. According to Sammes and others, the offspring of Gomer were the "Cimbri," who eventually settled Northern Europe. In the 1676 edition, a woodcut portrays the Cimbri (looking suspiciously like contemporary Bretons) making their way from somewhere north of Turkey to Britain.[37] These sons of Gomer were the original settlers of Britain, but civilization was brought to Britain by the Phoenicians, who came in search of tin. The culture hero of the Phoenicians is Hercules of Tyre, also illustrated by Sammes.

Thus, the reaction against Geoffrey of Monmouth involved an even more specifically Oriental thesis for the origin of British culture. According to Twyne in *De Rebus Albionicis*, the Carthiginian empire, founded by Phoenicians, expanded everywhere in search of raw materials, according to ancient sources, and certainly must have sought the rich tin reserves of Southern Britain. Twyne goes on to suggest archaeological evidence for Phoenician colonization, including housing types, clothing, facial adornments, and key words for sites and places. The unique dress of the Welsh is interpreted as Phoenician in origin. In addition, the Phoenicians introduce the hermetic magic of the East to the British Isles. Twyne also introduces negative stereotypes about the East into his scheme. The Phoenicians were "corrupt" and "cunning" and their life of luxury had led them from their original virility. In addition, the Phoenicians were dark in complexion. Invoking a familiar climactic theory, Twyne supposes that they grew paler after many winters, but painted themselves with the famous woad war paint. Twyne also suggested that Moorish blood was introduced into the racial makeup of certain parts of Britain.

While mid-seventeenth century antiquarians had developed a new and serious interest in medieval English history and an increasing skepticism toward theories of exogenous origin, such as the Trojan exiles as founders of Britain, the notion that England had some originary connection with Eastern cultures did not disappear. The most surprising of these arguments was by the eccentric Aylett Sammes, who, in his *Britannia Antiqua Illustrata* (1676), traced the origin of British culture to Phoenicia, and argued for an improbable coloring of Celtic and Welsh by Syrian influence.[38] He based his theory on largely linguistic ground, suggesting striking analogies between British place names and what he deduced to be Punic roots. For Sammes, Britain was probably not settled by Brutus and his Trojan exiles (though he does admit to the possibility of Aeneas having arrived) but by the Phoenicians. He also argues for an ultimately Black Sea origin for the Celts, and, since where the Phoenicians went the Greeks were not far behind, also prehistoric Greek visits to Britain. Layered over this historical geography were cultural or anthropological assumptions. The Druids, he suggests, served Phoenician gods (though he does not employ Selden's *De Diis Syriis*). The Bards were themselves actually Phoenician, and may have passed on the knowledge of Pythagorean mysteries and the Greek language to the Druids.

Sammes' anthropological assumptions had a long life in popular culture, even if their source went uncited. He illustrated his book with a striking print of a gigantic Wicker Man, being burned with sacrificial victims inside. He suggests that the origin of the Wicker Man may have been the great size of the Phoenicians themselves, who, being close to the First Age, were larger and more powerful than present-day humans. Following a disputed passage in Ptolemy, he describes a Phoenician Hercules, and proposes that Stonehenge may have been a temple to Hercules. Other anthropological evidence, such as the common brewing of barley by both Levantines and Britons and the employment of the chariot in warfare, were also called upon to support the Phoenician roots of British culture. The chariot thesis was variously debated through the centuries, because Caesar, in the Gallic Wars, expresses surprise at encountering chariots among the Britons, having encountered it nowhere else in Western Europe. For Sammes and others, the chariots were clear evidence of the "Asiatic" roots of British culture.

Sammes' theory was localized by Charles Leigh (1662–1701) in his survey of Lancashire.[39] Using largely etymological evidence, he portrayed a Lancashire colonized by Phoenicians and other Asian peoples, including Persians. Slightly earlier, Robert Sheringham's *De Anglorum Gentis* (1670) had discoursed on Phoenician and Germanic links, expanding the number of visiting peoples to include the Armenians.[40] Following others, Leigh proposed that the event that precipitated the Phoenician invasion of Britain had been the sack of Tyre by the Israelites, as described in the Biblical account. He does allow the post-Babel settlement of Britain earlier, and admits the presence of the descendants of Noah, Samothes, and Japhet. Arguing that previous (and later) cultures had no knowledge of gold handicraft, he points to all discoveries of gold objects in Lancashire as clear evidence of Phoenician presence.

The Phoenician thesis continued in various guises through the seventeenth century and into the eighteenth. Richard Cumberland (1632–1718) published a translation of the standard account of Phoenician history by Sanchoniathon, included in Greek in the works of Eusubius.[41] He identifies the Phoenicians as the lineage of Cain, while the Israelites descended from Seth. He proposes, interestingly, the thesis that the ancient pagan gods were in fact mortals, memorialized as deities. In keeping with the overtly occult and esoteric stream in much writing about Phoenician origins, he describes Hermes Trigesthus as a heathen counterpart to Moses. In the seventeenth-century account, Oriental civilization brings culture to the primitive Britons. In the eighteenth century, however, the Britons themselves acquire the status of Noble Savage. They are the result of a pre-Adamic settlement spared by the Deluge, which is consequently regarded as a localized Middle Eastern event rather than a world catastrophe.

Renaissance thinking about otherness had to grapple with the traditions of medieval anthropology. The Middle Ages had its own form of

Orientalism, even before the Crusades, and it expressed it in the combination of horror and fascination with the fabulous races of the world. According to de Bruyne, in his *Esthétique Médiévale*, the medieval world inherited this polarization from the ancient Greek contempt for civilizations that were not Greek, which by definition meant that they were Asiatic, and the motif of Asiatic otherness runs through Greek literature and philosophy, regarded as the violation of the Aristotelian emphasis on the mean as a standard of judgment, and all variations being judged grotesque.[42] The "monstrous races" in John Block Friedman's term, were not primitive societies graced by the nobility of nature as they would be after Rousseau. Nor were they frozen at an earlier stage in the great march of human history as they would be in nineteenth-century thinking. Instead, they were understood in terms of Biblical genealogies, which were unfortunately obscure or ambiguous. Exotic people may have descended from the children of Noah after the Flood. They may have been survivors of the Flood, carrying on the blood and traditions of the degenerated peoples the deluge was meant to wash from the earth. Even more disturbing, they may have been descendants of races that existed before Adam, and that may have been the result of fallen angels in human form and animalistic status. It remained for the seventeenth-century to expound on these possibilities at length.

The notion of a pre-Adamic creation was implicit in the influential works of Jean Bodin (1530–96) in the late sixteenth century, but was developed fully in the writings of Isaac de la Peyrère (1596–1676).[43] Sir Walter Raleigh, in his *History of the World*, had already questioned the literalness of post-Lapsarian Biblical chronology, assuming that events and actions would have been as difficult for Biblical peoples as for a Renaissance explorer.[44] But de la Peyrère went much further, questioning the Mosaic authorship of the Pentateuch, and arguing for the greater age of Phoenician and Egyptian over Hebrew civilizations, and repeating the deduction that the Flood was a localized disaster, aimed only at the Jews, since the sons of Noah had settled only the Levant. His point was that the Pentateuch was a summary or abridgement of what actually happened. More spectacularly, de la Peyrère interpreted the ambiguity of *Genesis* to suggest that a separate human creation predated Adam, and that the "gentiles" were the result of this earlier creation. The culture of Genesis after the Fall is in fact a culture of tools and clothing and agriculture developed by this older civilization, with which the progeny of Adam intermingled and intermarried.

Bodin's ideas were more flexible and subtle, for he presents the strongest case for environmental adaptation to change the nature of human society. As a result, cultural traits and human nature are by no means preordained, but are subject to local conditions. One important contribution of Bodin to the history of ideas is that the entropy of human decline as suggested in such medieval tropes as "The World Grown Old" is reversible. Another, less modern contribution, is that environment creates character, so that the nations of the world have vices and virtues that have developed as a result of adaptation. The people of the north are brave and stolid, but not very imaginative, or, in some schemes, even very intelligent; those of the south and east are more mercurial, imaginative but less reliable. It is an assumption that plays a role in some theories of medieval culture in the late eighteenth and early nineteenth centuries, in which an imaginative enhancement from Oriental culture is necessary to stimulate the industry of the North, producing the fictions of romance and the soaring structures of the Gothic.

The discovery of the New World and the American Indian peoples required some adjustment of either paradigm of settlement, pre-Adamic or post-Deluge. Explorers of Brazil thought that South America had been settled by none other than Noah himself.[45] Others took the state of Native American culture to reflect a separate creation. As with theories of the earliest settlement of Britain, explorers and geographers traced the origin of Native American peoples variously, in the words of Margaret Hodgen, "from the Welsh, some from the Greeks and Romans, some from the Carthaginians, the Scythians, the Egyptians, the Jews, the Ten Lost Tribes of Israel, the Africas, Ethiopians, French Kurlanders or Phoenicians."[46] Joseph de Acosta (1588–89) argued that it was obvious that the Indians descended from the Jews because their clothing is exactly parallel to that worn by Samson as described in the Bible.[47] Conversely, Hugo Grotius, according to John Ogilby, employed material as well as linguistic evidence to prove a kinship between the Norwegians and the peoples of the Americas, noting that Mexican peoples "wash'd their children as soon as they were born in cold water".[48]

The most arresting hypothesis, one that has a long history in American religious culture, argued that the American Indians were descended from the Ten Lost Tribes. In 1650, Manasseh ben Israel (1604–57), writing in Amsterdam in 1650 and translated into English in the following year, narrates a story of a Jewish explorer who had been led to a mysterious colony by Indians, who told him that they had been instructed in the Hebrew faith by the members of this colony.[49] Manassah proposes an overland journey through Asia with Jewish settlements being established by those who broke off from the main migration. The great structures of Peru, he suggests, were originally synagogues. Manasseh's ideas were reinforced by the similar argument of Thomas Thorowgood's *Jewes in America* published in 1650.[50] Thorowgood was a correspondent of Roger Williams, to whom he proposed the idea, and such notable figures as Cotton Mather and William Penn subscribed to the notion. There were of course skeptical tracts written in response that questioned the evidence of Manassah and Thorowgood or reasserted a more conventional position of post-Deluge settlement.

One of the most elaborate theories of American settlement also involved an Oriental element. Robertus Conteous Nortmannus in 1644 proposed that the Indians were the descendants of far sailing Phoenicians from Carthage or Tyre. In *De originibus Americanis libri quattor*, Giorgius Hornius (or Horn) dismisses the various proposals that preceded his, rightly noting that most of the apparent evidence consisted of coincidence or insufficient similarity.[51] He reduces the likely settlers of the Americas to three groups, Scythians from the North, Chinese from the East, and most importantly, Phoenicians from the West. He refined earlier Phoenician theses by suggesting at least three waves of settlement. Christian doctrine, he notes, may have influenced Mexican and Andean religions via Chinese settlements, which arrived with the knowledge of Christianity from Syrian Christian missionaries in India and China.

By the early eighteenth century, this species of antiquarianism had acquired a certain parodic air. Despite this, the work of William Stukeley and his celebration of Druidism was widely discussed.[52] Druids had been firmly established in the hermetic pantheon of Neoplatonic Humanism, carrying on a secret knowledge dating back to Pythagorean mysteries and the magic of the Egyptian Hermes. By the later seventeenth century, however, the Druids had taken a dive in status, and Sammes illustrates them involved in gruesome human sacrifices. Their stock rises in the eighteenth century, led largely by the polemics of William Stukeley. For Stukeley, the Druids arrived in Britain as part of an "oriental colony" led by Hercules and shared the religion of Abraham. Their religion was consistent with Christianity, though they still awaited the coming of the Messiah. He asserted that the Phoenicians were the first to bring agriculture to Britain. The Druids, moreover, were direct descendants of these "oriental" colonizers. If Bochart was relatively unknown to a wider lay audience and if Sammes was taken as eccentric as he was, the thesis of a Phoenician Britain was revived in spectacular form by Stukeley. Stukeley had been a physician and for some time one of the more respected archaeologists in England. But around 1729 he takes orders in the Church of England, because of, rather than in spite of, his belief that Druidic religion, as well as Plato and Moses, had deduced advance knowledge of the Trinity and other revealed Christian doctrines. This belief required a secret history of Druidism. The Druids had arrived in Britain, according to Stukeley, as part of an "oriental colony" of Phoenicians, shortly after Noah's deluge and were apparently "of *Abraham's* religion." Isolated in the West, they built on their patriarchal foundations a rational precursor of Christianity. The leader of the group was no other than the Hercules of Tyre described by Sammes. Where Sammes, however, firmly established the Druids as pagans, replete with human sacrifices and sacrificial bonfires, Stukeley imputes to them a proto-Christianity.

Sammes' influence was not limited to Stukeley. In 1723, a Reverend Henry Rowland published a *Mona Antiqua Restaurata*.[53] Like Bochart, Rowlands understands Welsh as a dialect of Hebrew, the original language, and argued that it preserves the original speech better than any other living language. Rowland, accepting the post-Babel diaspora of Noah's sons, suggests that this germ of "true religion" was brought to Britain, but was soon corrupted by a self-serving priesthood. But for Stukeley, the Druids play a heroic role, partly for their role as inheritors and conservators of ancient wisdom and true religion, and partly because of their resistance to Roman rule. Now the Druids become symbols of liberty and originary Britishness against Roman imperialism, reversing Stukeley's earlier contempt for any part of British history that did not reflect the greater glory of Greece and Rome.

In addition to his fascination with the theory of the Phoenician origins of British culture, Stukeley is also noteworthy for his early embrace of the "Gothick." In so doing, he represents a biographical shift from science to sentiment and from classicism to Gothicism. Nevertheless, he retained or expressed enthusiasms typical of both ends of his career at all times, suggesting that the shifts in subjectivity we impute to the eighteenth century cannot always be so clearly demarcated. In addition, his Druidic theories and his Gothicism are impelled by a similar concern to refute what he felt to be the atheistic tendencies of scientism and deism. Indeed, even his early, scrupulous archeological research did not preclude his religious orthodoxy (though his biographer Piggott finds him fiddling with measurements as the Phoenician–Druid link grew more elaborate in his imagination) and in this respect he resembled Sir Isaac Newton, who could simultaneously pursue the most rigorous calculations and speculate on religious mysteries on the other, seeing them as part of the same project.

In 1772, Charles Vallancey in *An Essay on the Antiquity of the Irish Language* could still assert that Irish was directly descended from Punic.[54] The many round towers of Ireland were in fact Phoenician astronomical observatories, the Phoenicians being famous for their astronomical skill. For Vallancey, the Phoenician connection was a claim for the antiquity of Irish culture and language and he claimed that a dialect of Irish was spoken in the Garden of Eden.

One of the peculiarities of these various arguments is the place of the Jews and of the Hebrew language in the schema of British origins. Romantic and nineteenth-century philology, with its heavy investment in the Aryan thesis, bracketed off the Semitic languages from the Indo-European family. This segregation led to some sinister arguments, such as the argument that the Phoenicians are Aryans rather than Semites, with the result that the Phoenician thesis of Sammes and others finds a place in the new White mythologies of late-twentieth-century racist ideology. But the earlier arguments, and even Sammes's eccentric book, actually argued for a close relationship of Phoenician and Hebrew in terms of language and culture. Biblical scholarship in the Renaissance and related Rabbinical commentary reinforced the thesis of an Eastern homeland for the Germanic people, but one linked to Jewish history. The world is settled by the sons of Noah after the deluge, and his son Japhet is regarded as the founder of the northern peoples. Such a geneology can be found in English as early as Aelfric.[55] Japhet's son Gomer is understood to have a had a special role in founding the German peoples. As Sir Walter Raleigh's *History of the World* has it, "Gomer . . . seated himself with Togorma, not far from Magog and Tubal, in the borders of Syria and Cilicia. Afterwards he proceeded further into Asia the less; and in long tract of time his valiant issue filled all Germany, rested long in France and Britain"[56] (78/rightcolumn London 11687). Gomer's name is transmuted into the "Cimbrians," inhabitants of Britain and eventually of Wales. The legend is repeated by various writers, including John Milton, in his *History of Britain*. Rabbinical tradition, referred to by Raleigh [p. 82/right column], cites Ashkenaz, Gomer's son, as founder of the German people. The battles between Brutus and Gog and Magog, familiar from Arthurian literature, are part of this legend.

The Phoenician thesis did not die out after the eighteenth century. It has been revived in quite different forms as recently as the twentieth century. In 1924, L. A. Waddell proposed that Phoenicians had founded most of the major cultures of the British Isles.[57] He argued for an "Aryan" status of the Phoenicians, quite different from earlier, and later, Semitic groupings. Virtually all of the cultural signifiers of British archeology, from stone circles through the attachment to St. George, turn out to have Phoenician roots. Waddell claims that his thesis in fact revives the older collective memory of British culture as enshrined in accounts such as Geoffrey of Monmouth, for the "Trojan" settlement of Britain was but a corruption of the actual fact of Phoenician colonization. Waddell's evidence is largely linguistic, in addition to an attempt to correlate physical remains from British excavations with known "Phoenician" objects. Everything that we know as civilization was brought to Britain by the Phoenicians, for "Civilization properly so-called is synonymous with Aryanization" (363) and introduced about 2800 B.C.[58] These Aryans over the centuries mixed with the non-Aryan aboriginal stock: "And it constitutes the leading Aryan element in the present-day population of these isles, the mass and substratum of which, although now Aryanized in speech and customs, still remain preponderatingly of the non-Aryan physical type of the 'Iberian' aborigines, and are racially neither Briton nor British, nor Anglo-Saxons, English, nor Scot, properly so-called" (364).[59] As alarming as Waddell's arguments sound, his conclusion is that Britain can no longer be considered a racially pure Aryan nation, though its culture is predominantly Aryan, yet it is more purely Aryan than "many continental countries which have secured or clamour for self-determination on 'racial' grounds, an idea derived from the spread of Western Aryan 'Nationalism' " (371).[60] Waddell's dismissal of German Nazism on the basis of the predominantly "round-headed" population of Germany is scarce comfort, however. He further observes that Aryan strains tend to rise to the top of the social ladder, and that movements against capitalism or other established forms of order, including religion, are traces of the old racial resentment of the aborigines against the Aryans. And he warns us that the increasing dilution of the old Aryan stock in Britain and America is "a problem for the Eugenicists"[61] Not surprisingly, Waddell's book is frequent recommended by White Power and anti-immigrant literature and Internet sites around the world.

If Waddell's book has had a disturbing afterlife in white supremacist communication and literature, Robert List takes much of the same data and takes it to a politically opposite conclusion.[62] Modelling his argument on Martin Bernal's influential and controversial *Black Athena*, List argues that British culture contains a suppressed strain of African and Near Eastern influence, to the point that many of the supposedly Celtic racial types of the British Isles contain African genes, a fact recognized in Scottish coats-of-arms containing the heads of "Moors."[63] Other widely recognized details of traditional British folklore in fact have striking parallels to Near Eastern non-Christian cults. Even the Arthurian and Grail legends reflect not only prehistoric contact between the East and Britain, but find reinforcement in the generally acknowledged influence of Islamic culture on a crusading and expanding Europe. List also surveys the evidence of African presence and African enthusiasms among British elites through the seventeenth century. His argument, however, is rendered less convincing by his idiosyncratic stress on comet crashes as crucial aspects of both Near Eastern and British popular religion and mythology.

In what the authors describe in their subtitles as "a radical reassessment," C. Scott Littleton and Linda A. Melcor in *From Scythia to Camelot*, propose that the ultimate origin of Arthurian legends were not Celtic at all, but were brought to Britain from the region of the Caucasus by the nomadic Alano-Sarmatians (ancestors of present-day Ossetians) serving in the

Roman legions.[64] While the thesis, proposed and developed in articles from the 1970s and 1980s, has never won wide acceptance, it attempts to account for some notably un-Celtic elements in Arthurian legend. From the point of view of method, Littleton and Melcor would seem to be reading lineal descent and influence into the generally diffusionist assumptions of late-nineteenth-century comparative mythology and folklore. The "Scythian" origins of Arthurian legend sit rather comfortably with medieval and Renaissance sources stretching back to Nennius, that cite an ultimately "Scythian" root for the historical inception of the British people, or at least British rulers.

As Maurice Olender observes in *The Languages of Paradise*, the search for mankind's original language and homeland was fraught with conjectural difficulties. The construction of a hypothetical proto-Indo-European resulted in a displacement of geography as well as of linguistics, shifting the origin of civilization from a Hebraic and Semitic point of human origin as found in Biblical sources, to an Indo-European and Aryan point of origin as promulgated in the new study of linguistics and the new definition of race and nation in the nineteenth century. For Herder, the Ganges could become the "river of Paradise."[65] In the articulation of German nationalism, Orientalism was employed to validate both the independence and the antiquity of the Barbarian past. For Herder, the oriental origin of the Germanic peoples is a way of freeing them from Roman dominance once and for all. Race, disguised as language, trumps culture.

The theories of the prehistory or early history of Britain surveyed in this chapter were motivated by a series of complex variables that change the status of these theories over time. The Early Modern antiquarians who sought to displace what they took to be the fanciful origins of Britain found in medieval accounts such as Geoffrey of Monmouth did so thinking they were holding the medieval versions to higher, more modern standards of evidence. At the same time, their investigations, and the histories constructed around their results, sought also to support new and sometimes conflicting institutional allegiances, such as defending the Church of England and parliamentary reform at the same time. In reaching back beyond the Middle Ages for fragments of information that had necessarily to be incorporated into a Biblical paradigm yet to be disaggregated by science, they eventually contributed to narratives presenting certain key idioms to colonial and imperial discourses. One of these idioms, which is emphasized in this chapter, is the delinking of the Oriental and the Medieval that served as a derogatory equation in the humanist critique of medieval culture in relation to the romance genre and Gothic architecture, which is emphasized in the previous chapter. Now, instead of an orientalized

Middle Ages being imagined as an insidious, decadent, or barbarous corruption of Western culture, the foundational Orient turns out to be in some sense the original West, the secret source of its arts, sciences and mythologies. As the archaic past of the East, and even that of the New World, is imagined as originally a white empire, its future could be imagined under the domination of its European incarnation.

CHAPTER THREE

THE MIDDLE AGES AS DISPLAY

The study of medieval literature at the end of the nineteenth century expands rapidly at the same time that the developing field of anthropology demonstrates a great interest in performances and rituals of what were regarded as primitive or decadent cultures, and in some subtle and some obvious ways, medieval literature and ethnic theatricality were thought of as analogous to one another. Moreover, at the same time that detailed literary scholarship was reconstructing the physical production of medieval drama, anthropology was engaged in a new practice of reconstruction by display. In the late nineteenth century, certain strands of high imperial culture quite literally exhibited a deeply ambiguous relation to the theatrical, and nowhere is this relation more strikingly demonstrated than in the developing field of anthropology. One of the topics in this chapter is the ways in which the concept of the medieval in the late nineteenth century is redefined by the rise of anthropology, an anthropology that owed a debt, if not directly to Nietzsche and Darwin, than to the popular understanding and appropriation of Nietzschean ideas, especially in regard to ideas of race and progress. I argue, therefore, that some of these analogies were visually expressed. At precisely the moment when the study of medieval literature and culture achieve academic institutionalization, the medieval is imagined again as both foreign and indigenous.

From the middle of the nineteenth through the early twentieth centuries, the great European powers mounted enormous international exhibitions, displaying both their technological and economic power and their newly acquired colonial possessions.[1] Over the past two decades an enormous scholarly literature has developed on what would have seemed an unlikely subject, that of world's fairs and international exhibitions, especially in the nineteenth century. A new interest in the symbolic and theatrical aspects of social history and of simulated environments, reflecting the state of our own cultural moment, has vitalized this previously understudied aspect of how the nineteenth century viewed itself. During the same two decades, literary and intellectual historians have turned their attention to another aspect of the same period—its obsession with the Middle Ages.[2] This new scholarly concern with medievalism also has a contemporary source, as the Middle Ages increasingly is pictured in both popular culture and academic discourse as an absolute historical opposite, as the last pre-modern moment in Western Civilization. Yet surprisingly these two distinct turns in recent scholarship turn out to have a link. As it turns out, world's fairs in the nineteenth century not only celebrated the triumph of European modernity, they also displayed aspects of Europe's own medieval past. From the Great Exhibition of 1851 onward, medieval reconstructions were among the most popular exhibits at world's fairs, and often the most difficult to assimilate to the fairs' modernizing agenda. A nearly complete collection of the official records of most of these fairs is available from the Smithsonian Institute on microfilm, and most of the descriptions that follow are based on materials from these reels.[3] For most of us today, for instance, the idea of the relation of these world's fairs to the Middle Ages is learned from Henry Adams (1838–1918), who in *The Autobiography of Henry Adams* extols the futurist power of the great hall of turbines, and contrasts these dynamos to the accepting grace of the cathedral, as developed in his dichotomy of "The Virgin and the Dynamo".[4] Yet one would not suspect from reading Adams's *Autobiography* or his essays or letters that it would have been possible for him to visit two medieval recreations at the Paris Exhibition of 1900, "Le Vieux Paris," and "Paris 1500," each with extensive reconstructions of buildings, costumed inhabitants and educational literature.[5]

My purpose here is not only to describe some of these examples of medieval installations at world's fairs, but also to uncover some hidden patterns and meanings in their display. Throughout the nineteenth century, we shall see, medieval installations played a complicated and unexpected part in world's fair planning. From the very first, however, the place of medieval exhibitions at world's fairs was unstable and contradictory. For as the nineteenth century progressed, these international exhibitions, which were being mounted as often as every five years on average, not only celebrated industrial wealth and technique, they also celebrated the growth of empire,— the imperial triumph of the West over the East and Africa. Installations and displays exhibited the raw materials, the handicrafts and the potential wealth of European colonial acquisitions, as well as those of independent Eastern states. This imperial theme, however, complicated the representation of Europe's own past, that of the Middle Ages. For since the late eighteenth century, the Medieval and the Oriental had been paired, as aesthetic styles, as points of linguistic origin, and, increasingly, as stages of cultural development.

While such structures could easily be dismissed precisely as curiosities, in the context of the ideology of world's fairs, they present the Middle Ages as both domestic and foreign. This dual interpretation of the Middle Ages has a prior history, from world's fairs to the Victorian anthropology than informed them and then further back to the strangely intertwined histories of medievalism and Orientalism in architecture, linguistics and literature. These images echo earlier eighteenth- and seventeenth-century theories of the "Oriental" origins of medieval architecture and literature that are the subjects of the previous chapters.

In the eighteenth century, antiquarianism, early Romanticism, and the picturesque, as well as direct knowledge of Eastern cultures had resulted in a shift in the negative valences accorded to the both the Middle Ages and the Orient. Garden architecture and landscape design collocated Oriental and medieval motifs as aspects of the picturesque. Intellectual history, according to Raymond Schwab, *The Oriental Renaissance*, "discovered" the East as the Renaissance itself "discovered" classical antiquity. Scholarship often migrated from Medieval to Oriental Studies, and back again. The Middle Ages represented in time what the Orient represented in space, an "other" to the present development of Western Civilization. The great moment in this enterprise was Sir William Jones' reconstruction of Sanskrit.[6] Suddenly a unity of world civilizations, frequently compared to the cultural unity of the Catholic Middle Ages, seemed possible through linguistic research. Medieval vernaculars themselves acquired a new antique prestige through their lineage to Sanskrit.

The "discovery" of Sanskrit meant not just deducing a system of parallels and descents and origins, but underlying these factors, a distinctly new sense of time. It led to the eventual discrediting of Biblical chronology, replacing the Biblical Orientalism we surveyed in the previous chapter with an anthropological Orientalism. Developed at the same time and inseparable from Romanticism, it accorded the archaic a status equivalent to the classical in terms of priority, complexity, and sophistication. Even without the fanciful imputations of a dimly understood trinitarianism, Sanskrit and Eastern civilizations in general now provided a sentinel on one side of classical antiquity as the Middle Ages did on the other, effectively bracketing off the classical as medial and interruptive, precisely as the classical revival of the Renaissance once did to the Middle Ages.

The enthusiasm for a mythic Celtic past reflected in the vogue of the Ossian poems flared at the same time that the first translations of the Asiatic Society appeared. Inevitably, the two "discoveries" were paired. As Schwab observes, "in the wake of Ossian, an already existing penchant for certain antiquities of the old world was to benefit the new sciences and enthusiasms; many scholars were members of both the Société Celtique and the

Société Asiatique. The two causes were first linked by mutual concerns, just as Jones had already claimed they were linked in their origins."[7] Sir William Jones himself, in his translation of the *Shakuntala*, explicitly compared the Sanskrit poem to the Ossian poems, at the time still deemed authentic.[8] The *Niebelungenleid* was also compared to Sanskrit works. A dissident from this view, Heinrich Heine (1797–1856), testifies to its widespread circulation. Heine was critical of the analogy, which he partly imputed to the Catholicism of Schlegel, who converted in 1808, and others. Heine praised Schlegel's Orientalism ("he became for Germany what William Jones was for England") but criticizes the frequent connections between Catholicism and Hinduism "uncovered" by Schlegel. "In the *Mahabharata* and the *Ramayana*," he complains, "they see the Middle Ages in elephantine form."[9] Heine claimed that the Schlegel brothers had been intimidated by Goethe's rejection of medievalism into redirecting their interests into Indic studies. This sublimated enthusiasm was nevertheless parallel in that it suggested an even greater antiquity for Germanic culture, through an ultimately Oriental, rather than occidental, descent.

Schwab cites as typical Victor Hugo's (1802–85) placement of the Middle Ages at the pinnacle of world culture, flanked by Persia and India on one side and Homeric Greece on the other. Hugo's image is influenced by Baron Eckstein. Eckstein was a tireless popularizer of the new Oriental studies in the salons of France, and was satirically lampooned "Baron Buddha." The Germanic North, with its instinctive appreciation of beauty, triumphs over the Latin South, with its anemic rationalism. And the great cultural moment of that North was medieval civilization. For the Germans, rationalism was to be associated with France and other foreign cultures. What Eckstein proposed was the displacement of French culture by the literature and culture of the East, which evolves into the triumph of German culture. It was a curious argument for one, like Eckstein, whose audience and country of residence was France. Eckstein, of course, was popularizing Herder's attempt to replace the Italian Renaissance with the German Middle Ages as the turning point of world culture. For Herder, far from being a dusty regression, the European Middle Ages represented the overthrow of classical tyranny and the reinvigoration of culture.

As Schwab points out, the implicit argument that the German Middle Ages represents a *translatio imperii* from ancient Indian antiquity continues as a leitmotif through the nineteenth century. Schwab detects the Orient even behind Wagner's vision of the Middle Ages.[10] Buddhism is filtered through the Grail, and the cycles of history in the *Ramayana* inform the great sweep of the Ring cycle. The very East that is the source of German civilization in linguistic (and racial) Aryanism only achieves its apotheosis in the Christian Middle Ages, or at least Wagner's representation of the period.

In the late nineteenth century, one finds scholars moving from Oriental to medieval studies as easily as an earlier generation of enthusiasts moved from medieval to Oriental studies. This shuttling had a marked effect on the earliest productions of what we would now call Comparative Literature, for in addition to Germanic and Romance philology, nineteenth century-literary research was marked by frequent associations and comparisons of motifs, plots, and characters among European and Eastern literatures, mythologies and folklore. The modern student turning to, say, Frazer's *The Golden Bough* or Stith Thompson's *Index of Folklore Motifs* is as likely to be impressed by their global scale as by their often divided allegiances between what we would now consider distinct genetic and structural explanations.

Romanticism obviously equated the Middle Ages and the Orient, but it kept them by and large on parallel tracks, with the possible exception of a German historical identity that saw its Middle Ages as the fulfillment of a development beginning in the Orient. For most thinkers, their appeal and their importance lay in their otherness, particularly in displacing the neoclassical paradigm of tracing all invention to Greece and Rome. In his early book of poems, *Les Orientales*, Victor Hugo, whose *Hunchback of Notre Dame* would be the most influential late-Romantic recreation of the Middle Ages, praises Oriental poetry, where "everything was great, rich, fruitful as in the Middle Ages, that other sea of poetry."[11] For Hugo, the power of both the Medieval and the Oriental was their separate but equal revision of histories past and present: "Would we not have a higher and broader view of this modern age by studying the Middle Ages, and of the ancient world by studying the Orient?" Implicit in Hugo's observation is a series of assumptions, which would resonate through the rest of the nineteenth century. The Middle Ages and the Orient are parallel universes, rather than part of a matrix of influences and invasions as in earlier connections. The preeminent contribution of these great past civilizations is their ability to stimulate our imaginations. But most strikingly, the Medieval is accorded a direct connection to modernity, explaining the origin of national and civil identity, while the Orient is a living museum of the past, bracketed off from modern development or even excluded from the potential for development.

Despite the prestige of Oriental origins in Romantic historiography, by the nineteenth century, a discourse of Western superiority begins to enter what had been a brief celebration of cultural relativism. It was the West that was to be the inheritor of the grandeur of Sanskrit and Indo-European (and other ancient) civilizations. Comparative studies began to emphasize the creative energy of the Gothic and the relatively static quality of Oriental architectures. If Islamic architecture was unchanging and uncreative, and Gothic architecture had distinct phases and a rich history of development, this would have come as no surprise to the Victorians familiar with nineteenth-century philology. For Von Humboldt and Schlegel, the organic and creative syntax of Indo-European contrasted with the inorganic and merely additive structure of the Semitic languages. Said's account of Renan's philology emphasizes the separation of East and West in language as well as in power.[12] The "original" languages of the sacred texts have no special status. Indeed, what philology reveals is the relative inadequacy of their conceptions which are only to be fully developed in Indo-European languages. Renan's project, that is, is not only to demonstrate the historicity and revisionism and multiple authorship of the Gospels, but to strip them of their original and sacred power. That power is now shifted to the interpreter, to the philologist, to a primarily Western form of knowledge. So in language, thus in architecture, or more properly, both were expressions of what would soon be understood as differences in race as well as in the languages of culture. Even the older category of Oriental languages was related to the Biblical diffusionist theory that linguistics slowly began to replace. "Semitic" languages, a category previously known as "Oriental" languages, were named in the eighteenth century for Shem, one of the other sons of Noah. In the nineteenth century, through the work of Renan and others, linguistic groupings are transformed into cultural, even political history. Aryans were supposedly polytheistic, migratory, dynamic, and transformative; Semites, especially Hebrews, never leave their historical homeland, turn inward, and insulate their religion and culture against change. Inheriting a mindset from neoclassicism, philology pictures Aryans as the new Greeks, the inventors and disseminators of culture.

Architectural history and criticism, developing into its recognizably modern form at the same time as the histories of language and of literature, also demonstrate complex and often contradictory parallels between the European Middle Ages and the East, both ancient and modern. Mark Crinson points out that while there were archeological attempts to understand classical architecture since the mid-seventeenth century and serious archaeology of Gothic architecture since the late eighteenth century, serious attempts to understand Islamic architecture were rare before the mid-nineteenth century:

> Those travellers who went to the Near East for cultural reasons, or those who mixed cultural with commercial or diplomatic purposes, usually wanted to understand the geography and civilizations of the Bible (seeing oriental customs as a continuation of Biblical life), and to explore Egypt as a palimpset still bearing the traces of European origins. In this sense, travelling in distance was also travelling in time, and the activity of description might

well be the translation of the enterprise of natural history into an observation
of the cultural past.[13]

Crinson links this new study to the increasing dominance of Europe over
the Ottoman Empire and to incursions into its dominions on the one hand
and to the rise of ethnography on the other.

Egyptologists, including the influential Edward Lane (1801–76), were as
drawn to the Islamic architecture of Cairo as they were to its ancient monuments. Islamic architecture was considered to be "medieval" because it
corresponded to that historical nomenclature in Northern and Western
civilization. Lane, in his *Manners and Customs of the Modern Egyptians*, was
acutely aware of the pressures of modernity, but for all that, conceived of
modern Egyptian life as constituting an unbroken and relatively unchanged
thread from "medieval" Cairo.[14] Lane criticized Muhammed Ali's industrialization efforts as alien to the essentially agricultural economy and society
of Egypt. Muhammad Ali, who came to power in 1836, like Ataturk almost
a century later, saw his role as modernizing and Europeanizing a
"medieval" and "oriental" Egypt. British architects visiting Istanbul or India
found themselves fascinated with architectural details that reminded them
of the craftsmanship of medieval Europe, and that they generalized to the
largely "medieval" state of Eastern economies and societies. William
Burges, the winner of the competition for the Crimean Memorial Church
in Istanbul, was especially attracted to the Northern regions of Istanbul,
including Galatea and the old city, which he compared to a sort of medieval
Pompeii.[15]

If there was a shift from the picturesque to the interpretation of the
Orient as essence, it was marked by the *Description de l'Egypte* (Commission
des Sciences et Arts d'Egypte 1809–28), the great post-invasion Napoleonic
inventory of Egyptian architecture and culture.[16] As Said points out in his
important discussion of the *Description*, its ideological strategy was to place
Revolutionary France in the lineage of the great empires of antiquity, relat-
ing to Egypt's past glories rather than its barbaric present.[17] Indeed, the
present state of Egypt was conceived of as "medieval" in the Enlightenment
pejorative sense of the word. As Mark Crinson observes:

> It was between the three images of ancient, medieval and modern Egypt that
> the study of Islam was to be stretched. Modern Egyptians were regarded as
> still medieval in their way of life, and yet pragmatic information about their
> country had to be gathered for the purposes of modernization. Ancient
> Egyptian civilization was still held to contain eternal verities, and yet the cul-
> ture of its descendants seemed alternatively time bound or corrupt, resulting
> from the teaching of a false prophet. The dazzling and beguiling image of
> that medieval culture had somehow to be mastered or rationalized, and yet

mastery of Egypt's past could perhaps only come about by mastery of her present.[18]

As early as 1835, it was still possible to locate a positive understanding of the expression of spirituality in both Islamic and Gothic architecture. In his 1835, "On the Influence of Religion upon Art," Owen Jones (1809–74) saw religious architecture as expressing a sort of racial memory, and he compares both Islamic and Gothic architecture to the present state of religious architecture in Britain:

> Who that has stood beside the fountain of the Mosque of Sultan Hassan in Grand Cairo, or has trod the golden halls of the fairy palace of the Alhambra, has not felt the calm, voluptuous translation of the Koran's doctrines? Who amidst the aisles of a Gothic cathedral has not felt materialism wither away, and awe-struck by the mysterious character of the building, cried out—Here, indeed, is the dwelling-place of the Christian's God! Here may He be worshipped in purity of spirit?[19]

Of course, Jones's rhetoric contrasts the spirituality of Gothic architecture with the sensuousness of Islamic architecture. The Gothic strikes awe, the Mosque echoes the calm voluptuousness of the Koran. The Gothic, and by extension the Western, is described in patriarchal language; Islamic architecture is feminized: "calm," "voluptuous," and "sensuous." Its implicit paganism and its connection with both romance and sexuality is suggested in the analogy to the "fairy palace," a common association. Nevertheless, Jones is according a certain power to Islamic architecture that at least allows a horizontal connection, however stretched, to its Western counterpart, the Gothic. Indeed, the Crystal Palace, for which Jones served as interior design architect, seems almost to express this dichotomy between a sober and inspiring exterior and a sensuously riotous interior.[20]

By the mid-nineteenth century, in writers such as James Fergusson (1808–86) in his *Illustrated Handbook of Architecture*, Islamic architecture is described with appreciation, but an appreciation that describes it in ways startlingly similar to some of the ambivalent accounts of the Gothic in the eighteenth century. Indeed, for mid-nineteenth century writers such as Fergusson, writing in the wake of the very different defenses of the Gothic in Pugin and in Ruskin, the Gothic is regarded as an architecture of rational repose, much like the classical architecture it was earlier contrasted with in the sixteenth and seventeenth centuries. It is now Islamic architecture that is uncontrolled, wildly exuberant and "barbaric" in its splendor:

> The Mahometan nations were led by their exuberance of fancy, and impatience of all restraint, to try every form, to attempt to fix every floating idea, and to take advantage of every suggestion either of nature or of art.[21]

As Fergusson says elsewhere, "I lived familiarly among a people who were still practicing their traditional art on the same principles as those which guided the architects of the Middle Ages in the production of similar but scarcely more beautiful or original works."[22] Fergusson insists on the importance of artifacts and buildings as documents of a lost culture. In the present, he says, "when nine-tenths of the population can read and every man who has anything to say rushes into print or makes a speech which is printed next morning, every feeling and every information regarding a people may be dug out of books. But it certainly was not so in the Middle Ages, nor in the early years of Greek or Roman history. Still less was this so in Egypt, nor is it the case in India, or in many other countries; and to apply our English nineteenth century experience to all these seems to me to be a mistake."[23] Fergusson's sense of relative historicism, as well as his defense of antiquarian research, is notable, but what is most striking is the parallel of the Middle Ages with the archaic, or with the East in the present day. In contrast to the ethnographic hierarchies Fergusson employs elsewhere, he reveals a respect for Islam and what it accomplished after the Hejirah. In a typically Western manner, dating to the crusades, he blames part of their success on the corruption and "perversion" of the Orthodox churches, particularly in Egypt and Syria.

Even more striking in Fergusson's preface is his defense of his own opinion that Gothic architecture cannot serve as a standard for judging world architecture: "It is very generally objected to my writings that I neither understand nor appreciate the beauties of Gothic architecture" (xiii) and worries that the enthusiasm for the Gothic may unduly compromise the reception of his argument.[24] But, he says, "if I cannot now speak of Gothic architecture with the same enthusiasm as others, this was not the case in the early part of my career as a student of art . . . I knew and believed in none but the mediaeval styles." He became, he says, a promoter of Gothic revival architecture, which, he hoped, would best even the Gothic of the Middle Ages. This faith in the Gothic, he said, was "first shaken" when he encountered the Mogul architecture of India, "and saw how many beauties of even the pointed style had been missed in Europe in the Middle Ages" (xiv).[25]

Even Thebes and Athens offer beauties unachieved by the Gothic, he says, inadvertently or explicitly returning to the neoclassic consensus that the picturesque Gothic of the eighteenth century reacted against. In the prefatory chapters of his book, he argues for a relatively timeless conception of formal aesthetics in one chapter (beauty, mass, stability, forms, proportion and so forth) and in another chapter argues that these various principles have been employed in different ways by different races (the Semitic, Aryan, and Celtic races especially). For Fergusson, the analysis of formal elements is a static, "scientific" enterprise, while ethnographic analysis is a form of dynamic history, telling the story of the people who made the architecture. Fergusson even seems to predict one of the tenets of modernism, that new forms should follow upon new technologies. Indeed, the buildings he praises from his own time, including the Crystal Palace and the warehouse rows in Manchester, will take their place in the genealogy of functionalist modernism.

If Fergusson's discussion of aesthetics strikes us as proto-modernist, his racial categories, despite their distribution of various vices and virtues to different races, is more compromised. He rejects the notion that civilization marches forward, in Comte's terms, from a "theological" childhood through a "metaphysical" adolescence to a "philosophical" maturity. Instead, Fergusson proposes that different forms of civilization, linked to racial characteristics, exist more or less simultaneously and gain attention through their relative domination of a particular historical moment. If it seems as if his definition of the Aryan as more "republican" and "self-determining" than other races is preferable to the Aryanism of twentieth-century fascism, Fergusson's stereotypes still end up as guiding the "scientific" analysis of buildings he had described earlier in his introductory chapters.

Despite Fergusson's critique of the Gothic, over a third of his four volumes in total are devoted to medieval architecture, and while the actual analysis of buildings is largely technical and aesthetic, his framing arguments reflect his ethnographic assumptions. A particularly revealing passage attempts to distinguish between French and German Gothic:

> As might be expected from the known difference of race, the history of architecture in Germany differs in the most marked degree from that of France . . . Had the Germans been as pure Aryans as they are sometimes supposed to be, they might under certain circumstances have resolved themselves into an aggregation of village communities under one paramount protector.[26]

What kept this from happening, however, was the presence of "a Celtic dominion on their Western Frontier." The aesthetic difference of Northern Germany may have been the result of "Wendish" blood. It is scarcely less comforting that racial mixture kept the Germans from being better medieval architects.

In our own time, we tend to think of eclecticism and revivalism as symptoms of an end of ideology, particularly modernist ideology. But in Victorian Britain and other nineteenth-century European countries, eclecticism and revivalism were themselves the basis for ideological debate. In nineteenth-century Germany, the question was "In Which Style Should We Build?" The choice of period style was understood as a rhetorical choice.

As Mark Crinson remarks in his study of Orientalism and Victorian architecture, "In Victorian Britain is was usually accepted that to build was to create meaning: architecture was 'phonetic', it had 'expressional character', and it exhibited 'particular moral or political ideas.' Choosing a style implied choosing meanings, but what meaning might be ascribed to a particular style was frequently a contested matter in Victorian architecture."[27]

Interestingly, debates developed about the suitability of the Gothic to Eastern locations as the Empire expanded. The Camden Society, with its liturgically based advocacy of a Pugin Gothic aesthetic, argued at first for the exportation of Gothic churches everywhere. But it soon became apparent that at least the strict ecclesiastically correct Camden Gothic, with its elaborate screens and plans, was inappropriate to many colonial climates. By midcentury, an adaptive eclecticism often reflecting local conditions and cultures, became more widely accepted. This eclecticism, often incorporating "Eastern" motifs, was justified by its readability by Islamic and other inhabitants and by familiarity with such designs by local workmen. The sternly Northern Gothic monument, proclaiming its isolation amid the heat and dust was replaced by more appreciation of local and regional styles, signalling also a shift from largely missionary to increasing commercial, diplomatic, and military functions of empire. Such eclecticism did, of course, receive the withering scorn of such journals as *The Ecclesiologist*, which continued to see Gothic not only as the reassertion of the true Church at home, but as an expression of the Church Militant abroad. Anything else would be going native. By mid-century, indeed, High Church Gothic was seen on all sides as militantly and uncompromisingly Western.[28] But the eclecticism, indeed, even the avoidance of Gothic in such projects as the British Church in Alexandria (1845–54) by James Wild avoided the Gothic in favor of an Early Christian plan decorated with non-figurative ornament, amid understandable controversy. Such eclecticism was defended as appropriate to communication with a largely non-Christian, non-Western population. Other debates about Imperial architecture would raise some of the same issues.

For the Crimean Memorial Church in Istanbul, however, the rules of the competition specified Gothic design, with a suggestion that "Southern Gothic" might suit the climate and setting, but specifically excluding Islamic or Byzantine references. In a gesture to Islamic sensibilities, no human representations were allowed as exterior decoration. The national associations of a Pugin-like Northern Gothic were to be modified by a more Ruskinian pan-European and ecumenically Christian Southern Gothic. Although the judge of the competition was to be A.J.B. Beresford Hope, who was closely associated with *The Ecclesiologist*, that journal predictably preferred the more explicitly Northern Gothic second-place design. The "Islamic" quality of Gothic vaulting itself, especially Southern Gothic with its polychrome banding, suggested allusions, either intended contextually or unintended, to the Eastern setting of a Western Church. Inevitably, anything other than the most rigidly Northern Gothic revivalism involved a form of double coding. The original competition's winning entry by William Burges was in any case modified and neutralized by the time of its final design. And by 1863, G.E. Street, the second-place winner, was appointed architect of the church.[29] Street's design is especially of interest because William Morris and Phillip Webb were his students. Unlike Burges, who was open to working with Istanbul's construction practices, Street insisted on British standards for masonry and construction, though he did attempt to design stonework with repetitive patterns supposedly appropriate to the simple skills of Oriental workmen. The result, instead of a dialogue with its Byzantine and Islamic setting, was a marker of religious and national identity, though somewhat modified to fit climate and building techniques.

There is some evidence that even in the last half of the nineteenth century, the Gothic and the Islamic could be regarded as styles appropriate to certain contexts, even by agents who identified with the nationalist and Anglican associations of the Gothic. Crinson describes the impact of the Oriental art historian Austen Henry Layard (1817–94), undersecretary of state for foreign affairs overseeing the ultimately unbuilt Alexandria Consulate in the early 1860s.[30] Layard had some appreciation for both medieval and ancient Middle Eastern architecture, but he had been responsible for some important Gothic projects in London, including George Gilbert Scott's Foreign Office proposal and G.E. Street's Gothic Law Courts. In 1868, Gladstone appointed him chief commissioner of works and Layard attempted to support Gothic designs for new public buildings in London. But for the Alexandria Consulate, Layard was interested in a rhetoric appropriate to local culture, and he encouraged the redesign of the original Italianate plan by the classically inclined T.L. Donaldson into an Islamicized facade, though the result resembled Venetian Gothic as a result.

An equally common assumption was the interpretation of Islamic architecture as a stage in the development of architecture toward the Gothic, particularly in the employment of the pointed arch. In Edward Freeman's 1849 *History of Architecture*, Islamic architecture is represented as frozen in time, never developing beyond one signal contribution to Western architecture, while the Gothic, like all things Western, successively transmuted itself through dynamic phases. In a set of images that are familiar from eighteenth century defenses of both the Gothic and the "Eastern," Freeman describes "Saracenic Fancy," which emphasizes delight, astonishment, and enchantment.[31] The lack of limits or control is especially emphasized, "the exuberance of a fancy, vivid and fertile to the last degree, but uncontrolled by any law of taste or consistency." In a dramatized image, Freeman describes the Norman palace at Palermo in Sicily, which "breathes the most Arabian spirit and calls up the same dreamy and romantic notions of Eastern splendor as the habitations of the Spanish Caliphs. One really feels that a stern-visaged, iron-clad Norman was out of place in such a light, sunny, lofty abode."[32]

In *The Shock of Medievalism*, Kathleen Biddick focuses on the debates over the question of Gothic ornament in the nineteenth century. She sees a split in the understanding of Gothic between a natural and organic style in late-eighteenth- and early-nineteenth-century understandings of Gothic, such as Sir James Hall's reconstructions of Gothic structures in wicker, and a tendency to regard Gothic ornament from a purely visual point of view, illustrating them in catalogues as "skin," and shifting the understanding of the Gothic from "the historical" to "the optic."[33] The resulting commodification of Gothic imagery allowed the "internal colonization" of Britain with neo-Gothic churches and other structures. If I understand Biddick correctly, she is implying a double movement, on the one hand surveying the past as if it were a visual panorama akin to the imperial gaze over foreign lands waiting for the taking, and on the other signifying the dehistoricized images of the Gothic with the semantics of Englishness. But to accomplish the latter, argues Biddick, requires the reintroduction of a somatics and interiority into the concept of the Gothic, which she discovers in the work of Freeman. Biddick's arresting analysis of Freeman is especially interesting considering Freeman's critique of Islamic architecture, which we observed above. In order to defend Gothic, that is, Freeman must purge it of its associations with the planar ornamentation of Islamic architecture.

What we see developing in the architectural languages, however different, of Fergusson and Freeman is something akin to an anthropology of architecture, taking into account race, climate, and geography. In this, they resemble Victorian students of medieval literature. Professional Victorian scholars inherited a tradition of amateur medievalism that developed from antiquarian and folklore studies, as important to English medieval studies as the rise of philology. The interest in folk customs and traditions continues in Victorian scholarship, and this interest continues well into the twentieth century, as folklore studies are central to politically charged scholarship on both the left and the right. At the end of the nineteenth century, however, the perspective on national folk traditions was transformed by the experiences of colonial domination. An anthropological perspective developed to interpret (and control) the culture of imperial subjects, but this perspective was eventually applied to the indigenous traditions of the colonizers' own culture. A similar process had occurred in the eighteenth century, though without the benefit of academic legitimization. As we have seen in chapter one, the Middle Ages constructed by eighteenth-century scholars was associated with both the exotic Orient and the primitive past, with both origin and alterity, and in so doing these writers were manipulating the categories that had been used to reject medieval literary and architectural achievements in Renaissance and neoclassical discourses.

We are familiar with critiques of Victorian literary history as being excessively dependent on evolutionary models. The most well known of these is O.B. Hardison's demolition of the assumptions behind such studies as E.K. Chambers' *The Mediaeval Stage*.[34] According to Chambers, fragments of the Easter service migrate as separate plays to the church porch and the churchyard and then, having been infected with secular and realistic qualities, are eventually expelled to the streets of the towns. There they flower but gradually lose their audience and their dramatic energies to the more sophisticated, and even more realistic and comic, Renaissance stage. Such an argument, Hardison brilliantly pointed out, was hopelessly Darwinian in its assumptions, and ignored both documentary evidence, parallel developments within dramatic traditions, and the dramatic structure of the liturgy itself.

There were, however, Victorian scientific models that competed with or complemented that of evolution. Such models suggested the complex layering of culture, changed only by glacially slow changes or by cataclysmic transformations. The most powerful of these alternative models was geological change. For Victorian and Edwardian thinkers, the science of geology was inescapably bound up with the adventures of exploration and empire. Geology allowed the creation of an imaginary landscape and anthropology filled that landscape with people. These models drew pictures that contrasted with the physical experience of an increasingly urbanized, mechanized, and industrialized modern world. Science provided an image of a world before the onset of human reordering, of industrial exploitation and urban transformation. As evolution rewrote the story of human creation, geology rewrote the story of its physical setting. E.K. Chambers, for instance, invokes this model of developmental form in his *Mediaeval Stage*: "The story is one of a sudden dissolution and a slow upbuilding."[35]

A similar contextual reconstruction was applied to the physical evidence of the human past. The excavation of Troy by Schliemann was typical of a new kind of archeology, one that attempted to reconstruct the context of a site rather than enumerate monuments. Winckelmann's Apollonian neoclassical reconstructions of the ancient world gave way to a fascination with a Dionysian version of classical culture, or, more properly, cultures, since the margins and borders of the ancient world, in a preview of our own debates about the origins of classical civilization, became increasingly central. In Greece itself, a concern with excavation and preservation began almost immediately after the establishment of the republic, but major excavations did not occur until the last decades of the nineteenth century and the beginning of the twentieth. Similarly, post-*resurgimento* Italy was also concerned with the control of antiquities, though by that time the major Etruscan sites had been dug and their artifacts removed. The clearing of the Roman Forum was begun and the excavations at Pompeii were initiated. Knossos and Ephesus were excavated by the British at the turn of the century. The German expeditions to Olympia and Pergamum took place in the 1880s and 1890s. The French digs at Delphi also took place in the 1890s. The romantic archeology of the late eighteenth and early nineteenth centuries followed procedures as concerned with aesthetics as with reconstruction. By the late Victorian era, however, a much more contextualized practice had developed. Ancient Greece and Rome still held a romantically charged fascination for Victorian culture, but archeology increasingly defined itself as a science, throwing light on the mystery of the past, and uncovering the connections between architecture, society, and religion. By the 1840s, the Society of Antiquaries had declined into inactivity, and some of its members, notably Thomas Wright, the editor of medieval texts, founded the British Archaeological Association, to channel the interest in new discoveries occasioned by the construction surrounding the railroads. At first still concerned, perhaps because of its own folkloric origins, with medieval remains, by the 1880s the Association concerned itself largely with prehistoric archaeology. The medieval, first imagined in textual reconstruction as a golden age, now becomes a stage of development, but a stage we have never quite grown out of. It is no accident that Freud should call upon Schliemann's Troy as a metaphor for the unconscious.

By the 1880s, the relation between anthropology and history becomes complicated by the impact of Social Darwinist ideas.[36] Popular anthropology was increasingly articulated as a justification for colonialism, as a paternalistic protection of the less by the more developed. Scholarly anthropology, which now articulates itself as an academic discipline, turns, however, both from this misguided interpretation of natural selection, and from the obsession with development itself, even as promulgated in very different ways by "respectable" anthropologists such as Spencer and Morgan. Instead, observation, fieldwork, and description from the perspective of the anthropologist, becomes its methodology. In the 1850s or so, someone like Max Müller (1823–1900) could address ethnological meetings as a colleague and coworker. By the 1880s, his position is distinctly that of an outsider. For by the later part of the century observation replaces philology as the procedure of ethnology. Both the scholarly development of anthropology and popular racial stereotypes intersect in the problematics of display. Phrenology, museums, the development of photography, and especially international exhibitions, identify the other, and the prior, as cultures of theatricality and display. The turning point, which looks both backward and forward, in these anthropological developments, was the massive and massively influential monument of late-nineteenth century and early twentieth-century anthropology, J.G. Frazer's *The Golden Bough*, with its emphasis on the magical. Inseparable from a context shaped both by Nietzsche and the popularizers who distorted his ideas, both by scientific and social Darwinism, Frazer's work, which provides the basis of modernist primitivism through its quotation in twentieth-century literature, also established the terms for the representation of the racial other. From one point of view the opposite of the rational and the scientific (as the medieval was thought to be), the primitive mind was also intensely practical in its concern with the application of magic and its impact on fertility. In fact, the celebration of fieldwork evidenced in anthropological exhibitions in world's fairs were motivated by a reaction against Frazer's synthetic anthropology, but the aesthetic of those exhibits did nothing but confirm Frazerian prejudices.

The largely structural suppositions of the earlier model of Aryan dispersal was replaced from the mid-nineteenth century on by evolutionary, and often Social Darwinist, premises. The obvious political and imperial assumption of European racial superiority at the same time was a problem for the image of the Middle Ages. Earlier Enlightenment and Whig notions of progress had always denigrated the Dark Ages, but the rise of anthropology and its unstable ideological affinity with colonialism also had an impact on the study and popular conception of the Medieval, which now began to be regarded with a combination of fascination and condescension. In the early nineteenth century, Romantic national self-definition had rewritten the medieval past as a site of origin and indigenous essence, but by the middle and late nineteenth century the security of this site becomes less certain. As anthropology developed as a way of understanding the alien objects of empire, its techniques could also be applied to the alterity of our own history, of the customs of the colonizers themselves in an earlier stage of development.

The development of anthropology, and its dual role as both science and ideology, its interest in performance and display, can be illustrated by references to the great nineteenth-century international exhibitions and world's fairs, which in the middle of the nineteenth-century themselves nearly always justified their existence by their lineage to medieval trade fairs, and which, by the end of the century were noted for their popular and scholarly anthropological exhibits. Moreover, the representation and display of the medieval, plays a minor but revelatory role in these developments,

developments that end up by marginalizing the symbolism of the medieval by the end of the century.

The publicity surrounding the Crystal Palace exhibition of 1851 emphasized the medieval roots of the Great Exhibition, as well as flattering Prince Albert's Arthurian self-representation. Indeed, the Exhibition of Ancient and Medieval Art of the year before, where medieval artifacts were displayed with the aim of inspiring modern manufacturers to higher standards of design and craftsmanship, virtually served as a dry run for the Great Exhibition of 1851.[37] Along with American technology and British goods, one of the most popular exhibits was the India section. Still informed by the notion of Aryan origins, the India exhibits emphasized luxury and undirected wealth. India at this point was not yet officially part of the British Empire. The Crystal Palace's India exhibitions were meant to emphasize the splendor of the East, impressing us with Britain's even greater superiority in its process of absorbing its culture "We enter the western division of the nave," says the illustrated catalogue, "We have here the Indian Court, Africa . . . the West Indies, the Cape of Good Hope, the Medieval Court . . . The long avenue leading from the Medieval Court to the end of the building is devoted to general hardware . . . of all kinds."[38] This interest probably represents something of a revival for medieval antiquities. The British public was probably still disenchanted by the memory of what were considered to be ludicrous, dangerous, and wasteful tournaments staged by Lord Eglenton and his cohorts twenty years before. In the 1840s, Sotheby's was glutted by medieval collectibles so fashionable a few years before.[39]

The Houses of Parliament and their medieval decoration, and a certain Arthurian aura cultivated by Prince Albert, had been responsible for a mid-century rise in popularity of medieval imagery and themes. International courts and displays were also popular, and these in general displayed handmade materials, such as the India Court and the Turkish Court. It was, however, the Medieval Court that drew the most attention because of Pugin's reputation and its relatively large scale. The Medieval Court consisted mostly of furnishings designed by Pugin and executed by his longtime associate firms. If Ruskin and Morris emphasized the process of building and making art, celebrating artisanal techniques and handicraft, Pugin was more concerned with the product rather than the process. He was by no means averse to industrial technology, as long as it was subservient to Gothic design. These firms included George Myers of London and John Hardman and Company of Birmingham, the latter owned by a prominent Catholic family. These included a Prie-Dieu, a cabinet, and various domestic items. Most controversial, however, was the sixteen-foot-high cross designed by a Ms. Kids of Bladensburg, Ireland, illustrated with busts of prophets and evangelists. Comprising largely, but not exclusively, manufactured rather than handcrafted items, the Exhibition drew the scorn of Ruskin and of his younger admirers who would form the core of the Pre-Raphaelite brotherhood. It may also have been Pugin's intense brand of Catholicism that placed the Medieval Court by association with a certain foreignness, although by the late 1840s Pugin's preference for esoteric liturgies had been largely rejected by Newman and his circle in favor of a more Baroque and Roman-inspired architecture and liturgy.[40] Indeed, Pugin's aesthetic by mid-century had been adapted by the Anglican Ecclessiological movement, which planted Pugin-inspired Gothic churches across the countries that contributed their exotic goods to the Great Exhibition, in something of a mirror inversion of the aesthetics of the Crystal Palace.

Medieval imitations, often explicitly religious, were not limited to the Medieval Court alone. Many were displayed in the non-English sections of the exhibition, and presumably were less controversial because of their placement in "foreign"-designated areas. One was a sculptured pietá with a German Gothic screen as background by Ernst Rietschel of Dresden, one of Saxony's most prolific sculptors. (Rietschel's contemporary reputation was itself controversial, since he often represented figures from the historical past in Northern European dress. Rietschel was in any case Lutheran.) Crusading imagery showed up elsewhere. A large statue of Godfrey of Bouillon, who died at Acre in the thirteenth century, was contributed by the Belgian sculptor Eugene Simonis, but was executed in Nineteenth Century neoclassical style. Crusade imagery would become a common theme in imperial and colonial art in a few decades, but it was represented as a synthesis of spiritual and temporal ideals in the mid-century. The Patent Wood Company of London exhibited a print of one of its products, a machine-made Gothic screen. Prince Albert's home duchy of Saxe-Coburg contributed a number of medieval objects to the Great Exhibition, presumably to reflect Albert's own interest in Arthurian imagery and the efforts to link his persona with the Arthurian revival. The woodcarvers Tobias Hoffmeister and Company, of Coburg, offered a German–Gothic style sideboard and four armchairs that made it look as if one were sitting in a Gothic cathedral. Despite the critical distance of the Pre-Raphaelites from the exhibit, a number of exhibited pieces reflected a certain Pre-Raphaelite influence. These included a decorative panel of Queen Eleanor by W.F. D'almaine, imitating "the style of Edward I," on a gold-patterned background as well as Waller Brothers' monumental brass of a female figure. Other medievalizing pieces, such as George Hedgeland's Gothic revival stained glass, lacked Pre-Raphaelite associations; as restorer of King's College, Cambridge, his Gothic frame enclosed a distinctly post-Raphaelite female figure.

A case could be made that the Crystal Palace itself was an orientalized fantasy, representing the industrial world as a light-filled New Jerusalem. From the late eighteenth century on, garden design and architecture borrowed heavily from prints of Oriental and Islamic architecture and buildings. The garden house was appropriately a little Garden of Eden and the Garden of Eden was a place in the East. The imagery of Victorian gardening thus had about it a millenialist iconography of an orientalized geography of revelation. If the Crystal Palace and Paxton's imagining of it struck many observers as related to a Gothic cathedral, its interior was programmatically related to Islamic architecture. Owen Jones, the architect responsible for most of the interior decoration of the Crystal Palace, was one of the first British architects to study Islamic architecture seriously and he used the light and color of the Alhambra as a model.[41]

One of the ironies of the aftermath of the Great Exhibition was a polarization in attitudes toward "oriental" design. Partly as a consequence of the Great Exhibition, Henry Cole and Owen Jones were involved with the establishment of the Department of Practical Art (1852) and the South Kensington Museum, one of the forerunners of the Victoria and Albert Museum. Cole and Jones were critical of the imitative, rather than functional nature of industrial design at the Great Exhibition, predicting modernist critiques. But what they preferred were the artisanal productions of Eastern and Middle Eastern countries, which they judged more functional, especially given the two-dimensional nature of Islamic ornament. Indeed, in his influential *The Grammar of Ornament*, Jones devoted far more space to Islamic design and ornament than to medieval European examples.

The Great Exhibition was already moving toward the presentation of other cultures in theatrical settings. The Turkish and Egyptian courts gestured toward some sense of architectural magnificence, albeit stuffed with products of delight and luxury. The Tunisian Court, however, had a tent made of animal skins, and it was presented as a bazaar, even down to a shopkeeper who could bargain over sales. After the success of the Great Exhibition of 1851, Paxton's building, meant to be temporary, was moved in order to create a permanent exhibition hall, a common move in future world's fairs. The shifting of the Crystal Palace to its site at Sydenham also involved a change of content and program. Instead of the industrial and technical focus of the Great Exhibition, the Crystal Palace was filled with architectural imitations and large-scale models. Art Historians such as James Fergusson and Owen Jones, instrumental in the installation of the Great Exhibition, now were explicit in their exoticism. Fergusson designed the Abyssinian court and Jones a model of the Alhambra. There was also a medieval court, now placed among a collection of architectural styles, including Islamic, Roman, Byzantine, Abyssinian, Pompeian, Egyptian,

Greek, Renaissance, Elizabethan, and Italian styles. The effect was less to emphasize historical development as it was to suggest an almost ahistorical panorama of cultural monuments. From the point of view of style, these sites were presented as equal, but the guidebooks and contemporary reactions distinguished sharply between the exotic and the familiar, the domestic and the foreign, the Western and the Eastern, now allowing influence and analogy, now moralizing and hierarchizing.

The Exhibition of 1851 was followed by several successful international exhibitions over the next few decades. Most of these were contained, as was the Great Exhibition, under one roof. However, as the fairs grew more popular, the number of exhibits soon grew too large for one building, and eventually auxiliary exhibits and buildings flanked or surrounded a central exhibit hall. But less than thirty years later, a different conception of history was evident. What had intervened was anthropology. At the 1867 International Exhibition in Paris, colonial and exotic pavilions created a park around the central and featured roofed area. Soon serious anthropological displays, exotic foreign cultures and crude entertainment were grouped together away from the exhibits of the technological and scientific achievements of the imperial powers.[42] Some European pavilions, with early modern and medieval themes, were placed among these. By the time of the Colonial and Indian Exhibition of 1886, which celebrated India's absorption into the Empire, a loose association between the medieval past of the home country and the present state of the colonies began to be noticeable. A cart drawn by bullocks patrolled up and down an "asian street," actually a reconstruction of a street scene from Sri Lanka, with appropriate facades. This street scene was matched by an "Old London" street, which combined medieval and Tudor elements of a pre-Great Fire London.[43] At the 1889 International Exhibition in Paris, the newly constructed Eiffel Tower was surrounded by "villages." One approached technological modernity through the past and the primitive. By the Paris International Exhibition of 1900, an entire section is devoted to the architectural past and to the colonial other. As mentioned above, two entire medieval theme parks were available at Paris 1900, one a meandering series of streets and buildings, "Vieux Paris," virtually reconstructing the Medieval Paris that had been obliterated by Haussmann's massive plan of urban renewal, and "Paris 1500," a plaza inspired by the literary Middle Ages of Victor Hugo.[44] Old London, Old Paris, Old Vienna, had become popular, even essential aspects of the world's fair by the turn of the century, at the same time that the industrial and economic forces celebrated in the main exhibits were transforming the material remains of the past beyond recognition.

If the medieval past of the European host countries was sometimes represented as if it were a colonized past, the present of the colonies was often presented as if it were the Middle Ages, continuing an attitude toward historical development that we saw articulated in the beginning of the nineteenth century. The "Streets of Cairo," with its overhanging balconies and camel rides, was so popular that it became a fixture at world's fairs from the 1880s on, evolving from an installation depicting Cairo to a generalized Oriental-themed entertainment complex. The image of the Oriental street inevitably was associated with the medieval streets of "Old London" and "Old Paris." At the 1867 Exhibition in Paris, the Khedive of Egypt arrived to find his country represented not by its modern progress, but by a royal palace from medieval Cairo, which he moved into and received "visitors with medieval hospitality."[45] At Paris 1889, Egyptian visitors were also embarrassed to find a reconstruction of medieval Cairo, decorated with artificial dirt.[46] Even in domestically focussed exhibitions, the Middle Ages was associated with kermess, carnival, and the oriental bazaar. The "Old London" area of the International Health Exhibit of 1884 was meant to illustrate a contrast of the medieval past with the elaborate waterworks, plumbing, and public health advantages of the present, but the medieval-themed exhibit turned out to be enormously popular.

In the grand international exhibitions, a clear pattern emerges of an association of the colonial and Oriental (and eventually the Medieval) with entertainment and recreation on the one hand and domestic and occidental architecture with business, industry, and progress on the other. But interesting variations on this pattern were played in some exhibitions held in places other than world capitals. The 1888 Exhibition in Glasgow, for instance, borrowed extensively from Islamic and Oriental architecture in its chief buildings. Even the most industrial and technological displays, and indeed the exhibits of Western nations, were held in a frankly orientalizing exhibition hall. The literature surrounding 1888 Glasgow does not clearly suggest the motivation for this design choice, but one aspect of it seemed to be to associate modern technology with ancient wonder. There were no obviously "medieval" villages at Glasgow 1888, save for a Russian village, which was at least as much exotically foreign as placed in a specific time period. At the more nationally oriented Glasgow Exhibition of 1911, however, which cloaked itself in Scottish Baronial architecture and included items from Scottish history and played much more directly to the Romantic image of Scotland, there was an "Auld Toon," a bit more architecturally consistent, though no less fanciful, than the similar villages exhibited earlier in Manchester and Edinburgh. One entered "Auld Toon" through a newly constructed castle keep which, interestingly, covered a Saracen fountain from an earlier installation.

Typically, even in later exhibitions like the Paris exhibition of 1878, European countries had their architecture represented by contemporary models and drawings, while non-Western countries, when they had architecture represented at all, had theirs represented by imitations of the past. This may be because, as some recent studies have suggested, the foreign stations were really meant to be places of performance, for dances, dramas, and rituals. The tools, clothing, and handicrafts apparently being presented for educational purposes in fact were little more than decontextualized theatrical props. As in American Fairs, which separated the Midway from the main buildings, science, technology, and progress are associated with the European present and future and with the didactic and inspirational celebration of industry. The exotic and foreign, and the past, are offered for entertainment and relaxation. At 1904 St. Louis World's Fair, "natives" staged their own lives in the Hall of Anthropology. In America, the world's fairs ethnographic exhibitions were used as anthropological laboratories, and anthropologists and their students actually used the displays as living laboratories.[47] In fact, in American fairs, Europe itself was treated as an earlier stage of civilization, and up through 1939, you could find German, Austrian, Belgian, Swedish and Dutch "villages."

That the "Old English" village should be placed in such a context suggests the duality of attitudes toward the imitation of the medieval past. At the International Health Exhibition of 1884, an "Old London Street" was constructed as a draw into a larger exhibition on devices, plans, and structures to improve public and personal health.[48] "Old London" was meant to represent the crowded, unsafe, and unhealthy past. In fact, however, it was enormously popular as a themed exhibit on its own, so that the sense of contrast with the clean, modern Victorian present may have been overwhelmed by nostalgia—or more properly, the time-machine experience of alternating between the modern and the medieval. The English village was always the conglomeration of medieval and Tudor architecture, complete with maypole and so forth, an ancestor of what in California at least is called the "Renaissance Pleasure Faire" and staged annually. But interestingly, from the late 1860s, the medieval sections, like Disneylands, had regular performances of mummings, masks and mimes, the sort of village or secular festivals that are the subject of Chambers' first volume with its stress on folkloric drama. Academic anthropology, with its emphasis on fieldwork, would eventually question crudely Social Darwinist assumptions, but the armchair anthropology of writers like J.G. Frazer, whose *The Golden Bough* described the magical outlook of the mind of prescientific cultures. Frazer makes a surprising number of allusions to medieval European culture, as if that culture could be analogous to the archaic worlds it seeks to describe. But the full expression of Frazerian anthropology appear shortly after the turn of the century in E.K. Chambers' *The Mediaeval Stage*. Chambers describes classical culture in racialized terms: "The mimetic instinct, which no race of mankind is wholly without, appears to have been unusually strong amongst the peoples of the Mediterranean stock" (1), but the Romans, "athletic rather than mimetic" highlight the spectacular, a tendency exaggerated by "slaves and foreigners" (2). But Chambers' heart is in folk drama. Chambers imagines a parallel agricultural folk culture, responding only to seasonal change, carrying on its practices under the surface veneer of Christianity. Fragments of the old religion attach themselves to the Church calendar. Fertility rites are disguised as village festivity: Maypoles and the village Maying; garlands and garlanding customs; rain-charms and sun-charms; bonfires and other holiday fires; animal and cereal sacrifices, many echoes of the Frazerian dying and reborn god. Even games and other ludic forms for Chambers are remnants of earlier agricultural and fertility rituals, such as races, wrestling matches, tug-of-wars, charivari, hock-tide capture, and ransom of men by women. Because of our own interest in the mystery plays, we have emphasized this part of Chambers's history, but his most characteristic arguments are articulated in terms of these folk forms and other plays, such as the Robin Hood plays, Mummers' Plays, and sword dances that owe strong allegiances to folk customs. The mystery plays were clearly out of bounds because of their doctrinal content . By the turn of the century and after in English fairs, Ireland and Scotland were typically represented by their romantic "medieval" past, complete with hand-weaving demonstrations and folk singing, while England was represented by manufacturing and science, representing the Celtic parts of England as if they were colonies. The Medieval–Tudor English village, however, escaped this condescension, rather suggesting a certain internal stereotype of English character—of "Englishness"—as having been established in the preindustrial age. Generally, however, the design allusions, especially after 1900, tended toward the Elizabethan and Tudor (and Shakespeare performances replace the earlier folk dances and skits) as the origins of the Empire itself, at the moment when the Imperial hold itself was becoming shaky.

At the 1900 Paris exhibition, England is represented by a Tudor-styled manor designed by Sir Edward Lutyens, the great architect of the Empire and the hero of contemporary postmodern historicism. Interestingly, Lutyens designed this as his friendship with Lady Sackville, Vita's mother, for whom he undertook many projects, was developing and the influence of these projects are noticeable in the pavilion. Lutyens's own wife had become a fanatic follower of theosophy and it consumed her whole life. Lutyens's relation with Lady Sackville continued until her own eventual mental deterioration.[49] In 1920 again, Lutyens provides a modernized Tudor, or more properly, a moderne building with Tudor overtones. Whereas nineteenth century America decorated its townscape with American

Gothic, the suburbs of the early twentieth century, peopled with flight from the newly mongrelized cities, chose the imperial comfort of the Tudor as its signature style.

Even if it seems as if these medieval exhibits were leading to our own employment of the Middle Ages as a theme for entertainment and a license for an almost child-like innocence (or, as in computer and video games, an excuse for a neo-Gothic anarchy), the evidence of their contemporary reception also suggests a good deal of seriousness, respect, and affection on the part of their audiences. Elizabeth Emery has extensively analyzed the development of "Vieux Paris" at the Paris 1900 Exhibition, and she finds that this more scholarly reconstruction (led by Albert Robida, the former science fiction illustrator and futurist) was vastly more popular than the frankly entertainment oriented competing exhibit at "Paris 1500," with its recreation of the world of Hugo's *Notre Dame de Paris*. Emery sees the reception of the "Vieux Paris" as part of a broad-based medievalism in late-nineteenth-century France, which attempted to provide a common ground for the highly polarized post-Dreyfus Affair political scene.[50] "Vieux Paris" was a preservationist reminder of what Paris had lost through its recent urban reconstruction, some of it occasioned by the Commune. Similarly, David Wayne Thomas has persuasively argued that "Old Manchester" at the 1886 Manchester Exhibition rewrote the history of the city in such a way as to attempt to heal the divisions occasioned by its brutal labor history and to offer an alternative to its stereotyping as a city of relentless industrialization.[51] MacKenzie points out that Oriental and Egyptian motifs were considered appropriate for engineering projects, as often were Gothic motifs. More generally, Oriental themes were applied to projects devoted to pleasure and leisure, though some of these, such as the great late Victorian entertainment piers, were also sophisticated engineering feats. Egyptian and Islamic styles were considered especially fitting for the newly emerging cinema. MacKenzie observes that Fergusson finds "Hindu" and "Moslem" forms appropriate to blend in with Gothic revival motifs. He also observes that in the influential categories developed in Owen Jones's *Grammar of Ornament* that the great majority are Oriental or Eastern and only about 5 or 6 were Western in provenance. He also points to the strong Oriental (though here really Japanese) influence on Art Nouveau, especially in Scotland.[52]

These different ways of reading the medieval exhibits at the great nineteenth-century world's fairs return us to the complex debate on the nature of the Middle Ages with which I began. For as I have argued, since the Renaissance there has been a sometimes implicit and sometimes explicit debate as to whether the Middle Ages was a continuation or an interruption in the development of Western culture, whether it was indigenous and local, the very point of origin of the modern nation on the one hand, or whether it was foreign and imposed, the result of contamination by outside forces on the other. Such questions, as Patrick Geary has recently reminded us in *The Myth of Nations* still resonate with sometimes destructive political force.[53] At the great nineteenth-century world's fairs, this implicit tension was literally staged through medieval pavilions, streets, and exhibitions, as another chapter in the unexpectedly related histories of Orientalism and medievalism

Historians and anthropologists have demonstrated in recent years the various ways in which the Empire came home. At the same time that westernizing habits and fashions were adapted by the elites in the colonies and dominions of the colonial powers, exotic taste began to mark the elites of the home countries. My point here is to suggest that this unequal crosspollination also existed in time as well as space. The present development of the colonized and the primitive was represented as "medieval," and conversely, the medieval past itself was pictured as exotic and primitive, as native and "native" at the same time. The identity of medieval performance and ethnic display and performance is one example of such a representation. From our own apparently superior position, it is easy enough to uncover these analogies. But there is another relatively unquestioned assumption in Victorian and Edwardian scholarship and in the exhibits I have mentioned, which we still retain. For even the most radical present-day analyses of medieval culture, borrowing from our own anthropology, have tended to replicate this same late-Victorian conception of medieval culture as essentially identical with its theatricality, to identify the medieval as the theatrical. In our own most vibrant and interesting analyses, we unconsciously have carried on a late-nineteenth century definition of medieval culture as one of display, spectacle, and excess. In so doing, our own historicisms have continued the task of an orientalizing ethnography, which imagines the medieval as both ancient and wise and childlike, and naive at the same time. I have no interest in establishing modern superiority over earlier conceptions of the Middle Ages. Indeed, what I suspect is that we have inherited precisely the contradictions I have analyzed here, for we still think of the Medieval, and its theatricality, as both comforting and strange, as simultaneously *gemütlich* and *unheimlich*.[54] It is that foreign land in which we are always at home.

NOTES

Introduction

1. Edward Said contributed a blurb to the publication of the novel. See, of course, Edward W. Said, *Orientalism* (New York: Pantheon Books, 1978). For an important, but very different, association of orientalism and "anglo-saxonism," see Allen J. Frantzen, *Desire for Origins: New Language, Old English, and Teaching the Tradition* (New Brunswick, N.J.: Rutgers University Press, 1990).
2. L.P. Hartley, *The Go-Between* (London: H. Hamilton, 1953), 1.
3. For an analysis of the instability of categories within Orientalist discourse, see Lisa Lowe, *Critical Terrains: French and British Orientalisms* (Ithaca: Cornell University Press, 1991). The following discussion obviously depends on the huge literature surrounding such influential studies as Benedict Anderson, *Imagined Communities: Reflections on the Origin and Spread of Nationalism* (London: Verso, 1983); and Homi K. Bhabha, *Nation and Narration*, ed. Homi K. Bhabha (London: Routledge, 1990) and Homi K. Bhabha, *The Location of Culture* (London: Routledge, 1994). Of the many books by Smith on national and ethnic identity, helpfully surveying different positions on these subjects, see Anthony D. Smith, *Myths and Memories of the Nation* (New York: Oxford University Press, 1999) and Anthony D. Smith, *The Ethnic Origins of Nations* (Oxford: Basil Blackwell, 1987).
4. In John Evelyn, tr. Roland Fréart, *A Parallel of the Ancient Architecture with the Modern* (London: J. Walthoe, 1733), 9.
5. Christopher Wren, "On the State of Westminster Abbey," in James Elmes, *Memoirs of the Life and Works of Sir Christopher Wren* (London: Priestley and Weale, 1823), 110.
6. The best guide to the rediscovery of romance in the eighteenth century remains Arthur Johnston, *Enchanted Ground: The Study of Medieval Romance in the Eighteenth Century* (London: Athlone Press, 1964). For a larger framework behind these literary ideas, see René Wellek, *The Rise of English Literary History* (Chapel Hill: University of North Carolina Press, 1941) and René Wellek, *A History of Modern Criticism: 1750–1950* (New Haven: Yale University Press, 1955).

7. Pierre-Daniel Huet, *A Treatise of Romances and Their Original* (London: Printed by R. Battersby for S. Heyrick, 1672).

8. Joseph Ritson, *Ancient Engleish Metrical Romanceës* (London: W. Bulmer and Company, for G. and W. Nicol, 1802), xxviii.

9. Richard Hurd, *Hurd's Letters on Chivalry and Romance, with The Third Elizabethan Dialogue* (New York: AMS Press, 1976), 154.

10. Edward W. Said, *The World, the Text, and the Critic* (Cambridge, MA.: Harvard University Press, 1983), 248–67.

11. George W. Stocking, *Victorian Anthropology* (New York: Free Press, 1987), 23; Thomas R. Trautmann, *Aryans and British India* (Berkeley: University of California Press, 1997). For a study of the impact of Aryan racial theories on the British Empire as a whole, see Tony Ballantyne, *Orientalism and Race: Aryanism in the British Empire*, Cambridge Imperial and Post-Colonial Studies Series (New York: Palgrave, 2002).

12. Raymond Schwab, *Oriental Renaissance: Europe's Rediscovery of India and the East, 1680–1880* (New York: Columbia University Press, 1984).

13. See R.J. Smith, *The Gothic Bequest: Medieval Institutions in British Thought, 1688–1863* (Cambridge: Cambridge University Press, 1987) especially on the politics of the "Norman Yoke" suppressing an essential Anglo-Saxon Englishness and its use as a way of justifying parliamentary power.

14. See George W. Stocking, *After Tylor: British Social Anthropology, 1888–1951* (Madison: University of Wisconsin Press, 1995); on Kemble, see Bruce Dickins, *J.M. Kemble and Old English Scholarship* (London: H. Milford, 1940) and Eleanor Nathalie Adams, *Old English Scholarship in England from 1566–1800* (New Haven: Yale University Press, 1917). For the discourse of India, frequently in terms of the past of the European empires, see Ronald B. Inden, *Imagining India* (Oxford: Basil Blackwell, 1990).

15. On the Great Exhibition, see Yvonne Ffrench, *The Great Exhibition, 1851.* (London: Harvill Press, 1950).

16. An interesting prehistory of the ethnic displays of the international exhibitions can be found in the standard study by Richard D. Altick, *The Shows of London* (Cambridge, MA.: Belknap Press, 1978).

17. See Alexander Joseph Denomy, *The Heresy of Courtly Love* (New York: D.X. McMullen Co., 1947); and Denis de Rougemont, *Love in the Western World* (New York: Harcourt, Brace and Company, 1940).

18. As Maria Rosa Menocal has pointed out, the exclusion, or the minimalization, of the possibility of non-Western sources of medieval culture is something of an obsession, even in comparative disciplines that should welcome it. See Maria Rosa Menocal, *The Arabic Role in Medieval Literary History: A Forgotten Heritage* (Philadelphia: University of Pennsylvania Press, 2003); and Maria Rosa Menocal, *Shards of Love: Exile and the Origins of the Lyric* (Durham: Duke University Press, 1994). Important studies of the medieval English literary tradition and its relation to the East and South are Dorothee Metlitzki, *The Matter of Araby in Medieval England* (New Haven: Yale University Press, 1977); and Alice E. Lasater, *Spain to England: A Comparative Study of Arabic, European, and English Literature of the Middle Ages* (Jackson: University Press of Mississippi, 1974).

19. See Roger Sherman Loomis, *Celtic Myth and Arthurian Romance* (New York: Columbia University Press, 1927) and ed. Roger Sherman Loomis, *Arthurian Literature in the Middle Ages: A Collaborative History* (Oxford: Clarendon Press, 1959).

20. To have Indiana Jones seek the Holy Grail in *Indiana Jones and the Last Crusade* is a coincidental summary image of my argument. Indiana Jones is, of course, named after "Oriental Jones," none other than Sir William Jones, who is credited with discovering the relation of Sanskrit to European languages. As with much eighteenth and nineteenth, and certain strands of twentieth century popular culture, the Eastern and the Medieval are parallel and often intertwined alternative histories. On Jones' life, see Garland Hampton Cannon, *The Life and Mind of Oriental Jones: Sir William Jones, the Father of Modern Linguistics* (Cambridge: Cambridge University Press, 1990).

21. For a convincing demonstration of such a position, see Michelle R. Warren, *History on the Edge: Excalibur and the Borders of Britain, 1100–1300*, Medieval Cultures (Minneapolis: University of Minnesota Press, 2000).

22. See Traian Stoianovich, *French Historical Method: The Annales Paradigm* (Ithaca, N.Y.: Cornell University Press, 1976); John M. Ganim, "The Literary Uses of the New History," in *The Idea of Medieval Literature: New Essays on Chaucer and Medieval Culture in Honor of Donald R. Howard*, ed. James M. Dean (Newark: University of Delaware Press; Associated University Presses, 1992), 209–26; Aron Gurevich, *Historical Anthropology of the Middle Ages*, ed. Jana Howlett (Chicago: University of Chicago Press, 1992); Aron Gurevich, *Medieval Popular Culture: Problems of Belief and Perception*, Cambridge Studies in Oral and Literate Culture (Cambridge: Cambridge University Press, 1988); Carlo Ginzburg, *The Cheese and the Worms: The Cosmos of a Sixteenth-Century Miller* (Baltimore: Johns Hopkins University Press, 1980); Natalie Zemon Davis, *Society and Culture in Early Modern France* (Stanford, CA.: Stanford University Press, 1975); Marshall David Sahlins, *Islands of History* (Chicago: University of Chicago Press, 1985); Clifford Geertz, *The Interpretation of Cultures: Selected Essays* (New York: Basic Books, 1973).

23. On Turner, see the excellent volume *Victor Turner and the Construction of Cultural Criticism: Between Literature and Anthropology*, ed. Kathleen M. Ashley (Bloomington: Indiana University Press, 1990).

24. Jeffrey Jerome Cohen, *The Postcolonial Middle Ages*, The New Middle Ages (New York: St. Martin's Press, 2000).

25. Bruce Holsinger, "Medieval Studies, Postcolonial Studies, and the Genealogies of Critique," *Speculum* 77 (2002): 1195–227.

26. John Dagenais and Margaret Greer, "Decolonizing the Middle Ages: Introduction," *Journal of Medieval and Early Modern Studies* 30, no. 3 (2000): 431–48. On Petrarch, see the important article by Nancy Bisaha, "Petrarch's Vision of the Muslim and Byzantine East," *Speculum* 76 (2001): 284–314.

27. See, for instance, the lively account by Maria Rosa. Menocal, *The Ornament of the World: How Muslims, Jews, and Christians Created a Culture of Tolerance in Medieval Spain* (Boston: Little, Brown, 2002); and the detailed chapters in Maria Rosa Menocal, *The Literature of Al-Andalus*, ed. Maria Rosa. Menocal,

Cambridge History of Arabic Literature (New York: Cambridge University Press, 2000). The many studies by Norman Daniel remain useful; see Norman Daniel, *The Arab Impact on Sicily and Southern Italy in the Middle Ages* (Cairo: Istituto italiano di cultura per la R.A.E., 1975); Norman Daniel, *The Arabs and Mediaeval Europe* (London: Longman, 1979); Norman Daniel, *Islam and the West: The Making of an Image* (Edinburgh: University Press, 1960); Norman Daniel, *Islam, Europe and Empire* (Edinburgh: Edinburgh University Press, 1966).

28. The scholarly literature on medieval orientalism (though much of that literature might question that term) has been steadily growing in recent years, perhaps most dramatically foregrounded by Cohen's *Postcolonial Middle Ages*. Some of these studies suggest how early the pattern of Western self-identification being formed in the mirror of the East articulates itself. Brenda Deen Schildgen, *Dante and the Orient*, Illinois Medieval Studies (Urbana: University of Illinois Press, 2002) argues that Dante transforms the tropes of the "Matter of the East" into an internal crusade and internal discovery, aimed at recapturing Europe as it were. The standard study of European identities in the later Middle Ages is Robert Bartlett, *The Making of Europe: Conquest, Colonization and Cultural Change 950–1350* (Princeton: Princeton University Press, 1993).

Chapter One   The Middle Ages as Genre

1. Huet, *A Treatise of Romances.*

2. Hippolyte Taine, *History of English Literature* (New York: H. Holt and Company, 1886), 43.

3. Horace, *Satires, Epistles, and Ars Poetica with an English Translation*, Loeb Classical Library (Cambridge: Harvard University Press, 1932), 450–51.

4. It is a passage which stands as a talisman to medieval rhetoricians such as Geoffrey of Vinsauf, who is not entirely precise as to its warnings: "Et ita vitabimus vitium illud quod apellatur incongrua partium positio . . . Quod vitium tangit Horatius in *Poetria* sub his verbis" (*Documentum de arte versificandi* II.3.154–5) in Edmond Faral, *Les Arts Poétiques Du XIIe et Du XIIIe Siècle* (Paris: É. Champion, 1924).

5. Giorgio Vasari, *Le Opere di Giorgio Vasari* (Firenze: Sansoni, 1973), 137.

6. An important history of ideas of the Gothic is Paul Frankl, *The Gothic* (Princeton, N.J.: Princeton University Press, 1960).

7. On the gendering of the imagination in general, see Marie Hélène Huet, *Monstrous Imagination* (Cambridge, MA.: Harvard University Press, 1993); for Bakhtin on Vasari, see M.M. Bakhtin, *Rabelais and His World* (Cambridge, MA.: MIT Press, 1968), 33.

8. Partha Mitter, *Much Maligned Monsters: History of European Reactions to Indian Art* (Oxford: Clarendon Press, 1977).

9. John Evelyn, *A Parallel of the Ancient Architecture with the Modern*, 9.

10. Wren, "On the State of Westminster Abbey," 110. Molière praised the paintings of his friend Pierre Mignard at Val-de-Grâce, which contrasted with "du fade

goût des ornements gothiques/Ces monstres odieux des siècles ignorants."
See Molière, Œvres de Molière., eds. Eugène André, Despois and Paul Mesnard (Paris: Hachette et cie., 1873), 541.

11. John Aubrey, *Chronologia Architectonica*, p. 186 cited in Michael Hunter, *John Aubrey and the Realm of Learning* (New York: Science History Publications, 1975), 162. I have relied on Hunter's transcriptions of the *Chronologia*, included in the manuscript of the widely known and published *Monumenta Britannica*, Bodleian MS Top. Gen. C. 25, ff-152–79. For an important contextualization of Aubrey in terms of the appreciation of Gothic architecture, see Howard Colvin, *Essays in English Architectural History* (New Haven: Published for the Paul Mellon Centre for Studies in British Art by Yale University Press, 1999), 206–16.

12. Hunter, *John Aubrey and the Realm of Learning*, 218.

13. James Beattie, *Dissertations Moral and Critical* (London: Printed for W. Strahan; and T. Cadell, in the Strand; and W. Creech at Edinburgh, 1783), 560.

14. Thomas Warton, *Observations on the Fairy Queen of Spenser* (London: R. and J. Dodsley, 1762), 322–23. See also Thomas Warton, *The History of English Poetry*, ed. Richard Price (London: Printed for T. Tegg, 1824).

15. Richard Hurd, *Letters on Chivalry and Romance*, 60–61.

16. Hurd, *Letters, on Chivalry and Romance*, 139–40.

17. "These Giants were oppressive feudal Lords, and every Lord was to be met with, like the Giant, in his strong hold, or castle. Their dependants of a lower form, who imitated the violence of their superiors, and had not their castles, but their lurking-places, were the Savages of Romance," Hurd, *Letters*, 96.

18. Hurd, *Letters, on Chivalry and Romance*, 152.

19. Hurd, *Letters, on Chivalry and Romance*, 154.

20. See Christopher Hill, *Puritans and Revolutionaries: Essays in Seventeenth-Century History Presented to Christopher Hill*, ed. D.H. Pennington (Oxford: Clarendon Press and Oxford University Press, 1982), 50–122; R.J. Smith, *The Gothic Bequest*.

21. See Samuel Kliger, " 'The 'Goths' in England: An Introduction to the Gothic Vogue in Eighteenth-Century Aesthetic Discussion,' " *Modern Philology* 43 (1945): 107–17.

22. Quoted in Stuart Piggott, *William Stukeley: an Eighteenth-Century Antiquary.* (Oxford: Clarendon Press, 1950), 24. See Alexander Gordon, *Itinerarium Septentrionale or, A Journey Thro' Most of the Counties of Scotland, and Those in the North of England* (London: Printed for the author and sold by G. Strahan etc., 1726).

23. Stuart Piggott, *William Stukeley*, 55.

24. Samuel Kliger, *The Goths in England*.

25. As Kliger observes in *The Goths in England*: "The equilibrum of opposites was more or less stable, but its constant tendency was towards instability in the direction of undue emphasis on either 'reason' or 'nature,' especially when such exterior forces as Tory politics with its intrenched [*sic*] beliefs in security and the *status quo*, or contrariwise, the force of whig politics with its stress on progress and on an expanding future, tended to upset the equilibrium in either of the two direction. The facts of Gothic freedom—the Whig

protests against monarchical restraints—Gothic energy—the picture of a youthful, ardent people supplanting the decadent Romans and rejuvenating the world thereby—depicted an opposition between 'nature' and 'reason'."

26. See Jordanes, *Iordanis Romana et Getica*, Monumenta Germaniae Historica Inde Ab Anno Christi Quingentesimo Usque Ad Annum Millesimum et Quingentesimum. (Berlin: Weidman, 1882). For a modern English translation, see Jordanes, *The Gothic History of Jordanes in English Version* (Cambridge; New York: Speculum Historiale; Barnes & Noble, 1966).

27. A convenient translation is Snorri Sturluson, *Heimskringla the Norse King Sagas*, trans. Samuel Laing (London: J.M. Dent, 1930).

28. Snorri Sturluson, *The Prose Edda*, trans. Arthur Brodeur (New York: The American-Scandinavian Foundation, 1916).

29. Widukind, *Rerum Gestarum Saxonicarum Libri Tres*, Monumenta Germaniae Historica (Hannover: Hahnsche Buchhandlung, 1989).

30. Aylett Sammes, *Britannia Antiqua Illustrata or, The Antiquities of Ancient Britain, Derived from the Phœicians* (London: Printed by T. Roycroft, for the author, 1676), 35.

31. Pierre-Daniel Huet, *A Treatise of Romances*, 10.

32. See Warburton's preface to Miguel de Cervantes Saavedra, *The Life and Exploits of the Ingenious Gentleman Don Quixote de la Mancha*, Charles Jarvis (London: Printed for J. and R. Tonson, and R. Dodsley, 1742), xv.

33. Thomas Percy, *Reliques of Ancient English Poetry* (London: L.A. Lewis, 1839), III, 8.

34. Thomas Warton, *History of English Poetry*, 1.

35. John Husbands, *A Miscellany of Poems by Several Hands* (Oxford: Printed by Leon. Lichfield, 1731), preface.

36. William Collins, *Oriental Eclogues* (London, 1760), 5.

37. Nathan Drake, *Literary Hours or, Sketches, Critical, Narrative, and Poetical* (London: Longman, Hurst, Rees, Orme, and Brown, 1820), I, 139.

38. Drake, *Literary Hours*, I, 147.

39. Most of these connections are carried through the history of romanticism and celebrated rather than denigrated. Victor Hugo, who writes as much about architecture as about anything, continued the obsession with the origins in the East, "L'ogive chez les goths de l'Orient venue," *Avant l'exil* in Victor Hugo, *Œvres Poétiques, Bibliothèque de la Pléiade* ([Paris]: Gallimard, 1964), I, 478. *Notre-Dame de Paris* literally represents the figuratively monstrous as identical with the Gothic. Interestingly, after about the 1850s, the Gothic becomes moralized and domesticated in America, and in contrast to the political valence of Palladian neoclassicism, the Gothic is championed as providing something like a church for every family; hence, Grant Wood's "American Gothic."

40. See Heinrich Hübsch, *In What Style Should we Build?: The German Debate on Architectural Style*, trans. Wolfgang Herrmann (Santa Monica, CA: Getty Center for the History of Art and the Humanities, 1992). Interestingly, the use of the adjective "Barbaric" in such contexts was proscribed during the Nazi era in Germany.

41. On Romanticism and Orientalism, especially in relation to the rise of empire, see Saree Makdisi, *Romantic Imperialism: Universal Empire and the Culture of Modernity*, Cambridge Studies in Romanticism (Cambridge: Cambridge University Press, 1998); Filiz Turhan, *The Other Empire: British Romantic Writings About the Ottoman Empire*, Literary Criticism and Cultural Theory (New York: Routledge, 2003); Tim Fulford and Peter J. Kitson, *Romanticism and Colonialism: Writing and Empire, 1780–1830*, ed. Tim Fulford (Cambridge: Cambridge University Press, 1998).

42. On the politics of medievalism, see Alice Chandler, *A Dream of Order: The Medieval Ideal in Nineteenth-Century English Literature* (Lincoln, Nebraska: University of Nebraska Press, 1970) and Mark Girouard, *The Return to Camelot* (New Haven: Yale University Press, 1981). The story of popular medievalism and chivalric nostalgia in the nineteenth century has been well told by Girouard. Girouard is especially helpful in detailing the influence of chivalric ideals upon the "Young Englanders" and the nostalgia, social as well as cultural, represented by the Middle Ages in their program. Chandler's *A Dream of Order* characterizes the high literary use of the medieval revival as a retreat from a critique of the present in its formulation of the Middle Ages as Golden Age. No matter how different the uses to which nineteenth-century writers and politicians put medieval romance, the ideal of romance remained more important than the individual works that made up the genre.

43. See Stephanie L. Barczewski, *Myth and National Identity in Nineteenth Century Britain: The Legends of King Arthur and Robin Hood* (Oxford: Oxford University Press, 2000). For a discussion of how Germanic nationalism is negotiated in the debates on the Celtic or Germanic origins of British national origins, see Maike Oergel, *The Return of King Arthur and the Nibelungen: National Myth in Nineteenth-Century English and German Literature*, European Cultures (New York: Walter de Gruyter, 1998). See also, in general, Hugh A. Mac-Dougall, *Racial Myth in English History: Trojans, Teutons, and Anglo-Saxons* (Hanover, N.H.: University Press of New England, 1982). On the shift towards a Saxon bias in Victorian historiography and literature, see Claire A. Simmons, *Reversing the Conquest: History and Myth in Nineteenth-Century British Literature* (New Brunswick, N.J.: Rutgers University Press, 1990).

44. Joseph Ritson, *Ancient Engleish Metrical Romanceës* (London: W. Bulmer and Company, for G. and W. Nicol, 1802), xxviii.

45. Ritson, p. xvi.

46. Ritson, p. (lix–lx).

47. Ritson, p. lxix.

48. Ritson, p. xciv.

49. In any case the relative lateness of British academic literary study meant that room was still left for men of letters and nonacademic scholars to play an important role in the establishment of the field. In the earlier part of the nineteenth century, this gap was filled by the book clubs, of which the Roxburghe club was the most productive, for which see Harrison R. Steeves, *Learned Societies and English Literary Scholarship in Great Britain and the United States* (New York: Columbia University Press, 1913). Composed largely of

aristocratic and gentlemanly amateurs, the clubs originally concerned them-selves with antiquarian matters of all kind, increasingly centering, however, on editions and literary miscellany. By mid-century, few of the clubs still functioned actively, and their place was taken by publishing societies. The tone of the clubs is best communicated by the rancor that met Sir Frederick Madden's edition of *Havelock the Dane*, largely because Madden was a non-member. Madden represents one aspect of nonacademic professionalism, through his appointment at the British Museum. Irascible and difficult, he combined an early fascination with medievalist antiquarianism with a sure sense of judgment, both textual and aesthetic. His work on the Pearl manu-script is best known to modern scholars, but he also produced important editions of *Havelock the Dane*, *William of Palerne*, the *Brut*, *Sir Gawayne*, the Wycliffe Bible and Mathew Paris' chronicle. In his dyspeptic dismissal of the efforts of other projects, he also predicts the judgments of modern editors upon nineteenth-century pioneering editorial efforts. Madden seemed attracted to the nexus of historiography and fictionalization that marks medieval literature for twentieth century rather than eighteenth-and nineteenth-century scholars. Even in treating the most exotic Middle English romances, he refrains from the rapture of his predecessors. His criti-cal observations are understandably lean, but the fact remains that the nature of his profession minimized the influence he would have other than in terms of the standards of his work. See Robert William Ackerman and Gretchen P. Ackerman, *Sir Frederic Madden: A Biographical Sketch and Bibliography* (New York: Garland Pub., 1979).

50. A recent biography is William Benzie, *Dr. F.J. Furnivall: Victorian Scholar Adven-turer* (Norman, OK.: Pilgrim Books, 1983); the best account of the study of Middle English is now David Matthews, *The Making of Middle English, 1765–1910*, Medieval Cultures (Minneapolis: University of Minnesota Press, 1999); an excellent related comparative account of Chaucer studies is now available in Richard J. Utz, *Chaucer and the Discourse of German Philology: A History of Reception and an Annotated Bibliography of Studies, 1793–1948*, Making the Middle Ages (Turnhout: Brepols, 2002).

51. W.P. Ker, *Epic and Romance* (London: Macmillan, 1897), a.

52. Ker, *Epic and Romance*, 371.

53. Ker, *Epic and Romance*, 3.

54. Ker, *Epic and Romance*, 5.

55. Ker, *Epic and Romance*, 5.

56. Ker, *Epic and Romance*, 5.

57. Ker, *Epic and Romance*, 7.

58. The most complete account of these structures and their context is Megan Aldrich, "Gothic Sensibility: The Early Years of the Gothic Revival," in *A.W.N. Pugin Master of Gothic Revival* (New Haven: Published for the Bard Graduate Center for Studies in the Decorative Arts, New York by Yale University Press, 1995).

59. A.W.N. Pugin, *The True Principles of Pointed or Christian Architecture* (London: J. Weale, 1841), 4.

60. A.W.N. Pugin, *Contrasts or, A Parallel Between the Noble Edifices of the Middle Ages, and Corresponding Buildings of the Present Day, Shewing the Present Decay of Taste. Accompanied by Appropriate Text* (London: C. Dolman, 1841), iii.

61. Pugin, *Contrasts*, v.

62. Pugin, *Contrasts*, 6.

63. Pugin, *Contrasts*, 12.

64. See Quatremère de Quincy, *The True, the Fictive, and the Real: The Historical Dictionary of Architecture of Quatremere de Quincy*, trans. Samir Younés (London: A. Papadakis, 1999) and Quatremère de Quincy, *Dictionnaire Historique d' Architecture* (Paris: Librairie d'Adrien le Clere, 1832).

65. See Hübsch, *In What Style Should we Build? the German Debate on Architectural Style*. See also W.D. Robson-Scott, *The Literary Background of the Gothic Revival in Germany: A Chapter in the History of Taste* (Oxford: Clarendon Press, 1965).

66. "The Stones of Venice" in John Ruskin, *The Works of John Ruskin*, ed. Edward Tyas Cook (London: G. Allen, 1903), IX, 40.

67. Crinson, Mark Crinson, *Empire Building: Opentalism and Victorian Architecture* (London: Routledge, 1996), 57, reads Ruskin's reaction as a primarily Protestant interest in medieval ornament, emphasizing its naturalism, not, as in Pugin, emphasizing the ritual function of medieval art and architecture.

68. "On the Unity of Art," *The Two Paths* in Ruskin, *The Works of John Ruskin*, XVI, 307.

69. Richard Ellmann, *Golden Codgers: Biographical Speculations* (London: Oxford University Press, 1973).

70. Crinson, *Empire Building* (73) points out that earlier French Romantic scholars regarded Byzantine architecture as "Neo-Greek," as connecting classical and Gothic architecture as part of the same historical lineage, rather than as the result of collision and contamination. See also David B. Brownlee, "Neugriechesch/Néo-Grec: The German Vocabulary of French Romantic Architecture," *Journal of the Society of Architectural Historians* 50 (1991): 18–21.

71. John Ruskin, *The Opening of the Crystal Palace Considered in Some of Its Relations to the Prospects of Art* (New York: J.B. Alden, 1973).

72. Ruskin, *The Opening of the Crystal Palace*, 10–11.

73. Ruskin, *The Opening of the Crystal Palace*.

74. Barczewski, *Myth and National Identity*, 219.

75. Allen J. Frantzen, " 'Chivalry, Sacrifice and The Great War: The Medieval Contexts of Edward Burne-Jones' 'The Miracle of the Merciful Knight'," in *Speaking Images Essays in Honor of V.A. Kolve* (Asheville, NC.: Pegasus Press, 2001), 611–35.

76. See T.E. Lawrence, *Seven Pillars of Wisdom: A Triumph* (London: J. Cape, 1935); a reedited version of Lean's classic film is available as David Lean, *Lawrence of Arabia*, Criterion Collection (United States: The Voyager Company, 1989).

77. Irving Howe, *A World More Attractive: A View of Modern Literature and Politics* (New York: Horizon Press, 1963), 1–40.

78. See John E. Mack, *A Prince of Our Disorder: The Life of T.E. Lawrence* (Boston: Little, Brown, 1976).

79. M.D. Allen, *The Medievalism of Lawrence of Arabia* (University Park, PA.: Pennsylvania State University Press, 1991).

80. Joseph Frank, "Spatial Form in Modern Literature," in *The Widening Gyre: Crisis and Mastery in Modern Literature* (Bloomington: Indiana University Press, 1968), 3–25, 49–62.

81. James Frazer, *The Golden Bough: A Study in Comparative Religion* (New York: Macmillan, 1894).

82. Roger Sherman Loomis, *Celtic Myth and Arthurian Romance*, 1.

83. See Roger Sherman Loomis, ed., *Arthurian Literature in the Middle Ages*.

84. John Speirs, *Medieval English Poetry: The Non-Chaucerian Tradition* (London: Faber and Faber, 1957); C.S. Lewis, "The Anthropological Approach," in *English and Medieval Studies Presented to J.R.R. Tolkien*, ed. Norman Davis (London: Allen, 1962), 219–30.

85. Lewis, "The Anthropological approach" 129.

86. See Traian Stoianovich, *French Historical Method: The Annales Paradigm*.

87. Northrop Frye, *Anatomy of Criticism: Four Essays* (Princeton: Princeton University Press, 1957), 191.

88. William Empson, *Some Versions of Pastoral* (London: Chatto & Windus, 1935).

89. Susan Crane, *Insular Romance: Politics, Faith, and Culture in Anglo-Norman and Middle English Literature* (Berkeley: University of California Press, 1986); Susan Wittig, *Stylistic and Narrative Structures in the Middle English Romances* (Austin: University of Texas Press, 1978).

90. Crane, *Insular Romance*, 1–3.

91. Lee Patterson, *Negotiating the Past the Historical Understanding of Medieval Literature* (Madison, Wis.: University of Wisconsin Press, 1987).

92. Jean-Pierre Mileur, *The Critical Romance: The Critic as Reader, Writer, Hero* (Madison, WI.: University of Wisconsin Press, 1990), discovers the quest romance not in modern literature but in modern criticism. The chief structuralist and post-structuralist critics, according to Mileur, carry on in their own writings the project of romanticism.

93. Especially M.M. Bakhtin, *Rabelais and His World* (Cambridge, MA.: MIT Press, 1968).

94. Wolfgang Kayser, *The Grotesque in Art and Literature* (Bloomington: Indiana University Press, 1963).

95. See John M. Ganim, *Chaucerian Theatricality* (Princeton: Princeton University Press, 1990).

96. Specifically in the essays collected as *The Dialogic Imagination*, ed. Michael Holquist and trans. Carly Emerson and Michael Holquist (Austin: University of Texas Press, 1981).

97. Marshall Berman, *All That is Solid Melts Into Air: The Experience of Modernity* (New York: Simon and Schuster, 1982).

98. C.S. Lewis, "De Descriptione Temporum," in *They Asked for a Paper: Papers and Addresses* (London: G. Bles, 1962), 11.

99. See the personal account by Yuri L. Bessmertny, "August 1991 as Seen by a Moscow Historian, or the Fate of Medieval Studies in the Soviet Era," *American Historical Review* (1992): 803–16.

100. See Aron Gurevich, *Categories of Medieval Culture* (London: Routledge & Kegan Paul, 1985); Gurevich, *Historical Anthropology of the Middle Ages*; Gurevich, *Medieval Popular Culture.*

Chapter Two   The Middle Ages as Genealogy, or, the White Orient

1. Geoffrey, Monmouth *The Historia Regum Britanniae of Geoffrey of Monmouth,* ed. Acton Griscom (London: Longmans, Green and Co., 1929).
2. James M. Dean, *The World Grown Old in Later Medieval Literature,* Medieval Academy Books (Cambridge, MA.: Medieval Academy of America, 1997).
3. See Robert W. Hanning, *The Vision of History in Early Britain from Gildas to Geoffrey of Monmouth* (New York: Columbia University Press, 1966). The obsession with migrations and origins that we find in Geoffrey of Monmouth, and then find again in a different form in the sixteenth and seventeenth-century accounts of Biblical and even Phoenician origin, which attempted to displace Geoffrey's myth, is not a late development. As Nicholas Howe has demonstrated in his, *Migration and Mythmaking in Anglo-Saxon England* (New Haven: Yale University Press, 1989) the transformation of ancestral migrations into epic and myth is part and parcel of English literature from its earliest, Anglo-Saxon days. Rather than mythicizing the tragedy of British defeat, as in the Arthurian legends, thereby lifting the events from history and rendering them reversible, Howe's thesis is that Old English literature memorializes the Anglo-Saxon triumph.
4. Hanning, *The Vision of History*, 105.
5. Hanning, *The Vision of History*, 106.
6. *An Anonymous Short English Metrical Chronicle,* ed. Ewald Zettl, Early English Text Society (Series) (London: Pub. for the Early English Text Society by H. Milford, Oxford University Press, 1935). For discussions of versions of the same tale in Anglo-Norman, see Lesley Johnson, "Return to Albion," in *Arthurian Literature XIII* (Woodbridge: D.S. Brewer, 1981), 19–40; for the latin translation from the Anglo-Norman, see James P. Carley and Julia Crick, "Constructing Albion's Past: An Annotated Edition of *De Origine Gigantum*," in *Arthurian Literature XIII* (Woodbridge: D.S. Brewer, 1981), 31–114; see also Ruth Evans, "Gigantic Origins: An Annotated Translation of *De Origine Gigantum*," in *Arthurian Literature XVI* (Woodbridge: D.S. Brewer), 197–211.
7. Ewald Zettl, *An Anonymous Short English Metrical Chronicle.* See Jeffrey Jerome Cohen, *Of Giants Sex, Monsters, and the Middle Ages,* Medieval Cultures (Minneapolis, MN: University of Minnesota Press, 1999). A full discussion of the prologue to the Prose *Brut* is now available in Tamar Drukker, "Thirty-Three Murderous Sisters: A Pre-Trojan Foundation Myth in the English Prose *Brut* Chronicle," *Review of English Studies* 54, no. 216 (September 2003): 449–63.

8. See Hector Boece, *A Description of Scotland*, John Bellenden (London, 1587). The best study of the late-medieval Scottish historiographic tradition is R. James Goldstein, *The Matter of Scotland: Historical Narrative in Medieval Scotland*, Regents Studies in Medieval Culture (Lincoln: University of Nebraska Press, 1993). An accessible article on the tradition of the linkage of Egypt and Scotland is William Matthews, "The Egyptians in Scotland: The Political History of a Myth," *Viator* 1 (1970): 289–306.

9. See the edition and subsequent translation by Skene, John Fordun, *John of Fordun's Chronicle of the Scottish Nation*, ed. William Forbes Skene (Edinburgh: Edmonston and Douglas, 1872) and John Fordun, *Johannis de Fordun Chronica Gentis Scotorum*, ed. William F. Skene, Historians of Scotland (Edinburgh: Edmonston & Douglas, 1871).

10. Ranulf Higden, *Polychronicon Ranulphi Higden Monachi Cestrensis Together with the English Translations of John Trevisa and of an Unknown Writer of the Fifteenth Century*, Rerum Britannicarum Medii Aevi Scriptores (London: Longman, 1865).

11. See Hanning, *The Vision of History*, 107.

12. John Stow and Edmund Howes, *The Annales, or, Generall Chronicle of England* (Londini: Impensis Thomae Adams, 1615).

13. See Raphael Holinshed, *Holinshed's Chronicles—England, Scotland, and Ireland; with a New Introd. by Vernon F. Snow* (New York: AMS Press, 1976).

14. See Polydore Vergil, *Historia Anglica, 1555* (Menston: Scolar Press, 1972); and Polydore Vergil, *Polydore Vergil's English History*, ed. Henry Ellis (London: J.B. Nichols, 1846).

15. John Bale, *The Vocacyon of Johan Bale*, ed. Peter. Happé (Binghamton, N.Y.: Medieval & Renaissance Texts & Studies in conjunction with Renaissance English Text Society, 1990), XII, 14.

16. See May McKisack, *Medieval History in the Tudor Age* (Oxford: Clarendon Press, 1971), 22. A helpful account of the careers of the early antiquaries is Graham Parry, *The Trophies of Time: English Antiquarians of the Seventeenth Century* (Oxford: Oxford University Press, 1995); and, for a slightly longer time-line, Joseph M. Levine, *Humanism and History: Origins of Modern English Historiography* (Ithaca: Cornell University Press, 1987).

17. Holinshed, *Chronicles* II. 136–37.

18. See T.D. Kendrick, *British Antiquity* (London: Methuen, 1950), 69–73.

19. See William Camden, *Camden's Britannia, 1695*, ed. Edmund Gibson (New York: Johnson Reprint Corp., 1971).

20. Arthur B. Ferguson, *Utter Antiquity: Perceptions of Prehistory in Renaissance England* (Durham: Duke University Press, 1993).

21. Bedwell's knowledge of Arabic, despite his interest in scientific knowledge beholden to Arabic tradition, was most widely received in his attack on the Koran. See William Bedwell, *Mohammedis Imposturae That is, a Discouery of the Manifold Forgeries, Falshoods, and Horrible Impieties of the Blasphemous Seducer Mohammed: With a Demonstration of the Insufficiencie of His Law, Contained in the Cursed Alkoran, Deliuered in a Conference Had Betweene Two Mohametans, in Their Returne from Mecha* (London: Imprinted by Richard Field, 1615). For

Andrewes' various controversial interests, see Lancelot Andrewes, *Selected Writings*, ed. P.E. Hewison, Fyfield Books (Manchester: Carcanet Press, 1995).

22. Robert Cotton, *The Danger Wherein the Kingdome Now Standeth*, The English Experience (Amsterdam: Theatrum Orbis Terrarum, 1975).

23. See James Ussher, *The Annals of the World. Deduced from the Origin of Time* (London: Printed by E. Tyler 1658); James Ussher, *Britannicarum Ecclesiarvm Antiqvitates*. (Dublinii: Ex Officina Typographica Societatis Bibliopolarum, 1639). On Ussher in general, see Parry, *The Trophies of Time* 130–56.

24. John Evelyn, *Diary. Now First Printed in Full from the Mss. Belonging to John Evelyn* (Oxford: Clarendon Press, 1955), 21 August 1655.

25. Nathaniel Bacon and John Selden, *An Historical and Political Discourse of the Laws & Government of England from the First Times to the End of the Reign of Queen Elizabeth. With a Vindication of the Antient Way of Parliaments in England, Collected from Some Manuscript Notes of John Selden, Esq.* (London: Printed for J. Starkey, 1689).

26. John Fortescue, John Selden, and Ralph de Hengham, *De Laudibus Legum Angliae*, ed. John Selden, illus. John Selden, trans. John Selden (London: Printed by E. and R. Nutt, and R. Gosling for R. Gosling, 1737).

27. Richard Verstegan, *A Restitution of Decayed Intelligence*, English Recusant Literature, 1558–1640 (Ilkley UK: Scolar Press, 1976).

28. For a discussion of Verstegan's overall program, see Parry, *Trophies of Time*, 49–69.

29. Strabo, *Strabonis Revm Geographicarvm Libri XVII* (Lutetiæ Parisiorum: Typis regüs, 1620).

30. John Twyne, *De Rebvs Albionicis, Britannicis Atqve Anglicis, Commentariorum Libri Duo . . .*, ed. Thomas Twyne (Londini: Excudebat E. Bollifantus, pro R. Watkins, 1590).

31. Samuel Bochart, *Samuelis Bocharti Geographia Sacra* (Excusum Francofurti ad Moenum: Impensis Johannis Davidis Zunneri, typis Balthasaris Christophori Wustii., 1674); Samuel Bochart, *Samuelis Bocharti Opera Omnia* (Lugduni Batavorum Trajecti ad Rhenum: Apud Cornelium Boutesteyn, & Samuelem Luchtmans. Apud Guilielmum vande Water, 1712).

32. John Selden, *De Dis Syris Syntagmata II* (Lipsiae: Impensis J. Brendeli, 1662); a partial English translation was published as John Selden and W.A. Hauser, *The Fabulous Gods Denounced in the Bible* (Philadelphia: J.B. Lippincott & Co., 1880).

33. William Burton, *A Commentary on Antoninus* (London: Printed by T. Roycroft, 1658).

34. John Milton, *Complete Prose Works* (New Haven: Yale University Press, 1953).

35. For a lively description of some of these debates, see Stuart Piggott, *Ancient Britons and the Antiquarian Imagination: Ideas from the Renaissance to the Regency* (London: Thames and Hudson, 1989).

36. Most famously in V. Gordon Childe, *What Happened in History*, Pelican Books (Harmondsworth: Penguin Books, 1942) and V. Gordon Childe, *Man Makes Himself*, The Library of Science and Culture (London: Watts & Co., 1936).

37. The visualization of the archaic past, and of prehistory in the history of anthropology, reveals how often cultural imagery is conflated, most famously

in the woodcuts of American Indians and ancient celts. See Stephanie Moser, *Ancestral Images: The Iconography of Human Origins* (Ithaca, N.Y.: Cornell University Press, 1998).

38. Sammes, *Britannia Antiqua*.

39. Charles Leigh, *The Natural History of Lancashire, Cheshire, and the Peak, in Derbyshire with an Account of the British, Phoenician, Armenian, Gr. and Rom. Antiquities in Those Parts* (Oxford: Printed for the author, etc., 1700).

40. Robert Sheringham, *De Anglorum Gentis* (Cantabrigiæ: Excudebat J. Hayes, impensis E. Story, 1670).

41. Richard Cumberland, *Sanchoniatho's Phœnician History* (London: Printed by W.B. for R. Wilkin, 1720).

42. Edgar de Bruyne, *Études d'Esthétique Médiévale*, Werken Uitgegeven Door de Faculteit Van de Letteren en Wijsbegeerte (Brugge: De Tempel, 1946).

43. See Isaac de La Peyrère, *Men Before Adam. Or, A Discourse Upon the Twelfth, Thirteenth, and Fourteenth Verses of the Fifth Chapter of the Epistle of the Apostle Paul to the Romans. [Followed by] A Theological Systeme Upon That Presupposition, That Men Were Before Adam*. London: [s.n.] 1656).

44. Walter Raleigh, *The History of the World*, ed. C.A. Patrides (London: Macmillan, 1971).

45. For a classic account of the legend of Noah in the sixteenth century and after, see Don Cameron Allen, *The Legend of Noah: Renaissance Rationalism in Art, Science, and Letters*, Illinois Studies in Language and Literature (Urbana: University of Illinois Press, 1949); see also Norman Cohn, *Noah's Flood: The Genesis Story in Western Thought* (New Haven: Yale University Press, 1996); on the relation these ideas to the science of the time, see Paolo Rossi, *The Dark Abyss of Time: The History of the Earth & the History of Nations from Hooke to Vico* (Chicago: University of Chicago Press, 1984).

46. Margaret Trabue Hodgen, *Early Anthropology in the Sixteenth and Seventeenth Centuries* (Philadelphia: University of Pennsylvania Press, 1964), 312.

47. Hodgen, *Early Anthropology*, 313–14.

48. John Ogilby, *America: Being the Latest, and Most Accurate Description of the New World* (London: Printed by the author, 1671), 29–32. See Hodgen, *Early Anthropology*, 314–15.

49. A recent edition is available as Manasseh ben Israel, *The Hope of Israel*, ed. Henry Méchoulan, trans. Henry Méchoulan (Oxford: Published for the Littman Library by Oxford University Press, 1987).

50. Thomas Thorowgood, *Ievves in America, or, Probabilities That the Americans Are of That Race* (London: Printed by W[illiam]. H[unt]. for Tho. Slater, and are to be [sic] sold at his shop at the signe of the Angel in Duck lane, 1650).

51. Georg Horn, *De Originibus Americanis Libri Quatuor* (Hagae Comitis: Sumptibus Adriani Vlacq, 1652).

52. For Stukeley's most notorious writings, see William Stukeley, *Stonehenge, a Temple Restor'd to the British Druids; Abury, a Temple of the British Druids*, Myth & Romanticism (New York: Garland, 1984); and William Stukeley, *Abury, a Temple of the British Druids, with Some Others, Described. Wherein is a More Particular Account of the First and Patriarchal Religion; and of the Peopling the*

British Islands, illus. William Stukeley (London: Printed for the author and sold by W. Innys, R. Manby, B. Dod, J. Brindley, and the booksellers in London, 1743). On Stukeley in general, see the definitive study by Stuart Piggott, *William Stukeley: An Eighteenth-Century Antiquary* (Oxford: Clarendon Press, 1950); an interesting illustrated description of the ideas of Stukeley and others is Sam Smiles, *The Image of Antiquity: Ancient Britain and the Romantic Imagination* (New Haven: Published for the Paul Mellon Centre for Studies in British Art by Yale University Press, 1994).

53. Henry Rowlands, *Mona Antiqua Restaurata* (Dublin: Printed by Aaron Rhames, for Robert Owen, 1723).

54. Charles Vallancey, *An Essay on the Antiquity of the Irish Language* (Dublin: Printed by and for S. Powell, 1772).

55. Aelfric, *The Old English Version of the Heptateuch Aelfric's Treatise on the Old and New Testament, and His Preface to Genesis*, ed. Aelfric (London: Published for Early English Text Society by the Oxford University Press, 1969), 27.

56. Raleigh, *History of the World*.

57. L.A. Waddell, *The Phoenician Origin of Britons, Scots & Anglo-Saxons Discovered by Phoenician & Sumerian Inscription in Britain, by Pre-Roman Briton Coins & a Mass of New History* (London: Williams and Norgate, 1924).

58. Waddell, *Phoenician Origins*, 363.

59. Waddell, *Phoenician Origin*, 364.

60. Waddell, *Phoenician Origin*, 371.

61. Waddell, *Phoenician Origin*, 376. Waddell is still cited as an expert on Tibetan Buddhism. For an account of his place in Tibetan Religous Studies, see *Curators of the Buddha: The Study of Buddhism Under Colonialism*, ed. Donald S. Lopez (Chicago, II: University of Chicago Press, 1995).

62. Robert N. List, *Merlin's Secret: The African and Near Eastern Presence in the Ancient British Isles* (Lanham, Md.: University Press of America, 1999).

63. See Martin Bernal, *Black Athena: The Afroasiatic Roots of Classical Civilization* (New Brunswick, N.J.: Rutgers University Press, 1987). For critiques and a response by Bernal, see Mary R. Lefkowitz, *Black Athena Revisited*, ed. Mary R. Lefkowitz (Chapel Hill: University of North Carolina Press, 1996); and Martin Bernal, *Black Athena Writes Back: Martin Bernal Responds to His Critics*, ed. David Chioni Moore (Durham: Duke University Press, 2001).

64. C. Scott Littleton and Linda A. Malcor, *From Scythia to Camelot: A Radical Reassessment of the Legends of King Arthur, the Knights of the Round Table, and the Holy Grail*, Garland Reference Library of the Humanities (New York: Garland, 1994).

65. Maurice Olender, *The Languages of Paradise: Aryans and Semites, a Match Made in Heaven* (New York: Other Press, 2002), 3.

Chapter Three   The Middle Ages as Display

1. For heavily illustrated studies of international exhibitions and world's fairs in general, see John Allwood, *The Great Exhibitions* (London: Studio Vista, 1977); and Wolfgang Friebe, *Buildings of the World Exhibitions* ([Leipzig, East

Germany]: Edition Leipzig, 1985). For an extended analysis of the relation of world's fairs to imperial politics, see the important study by Paul Greenhalgh, *Ephemeral Vistas: The Expositions Universelles, Great Exhibitions, and World's Fairs, 1851–1939* (Manchester: Manchester University Press, 1988). Approaching American fairs from a similar perspective is Robert W. Rydell, *All the World's a Fair: Visions of Empire at American International Expositions, 1876–1916* (Chicago: University of Chicago Press, 1984). A record of documentation concerning the fairs is available from the Smithsonian on microfilm reels, and much of the following depend on documents bibliographed in Robert W. Rydell, *The Books of the Fairs: Materials About World's Fairs, 1834–1916, in the Smithsonian Institution Libraries* (Chicago: American Library Association, 1992). I am deeply indebted to the important study by P.A. Morton, *Hybrid Modernities: Architecture and Representation at the 1931 Colonial Exposition, Paris* (Cambridge, MA.: MIT Press, 2000) for the germ of many of the ideas that follow.

2. See, for instance, R. Howard Bloch and Stephen G. Nichols, *Medievalism and the Modernist Temper*, ed. R. Howard Bloch and Stephen G. Nichols (Baltimore: Johns Hopkins University Press, 1996); Umberto Eco, *Travels in Hyper Reality: Essays* (San Diego: Harcourt Brace Jovanovich, 1986); Laura Morowitz and Elizabeth Emery, *Consuming the Past: The Medieval Revival in Fin-de-Siècle France* (Aldershot: Ashgate, 2003); Angela Jane Weisl, *The Persistence of Medievalism: Narrative Adventures in Contemporary Culture*, New Middle Ages (New York: Palgrave, 2003); Janine Rosalind Dakyns, *The Middle Ages in French Literature 1851–1900* (London: Oxford University Press, 1973); Alice Chandler, *A Dream of Order: The Medieval Ideal in Nineteenth-Century English Literature* (Lincoln: University of Nebraska Press, 1970); Kathleen Biddick, *The Shock of Medievalism* (Durham London: Duke University Press, 1998); and Kathleen Biddick, *The Typological Imaginary: Circumcision, Technology, History* (Philadelphia: University of Pennsylvania Press, 2003). The series *Studies in Medievalism* has been essential to this enterprise.

3. Rydell, *The Books of the Fairs*.

4. See Henry Adams, *The Education of Henry Adams: An Autobiography*, ed. Henry Cabot Lodge (Boston: Houghton Mifflin Co., 1918); Henry Adams, *Mont-Saint-Michel and Chartres* (Boston: Houghton Mifflin Company Riverside Press, 1913); Henry Adams, *The Letters of Henry Adams*, ed. J.C. Levenson (Cambridge, MA.: Belknap Press of Harvard University Press, 1982); Henry Adams, *Supplement to the Letters of Henry Adams: Letters Omitted from the Harvard University Press Edition of the Letters of Henry Adams*, ed. J.C. Levenson (Boston: Massachusetts Historical Society, 1989).

5. For an overview of Paris 1900, see Richard D. Mandell, *Paris 1900: The Great World's Fair* (Toronto: University of Toronto Press, 1967). For an idea of what an American visitor was expected to see at Paris 1900, see the guidebook by Barrett Eastman, *Paris, 1900: The American Guide to City and Exposition* (New York: Baldwin & Eastman, 1899). Paris 1900 is well documented in photographs and most major American archives such as the Smithsonian and the Library of Congress have extensive holdings. For a contemporary view,

see Marius Bar, *The Parisian Dream City: A Portfolio of Photographic Views of the World's Exposition at Paris* (St. Louis, MO.: N.D. Thompson Publishing Co., 1900); *L'Architecture à l'Exposition Universelle de 1900* (Paris: Librairies-imprimeries réunies, 1902) and *L'Architecture & la Sculpture à l'Exposition de 1900* (Paris: A. Guérinet, 1904).

6. For an argument that some of the thinkers described in the previous chapter predicted Jones's thesis, see George J. Metcalf, "The Indo-European Hypothesis in the Sixteenth and Seventeenth Centuries," in *Studies in the History of Linguistics: Traditions and Paradigms*, Dell Hymes (Bloomington: Indiana University Press, 1974), 233–57.

7. Schwab, *Oriental Renaissance*, 83. Schwab here is paraphrasing François Joseph Picavet, *Les Idéologues: Essai sur l'Histoire Des Idées* (Paris: F. Alcan, 1891).

8. Kalidasa, *Sacontalá, or, The Fatal Ring*, trans. William Jones (Calcutta, 1789). Chateaubriand also compared the *Sacontalá* to the *Ossian* poems.

9. See Schwab, *Oriental Renaissance*, 75; Heinrich Heine, *The Romantic School and Other Essays*, ed. Jost Hermand, The German Library (New York: Continuum, 1985).

10. Schwab, *Oriental Renaissance*, 438–52.

11. Victor Hugo, *Les Orientales*, Collection Poésie ([Paris]: Gallimard, 1964).

12. Said, *Orientalism*, 139–43. On language study in England, and in general, see the standard works by Hans Aarsleff, *The Study of Language in England, 1780–1860* (Princeton, N.J.: Princeton University Press, 1967); and Hans Aarsleff, *From Locke to Saussure: Essays on the Study of Language and Intellectual History* (Minneapolis: University of Minnesota Press, 1982).

13. Crinson, *Empire Building*, 16. For heavily illustrated examples, see Patrick Conner, *Oriental Architecture in the West* (London: Thames and Hudson, 1979) and Patrick Conner, *The Inspiration of Egypt: Its Influence on British Artists, Travellers, and Designers, 1700–1900*, ed. Patrick Conner (Brighton: Brighton Borough Council, 1983).

14. Edward William Lane, *An Account of the Manners and Customs of the Modern Egyptians* (London: C. Knight and Co., 1837). Lane's work has been reprinted many times, including recent editions.

15. On Burges and the Istanbul competition, see Crinson, *Empire Building*, 154–55.

16. For an edition and translation of the original 1809–28 report of the Commission des Sciences et Arts d'Egypte, see Gilles Néret, *Description de l'Egypte* (Köln: Benedikt Taschen, 1994). For a splendid edition of the prints, see Charles Coulston Gillispie, ed. *Monuments of Egypt The Napoleonic Edition: The Complete Archaeological Plates from la Description de l'Egypte* (Princeton, NJ: Princeton Architectural Press in association with the Architectural League of New York, the J. Paul Getty Trust, 1987).

17. The most sustained critique of Said's *Orientalism* in relation to nineteenth century cultural productions is John M. *MacKenzie, Orientalism: History, Theory, and the Arts* (New York: St. Martin's Press, 1995). Careful to place his larger political sympathies on the side of rather than against Said, he nevertheless attempts to assemble evidence to dispute Said's thesis that Orientalism

as it developed in the nineteenth century accompanied, and even justified, the expansion of imperialism. Even above and beyond his lengthy critique of Said's historiography, however, Mackenzie is even more concerned with a postcolonial studies agenda that he claims follows in Said's wake that assumes that all orientalist representations by Western artists and writers are condescending, dismissive, or hostile to Eastern and Islamic culture. In fact, as Mackenzie acknowledges, postcolonial studies accomodate a wide range of positions on the relative agency and hegemony of colonizer and colonized; however, he insufficiently acknowledges Said's own concern to distinguish sympathetic from condemnatory attitudes. Mackenzie assumes that any sympathy displayed by a Western artist toward an Eastern subject or topic absolves them of Said's critique. However that may be, Mackenzie amasses a good deal of extremely helpful evidence and data, and is attentive to the complexity of the occidental perspective on the Orient, usually when he drops his mission of refuting Said. As Mackenzie notes, the violence often portrayed in Orientalist paintings, even when dealing with animal rather than human subjects, is in many ways an inheritance of Romanticism, and the Romantic conception of the violence sublime, as much as it is a projection of violence onto the East. One might observe, however, that Romantic portrayals of Eastern barbarism and violence, however celebratory and fascinated, do in fact associate barbarism and violence with the East. More to our point, however, MacKenzie observes that such barbarism and violence is also associated with Gothic and medieval themes. On the positive side, Mackenzie notes the obsession with horses and hunting in many nineteenth-century Orientalist paintings. He correctly identifies the association of the British aristocracy (and gentry) with their counterparts in Arabian, and especially Bedouin, cultures. This bond is reinforced by the breeding of Arabian horse livestock in the West, and especially in Britain. Interestingly, this association is also noted by later commentators, including T.E. Lawrence, who makes a distinction between noble desert Arabs and decadent city Arabs. It is also a cultural connection noted by some of the travel writers and diplomats who open British communication with the newly important Arab states with the rise of oil economies in the early to mid-twentieth century. Along with other scholars, Mackenzie notes the fascination with the ambivalent gender and sexual relations sought after in Orientalist fiction and to some extent, art. Such a fascination is at least partly in reaction to the rigid gender categories of nineteenth-century Western Europe. But at the same time, Mackenzie also correctly observes that the fascination with the Middle Ages, and with the themes of courtly love as they are focussed upon during the same period is also a fascination with a different and more complex set of sexual and gender roles, and are also often as much projection as discovery of medieval practice. Where Said and others have criticized the imagery of the "empty" desert as a justification of conquest and possession—what could be wrong with claiming and cultivating an empty and unappreciated land?—Mackenzie observes that the timelessness and purity of the desert landscape in fact offered an alternative to the historically transformed industrial landscape of nineteenth-century Europe. The pure and empty desert was therefore an alternative, an escape and a critique of European environmental degredation. Other helpful debates with what their authors take to be too broad a brush, and too one-sided a version of Said's account are Julie F. Codell and Dianne Sachko Macleod, eds, *Orientalism Transposed: The Impact of the Colonies on British Culture* (Aldershot: Ashgate, 1998); and Jill Beaulieu and Mary Roberts, eds. *Orientalism's Interlocutors: Painting, Architecture, Photography*, Objects/Histories (Durham: Duke University Press, 2002).

18. Crinson, *Empire Building*, 26.

19. Owen Jones, *Lectures on Architecture and the Decorative* Arts ([S.l.]: Printed for private circulation, 1863), 20–21. See the discussion of this passage in Crinson, *Empire Building*, 34.

20. See Jones' most famous work, Owen Jones, *The Grammar of Ornament* (London: Day and son, 1856). For a sense of his appreciation of non-Western traditions, see Owen Jones, *The Alhambra Court in the Crystal Palace.*, Guides and Handbooks, Crystal Palace (London, 1854); Owen Jones, *The Complete "Chinese Ornament": 100 Plates*, Dover Pictorial Archive Series (New York: Dover, 1990).

21. James Fergusson, *The Illustrated Handbook of Architecture Being a Concise and Popular Account of the Different Styles of Architecture Prevailing in All Ages and All Countries* (London: J. Murray, 1855), 469–70. See also James Fergusson, *A History of Architecture in All Countries from the Earliest Times to the Present Day* (London: J. Murray, 1862); James Fergusson, *History of Indian and Eastern Architecture* (New York: Dodd, Mead & Company, 1891).

22. Fergusson, *Illustrated Handbook*, I: ii.

23. Fergusson, *Illustrated Handbook*, I: xii–xiii.

24. Fergusson, *Illustrated Handbook*, I: xiii.

25. Fergusson, *Illustrated Handbook*, I: xiii–xiv.

26. Fergusson, *Illustrated Handbook*, II: 1–2.

27. Crinson, *Empire Building*, 9.

28. I have been presenting the Gothic revival as part of a complex and vexed history dating to the sixteenth century, but we should be reminded that E.J. Hobsbawm and T.O. Ranger, *The Invention of Tradition*, ed. E.J. Hobsbawm (Cambridge: Cambridge University Press, 1983) cites the decision to build the Houses of Parliament in the Gothic Style as a prime example of an invented tradition. As with most invented traditions, it was an effort to establish "the continuity with a suitable historic past" (1). As Hobsawm points out, however, the decision to rebuild the Chambers on the same plan after the devastation of World War II was also an establishment of a new tradition in the guise of connecting with an older one.

29. See Crinson, *Empire Building*, 139.

30. Crinson, *Empire Building*, 185–86.

31. Edward Augustus Freeman, *A History of Architecture* (London: J. Masters, 1849), 271–72.

32. Freeman, *History of Architecture*, 291.

33. Kathleen Biddick, *The Shock of Medievalism* (Durham: Duke University Press, 1998).

34. O.B. Hardison, *Christian Rite and Christian Drama in the Middle Ages: Essays in the Origin and Early History of Modern Drama* (Baltimore: Johns Hopkins Press, 1965); E.K. Chambers, *The Mediaeval Stage* (London: Oxford University Press, 1903).

35. Chambers, *Mediaeval Stage*, I, vi.

36. In addition to Stocking, *Victorian Anthropology*, see Henrika Kuklick, *The Savage Within: The Social History of British Anthropology, 1885–1945* (Cambridge: Cambridge University Press, 1991).

37. Ffrench, *The Great Exhibition, 1851* remains a good account of the development of the exhibition.

38. *Official Descriptive and Illustrated Catalogue of the Great Exhibition of the Works of Industry of All Nations*, 1851 (London: Spicer Brothers, 1851).

39. The best account of these manifestations of popular medievalism remains Girouard, *The Return to Camelot*.

40. See the excellent discussion of the Mediaeval Court and the controversy over Pugin's Catholicism in Jeffrey A. Auerbach, *The Great Exhibition of 1851: A Nation on Display* (New Haven, CT: Yale University Press, 1999).

41. See Jones, *The Alhambra Court*.

42. An interesting prehistory of the ethnic displays of the international exhibitions can be found in the standard study by Altick, *The Shows of London*, especially pp. 268–301.

43. See the description in Frank Cundall, *Reminiscences of the Colonial and Indian Exhibition*, illus. Frank Cundall (London: W. Clowes & Sons, 1886), and Ernest T. Hamy, *Études Ethnographiques et Archéologiques sur l'Exposition Coloniale et Indienne de Londres* (Paris: E. Leroux, 1887).

44. See Morowitz and Emery, *Consuming the Past*.

45. As described in Timothy Mitchell, *Colonising Egypt* (Berkeley: University of California Press, 1988), 220.

46. For a description of the various "Streets of Cairo," see Zeynep Çelik, *Displaying the Orient: Architecture of Islam at Nineteenth-Century World's Fairs*, Comparative Studies on Muslim Societies (Berkeley: University of California Press, 1992).

47. On the slightly later use of world's fairs as anthropological laboratories, see Burton Benedict, *The Anthropology of World's Fairs: San Francisco's Panama Pacific International Exposition of 1915* (Berkeley: Lowie Museum of Anthropology; Scolar Press, 1983).

48. See the excellent account of the exhibition by Annmarie Adams, *Architecture in the Family Way: Doctors, Houses, and Women, 1870–1900*, McGill-Queen's/Hannah Institute Studies in the History of Medicine, Health, and Society (Montreal: McGill-Queen's University Press, 1996), 9–35.

49. See the standard study by Jane Brown, *Lutyens and the Edwardians: An English Architect and His Clients* (London: Viking, 1996).

50. See Emery and Morowitz, *Consuming the Past*.

51. David Wayne Thomas, "Replicas and Originality: Picturing Agency in Daniel Gabriel Rossetti and Victorian Manchester," *Victorian Studies* 43, no. 1

(2000): 67–102. For an illustration of some of the recreations of medieval and early modern Manchester, see Alfred Darbyshire, *A Booke of Olde Manchester and Salford*, ed. George Milner (Manchester: John Heywood, 1887).

52. See MacKenzie, *Orientalism: History, Theory, and the Arts*.

53. Patrick J. Geary, *The Myth of Nations: The Medieval Origins of Europe* (Princeton: Princeton University Press, 2002).

54. The most eloquent analysis of the desire implicit in medievalism is L.O. Aranye Fradenburg, *Sacrifice Your Love: Psychoanalysis, Historicism, Chaucer* (Minneapolis: University of Minnesota Press, 2002).

BIBLIOGRAPHY

Aarsleff, Hans. *The Study of Language in England, 1780–1860*. Princeton: Princeton University Press, 1967.

———. *From Locke to Saussure: Essays on the Study of Language and Intellectual History*. Minneapolis: University of Minnesota Press, 1982.

Ackerman, Robert William, and Gretchen P. Ackerman. *Sir Frederic Madden a Biographical Sketch and Bibliography*. New York: Garland Pub., 1979.

Adams, Annmarie. *Architecture in the Family Way: Doctors, Houses, and Women, 1870–1900*. McGill-Queen's/Hannah Institute Studies in the History of Medicine, Health, and Society. Montreal: McGill-Queen's University Press, 1996.

Adams, Eleanor Nathalie. *Old English Scholarship in England from 1566–1800*. New Haven: Yale University Press, 1917.

Adams, Henry. *Mont-Saint-Michel and Chartres*. Boston, Cambridge: Houghton Mifflin Company Riverside Press, 1913.

———. *The Education of Henry Adams: An Autobiography*. Edited by Henry Cabot Lodge. Boston: Houghton Mifflin Co., 1918.

———. *The Letters of Henry Adams*. Edited by J.C. Levenson. Cambridge: Belknap Press of Harvard University Press, 1982.

———. *Supplement to the Letters of Henry Adams Letters Omitted from the Harvard University Press Edition of the Letters of Henry Adams*. Edited by J.C. Levenson. Boston: Massachusetts Historical Society, 1989.

Aelfric. *The Old English Version of the Heptateuch: Aelfric's Treatise on the Old and New Testament, and His Preface to Genesis*. London: Published for Early English Text Society by the Oxford U.P., 1969.

Aldrich, Megan. "Gothic Sensibility: The Early Years of the Gothic Revival." In *A. W.N. Pugin Master of Gothic Revival*. New Haven: Published for the Bard Graduate Center for Studies in the Decorative Arts, New York by Yale University Press, 1995.

Ali, Tariq. *Shadows of the Pomegranate Tree*. London: Verso, 1993.

———. *The Book of Saladin*. London: Verso, 1999.

Allen, Don Cameron. *The Legend of Noah: Renaissance Rationalism in Art, Science, and Letters*. Illinois Studies in Language and Literature. Urbana: University of Illinois Press, 1949.

Allen, M.D. *The Medievalism of Lawrence of Arabia*. University Park, PA: Pennsylvania State University Press, 1991.

Allwood, John. *The Great Exhibitions*. London: Studio Vista, 1977.

Altick, Richard D. *The Shows of London*. Cambridge, MA: Belknap Press, 1978.

Altick, Richard Daniel. *The Shows of London*. Cambridge, MA: Belknap Press, 1978.

Anderson, Benedict. *Imagined Communities: Reflections on the Origin and Spread of Nationalism*. London: Verso, 1983.

Andrewes, Lancelot. *Selected Writings*. Edited by P.E. Hewison. Fyfield Books. Manchester: Carcanet Press, 1995.

L'Architecture & la Sculpture à l'Exposition de 1900. Paris: A. Guérinet, 1904.

L'Architecture à l'Exposition Universelle de 1900. Paris: Librairies-imprimeries réunies, 1902.

Arden, Heather. *Medievalism in France*. Edited by Heather Arden. Studies in Medievalism. Michigan: Studies in Medievalism, 1983.

Art Journal. *The Illustrated Catalogue of the Great Exhibition of London, 1851*. Kennebunkport: Milford House, 1970.

———. *The Illustrated Catalogue of the Great Exhibition of London, 1851*. Kennebunkport: Milford House, 1970.

Ashley, Kathleen M. *Victor Turner and the Construction of Cultural Criticism: Between Literature and Anthropology*. Edited by Kathleen M. Ashley. Bloomington: Indiana University Press, 1990.

Atterbury, Paul. *A.W.N. Pugin Master of Gothic Revival*. New Haven: Published for the Bard Graduate Center for Studies in the Decorative Arts, New York by Yale University Press, 1995.

Auerbach, Jeffrey A. *The Great Exhibition of 1851: A Nation on Display*. New Haven: Yale University Press, 1999.

Bacon, Nathaniel, and John Selden. *An Historical and Political Discourse of the Laws & Government of England from the First Times to the End of the Reign of Queen Elizabeth. With a Vindication of the Antient Way of Parliaments in England, Collected from Some Manuscript Notes of John Selden, Esq*. London: Printed for J. Starkey, 1689.

Bakhtin, M.M. *Rabelais and His World*. Cambridge: MIT Press, 1968.

Bakhtin, M.M. and Michael Holquist. *The Dialogic Imagination: Four Essays*. Edited by Michael Holquist. Translated by Michael Holquist. University of Texas Press Slavic Series. Austin: University of Texas Press, 1981.

Bakhtin, M.M., and Caryl Emerson. *Problems of Dostoevsky's Poetics*. Edited by Caryl Emerson. Translated by Caryl Emerson. Theory and History of Literature. Minneapolis: University of Minnesota Press, 1984.

Bakhtin, M.M., V.N. Voloshinov, P.N. Medvedev, and Pam Morris. *The Bakhtin Reader: Selected Writings of Bakhtin, Medvedev, and Voloshinov*. Edited by Pam Morris. London: E. Arnold, 1994.

Bale, John. *The Vocacyon of Johan Bale*. Edited by Peter. Happé. Binghamton: Medieval & Renaissance Texts & Studies in conjunction with Renaissance English Text Society, 1990.

Ballantyne, Tony. *Orientalism and Race: Aryanism in the British Empire*. Cambridge Imperial and Post-Colonial Studies Series. New York: Palgrave, 2002.

Barczewski, Stephanie L. *Myth and National Identity in Nineteenth Century Britain: The Legends of King Arthur and Robin Hood*. Oxford: Oxford University Press, 2000.

Bar, Marius. *The Parisian Dream City: A Portfolio of Photographic Views of the World's Exposition at Paris*. St. Louis, MO: N.D. Thompson Publishing Co., 1900.

Beattie, James. *Dissertations Moral and Critical*. London: Printed for W. Strahan; and T. Cadell, in the Strand; and W. Creech at Edinburgh, 1783.

Beaulieu, Jill and Mary Roberts. *Orientalism's Interlocutors: Painting, Architecture, Photography*. Edited by Jill. Beaulieu. Objects/Histories. Durham: Duke University Press, 2002.

Bedwell, William. *Mohammedis Imposturae That is, a Discouery of the Manifold Forgeries, Falshoods, and Horrible Impieties of the Blasphemous Seducer Mohammed: With a Demonstration of the Insufficiencie of His Law, Contained in the Cursed Alkoran, Deliuered in a Conference Had Betweene Two Mohametans, in Their Returne from Mecha*. London: Imprinted by Richard Field, 1615.

Benedict, Burton. *The Anthropology of World's Fairs: San Francisco's Panama Pacific International Exposition of 1915*. Berkeley: Lowie Museum of Anthropology; Scolar Press, 1983.

Benzie, William. *Dr. F.J. Furnivall: Victorian Scholar Adventurer*. Norman, Okla: Pilgrim Books, 1983.

Berman, Marshall. *All That is Solid Melts Into Air: The Experience of Modernity*. New York: Simon and Schuster, 1982.

Bernal, Martin. *Black Athena: The Afroasiatic Roots of Classical Civilization*. New Brunswick: Rutgers University Press, 1987.

———. *Black Athena Writes Back: Martin Bernal Responds to His Critics*. Edited by David Chioni Moore. Durham: Duke University Press, 2001.

Bessmertny, Yuri L. " 'August 1991 as Seen by a Moscow Historian, or the Fate of Medieval Studies in the Soviet Era.' " *American Historical Review* (1992), 803–16.

Bhabha, Homi K. *Nation and Narration*. Edited by Homi K. Bhabha. London: Routledge, 1990.

———. *The Location of Culture*. London: Routledge, 1994.

Biddick, Kathleen. *The Shock of Medievalism*. Durham: Duke University Press, 1998.

Biddick, Kathleen. *The Typological Imaginary: Circumcision, Technology, History*. Philadelphia: University of Pennsylvania Press, 2003.

Bisaha, Nancy. "Petrarch's Vision of the Muslim and Byzantine East." *Speculum* 76 (2001): 284–314.

Bloch, R. Howard. and Stephen G. Nichols. *Medievalism and the Modernist Temper*. Baltimore: Johns Hopkins University Press, 1996.

Bochart, Samuel. *Samuelis Bocharti Opera Omnia. Hoc Est Phaleg, Canaan, et Hierozoicon. Quibus Accesserunt Dissertationes Variae Ad Illustrationem Sacri Codicis Aliorumque Monumentorum Veterum. Praemittitur Vita Auctoris à Stephano Morino Descripta et Paradisi Terrestris Delineatio Ad Mentem Bocharti*. Lugduni Batavorum Trajecti ad Rhenum: Apud Cornelium Boutesteyn, & Samuelem Luchtmans. Apud Guilielmum vande Water, 1712.

Bochart, Samuel, *Wust. Samuelis Bocharti Geographia Sacra Cujus Pars Prior Phaleg de Dispersione Gentium & Terrarum Divisione Facta in Æificatione Turris Babel*. Excusum

Francofurti ad Moenum: Impensis Johannis Davidis Zunneri, typis Balthasaris Christophori Wustii., 1674.

Bodin, Jean. *Selected Writings on Philosophy, Religion, and Politics.* Edited by Paul Lawrence. Rose. Les Classiques de la Pensée Politique. Genève: Librairie Droz, 1980.

Boece, Hector. *A Description of Scotland.* John Bellenden. London, 1587.

Boos, Florence Saunders. *History and Community: Essays in Victorian Medievalism.* Edited by Florence Saunders Boos. Garland Reference Library of the Humanities. London: Garland, 1992.

Brown, Jane. *Lutyens and the Edwardians: An English Architect and His Clients.* London: Viking, 1996.

Brownlee, David B. "Neugriechesch/Néo-Grec: The German Vocabulary of French Romantic Architecture." *Journal of the Society of Architectural Historians* 50 (1991): 18–21.

Bruyne, Edgar de. *Études d'Esthétique Médiévale.* Werken Uitgegeven Door de Faculteit Van de Letteren en Wijsbegeerte. Brugge: De Tempel, 1946.

Burke, Peter *Popular Culture in Early Modern Europe.* New York: Harper and Fow, 1978.

Burton, William. *A Commentary on Antoninus.* London: Printed by T. Roycroft, 1658.

Burton, William. *The Description of Leicester Shire.* London: Printed for John White, 1622.

Camden, William. *Camden's Britannia, 1695.* Edited by Edmund Gibson. New York: Johnson Reprint Corp., 1971.

Cannon, Garland Hampton. *The Life and Mind of Oriental Jones: Sir William Jones, the Father of Modern Linguistics.* Cambridge: Cambridge University Press, 1990.

Carley, James P. and Julia Crick. "Constructing Albion's Past: An Annotated Edition of *De Origine Gigantum.*" In *Arthurian Literature XIII,* 31–114. Woodbridge: D.S. Brewer, 1981.

Cervantes Saavedra, Miguel de. *The Life and Exploits of the Ingenious Gentleman Don Quixote de la Mancha.* Charles Jarvis. London: Printed for J. and R. Tonson and R. Dodsley, 1742.

Chambers, E.K. *The Mediaeval Stage.* London: Oxford University Press, 1903.

Chandler, Alice. *A Dream of Order: The Medieval Ideal in Nineteenth-Century English Literature.* Lincoln: University of Nebraska Press, 1970.

Chateaubriand, François Auguste René. *Génie Du Christianisme.* Paris: Stéréotype d'Herhan, 1807.

Chateaubriand, François Auguste René, and Charles Augustin Sainte-Beuve. *Œvres Complètes de Chateaubriand.* Paris: Garnier frères, 1929.

Childe, V. Gordon. *The Aryans: A Study of Indo-European Origins.* History of Civilization. London: Kegan Paul, Trench, Trübner, 1926.

———. *The Dawn of European Civilization.* History of Civilization. London: K. Paul, Trench, Trübner, 1927.

———. *Man Makes Himself.* The Library of Science and Culture. London: Watts & Co., 1936.

———. *What Happened in History.* Pelican Books. Harmondsworth: Penguin Books, 1942.

————. *Prehistoric Migrations in Europe*. Serie A—Forelesninger. Oslo; Cambridge, MA; London: Aschehoug; Harvard University Press; Kegan Paul, Trench, Trübner & Co., 1950.

Clark, Kenneth. *The Gothic Revival: An Essay in the History of Taste*. New York: Humanities Press, 1970.

Codell, Julie F., and Dianne Sachko Macleod (eds). *Orientalism Transposed: The Impact of the Colonies on British Culture*. Aldershot: Ashgate, 1998.

Cohen, Jeffrey Jerome. *Of Giants: Sex, Monsters, and the Middle Ages*. Medieval Cultures. Minneapolis: University of Minnesota Press, 1999.

————. *The Postcolonial Middle Ages*. The New Middle Ages. New York: St. Martin's Press, 2000.

Cohen, Jeffrey Jerome. *Medieval Identity Machines*. Medieval Cultures. Minneapolis: University of Minnesota Press, 2003.

Cohn, Norman. *Noah's Flood: The Genesis Story in Western Thought*. New Haven: Yale University Press, 1996.

Collins, William. *Oriental Eclogues [by W.Collins]*. London, 1760.

Collins, William, Richard. Wendorf, and Charles. Ryskamp. *The Works of William Collins*. Edited by Richard. Wendorf. Oxford: Clarendon Press; Oxford University Press, 1979.

Colvin, Howard. *Essays in English Architectural History*, New Haven: Published for the Center for Studies in British Art by Yale University Press, 1999.

Conner, Patrick. *Oriental Architecture in the West*. London: Thames and Hudson, 1979.

————. *The Inspiration of Egypt: Its Influence on British Artists, Travellers, and Designers, 1700–1900*. Edited by Patrick Conner. [Brighton]: Brighton Borough Council, 1983.

Cotton, Robert. *The Danger Wherein the Kingdome Now Standeth*. The English Experience. Amsterdam: Theatrum Orbis Terrarum, 1975.

Crane, Susan. *Insular Romance: Politics, Faith, and Culture in Anglo-Norman and Middle English Literature*. Berkeley: University of California Press, 1986.

Crinson, Mark. *Empire Building: Orientalism and Victorian Architecture*. London: Routledge, 1996.

Cumberland, Richard. *Sanchoniatho's Phœician History*. London: Printed by W.B. for R. Wilkin, 1720.

Cundall, Frank. *Reminiscences of the Colonial and Indian Exhibition*. Edited by Frank. Cundall. Illustrated by Frank. Cundall. London: W. Clowes & Sons, 1886.

Çelik, Zeynep. *Displaying the Orient: Architecture of Islam at Nineteenth-Century World's Fairs*. Comparative Studies on Muslim Societies. Berkeley: University of California Press, 1992.

Dakyns, Janine Rosalind. *The Middle Ages in French Literature 1851–1900*. London: Oxford University Press, 1973.

Daniel, Norman. *Islam and the West: The Making of an Image*. Edinburgh: University Press, 1960.

Daniel, Norman. *Islam, Europe and Empire*. Edinburgh: Edinburgh University Press, 1966.

————. *The Arab Impact on Sicily and Southern Italy in the Middle Ages*. Cairo: Istituto italiano di cultura per la R.A.E., 1975.

Daniel, Norman. *The Arabs and Mediaeval Europe*. London: Longman, 1979.

Darbyshire, Alfred. *A Booke of Olde Manchester and Salford*. Edited by George Milner. Manchester: John Heywood, 1887.

Davis, Kathleen. "National writing in the Ninth Century: A Reminder for Post Colonial Thinking about the Nation," *Journal of Medium and Early Modern Studies* 28 (1998): 611–37.

Davis, Natalie Zemon. *Society and Culture in Early Modern France*. Stanford: Stanford University Press, 1975.

———. *The Return of Martin Guerre*. Cambridge: Harvard University Press, 1983.

———. *Fiction in the Archives: Pardon Tales and Their Tellers in Sixteenth-Century France*. The Harry Camp Lectures at Stanford University. Stanford: Stanford University Press, 1987.

Davis, Norman, and C.L. Wrenn. *English and Medieval Studies Presented to J.R.R. Tolkien on the Occasion of His Seventieth Birthday*. London: Allen & Unwin, 1962.

Dean, James M. *The World Grown Old in Later Medieval Literature*. Medieval Academy Books. Cambridge: Medieval Academy of America, 1997.

Denomy, Alexander Joseph. *The Heresy of Courtly Love*. New York: D.X. McMullen Co., 1947.

Dickins, Bruce. *J.M. Kemble and Old English Scholarship*. London: H. Milford, 1940.

Dobin, Howard. *Merlin's Disciples: Prophecy, Poetry, and Power in Renaissance England*. Stanford: Stanford University Press, 1990.

Drake, Nathan. *Literary Hours or, Sketches, Critical, Narrative, and Poetical*. London: Longman, Hurst, Rees, Orme, and Brown, 1820.

Drukker, Tamar. "Thirty-Three Murderous Sisters: A Pre-Trojan Foundation Myth in the English Prose *Brut* Chonicle." *Review of English Studies* 54, no. 216 (September 2003): 449–63.

Drukker, Tamara. "Thirty-Three Murderous Sisters: A Pre-Trojan Foundation Myth in the Middle English Prose *Brut* Chronicle." *Review of English Studies* 54, no. 216 (September 2003): 449–63.

Eastlake, Charles L. and J. Mordaunt Crook. *A History of the Gothic Revival*. Edited by J. Mordaunt Crook. Leicester: Leicester University Press, 1970.

Eastman, Barrett. *Paris, 1900: The American Guide to City and Exposition*. New York: Baldwin & Eastman, 1899.

Eco, Umberto. *Travels in Hyper Reality: Essays*. San Diego: Harcourt Brace Jovanovich, 1986.

Ellis, Steve. *Chaucer at Large: The Poet in the Modern Imagination*. Medieval Cultures. Minneapolis London: University of Minnesota Press, 2000.

Ellmann, Richard. *Golden Codgers: Biographical Speculations*. London: Oxford University Press, 1973.

Elmes, James. *Memoirs of the Life and Works of Sir Christopher Wren*. London: Priestley and Weale, 1823.

Empson, William. *Some Versions of Pastoral*. London: Chatto & Windus, 1935.

Evans, Ruth. " 'Gigantic Origins: An Annotated Translation of *De Origine Gigantum*.' " *In Arthurian Literature XVI* 197–211. Woodbridge: D.S. Brewer, 1981.

Evelyn, John. *Diary*. Oxford: Clarendon Press, 1955.

Faral, Edmond. *Les Arts Poétiques Du XIIe et Du XIIIe Siècle*. Paris: É. Champion, 1924.

Federico, Sylvia. *New Troy: Fantasies of Empire in the Late Middle Ages*. Medieval Cultures. Minneapolis: University of Minnesota Press, 2003.

Ferguson, Arthur B. *Utter Antiquity: Perceptions of Prehistory in Renaissance England*. Durham: Duke University Press, 1993.

Fergusson, James. *An Essay on the Ancient Topography of Jerusalem, with Restored Plans of the Temple, &c., and Plans, Sections, and Details of the Church Built by Constantine the Great Over the Holy Sepulchre, Now Known as the Mosque of Omar*. London: J. Weale, 1847.

———. *The Illustrated Handbook of Architecture: Being a Concise and Popular Account of the Different Styles of Architecture Prevailing in All Ages and All Countries*. London: J. Murray, 1855.

———. *A History of Architecture in All Countries from the Earliest Times to the Present Day*. London: J. Murray, 1862.

———. *History of Indian and Eastern Architecture*. New York: Dodd, Mead & Company, 1891.

Fergusson, James, and James Burgess. *The Cave Temples of India*. London: W.H. Allen & Co., etc., 1880.

Ffrench, Yvonne. *The Great Exhibition, 1851*. London: Harvill Press, 1950.

Fordun, John. *Johannis de Fordun Chronica Gentis Scotorum*. Edited by William F. Skene. Historians of Scotland. Edinburgh: Edmonston & Douglas, 1871.

———. *John of Fordun's Chronicle of the Scottish Nation*. Edited by William Forbes Skene. Edinburgh: Edmonston and Douglas, 1872.

Fortescue, John, John Selden, and Ralph de Hengham. *De Laudibus Legum Angliae*. Edited by John Selden. Illustrated by John Selden, translated by John Selden. In the Savoy [London]: Printed by E. and R. Nutt, and R. Gosling (assigns of E. Sayer, Esq.) for R. Gosling, 1737.

Fradenburg, L.O. Aranye. *Sacrifice Your Love: Psychoanalysis, Historicism, Chaucer*. Medieval Cultures, 31. Minneapolis: University of Minnesota Press, 2002.

France. *L'Exposition Universelle de 1989 et les Grands Projets de l'Etat à Paris* [Paris]: Ministère de l'urbanisme et du logement, Mission de coordination des grandes opérations d'architecture et d'urbanisme, 1983.

Frank, Joseph. "Spatial Form in Modern Literature." In *The Widening Gyre: Crisis and Mastery in Modern Literature*. Bloomington: Indiana University Press, 1968.

Frankl, Paul. *The Gothic*. Princeton: Princeton University Press, 1960.

Frantzen, Allen J. " 'Chivalry, Sacrifice and The Great War: The Medieval Contexts of Edward Burne-Jones' 'The Miracle of the Merciful Knight'." In *Speaking Images: Essays in Honor of V.A. Kolve* 611–35. Asheville: Pegasus Press, 2001.

Frantzen, Allen J. *Desire for Origins: New Language, Old English, and Teaching the Tradition*. New Brunswick: Rutgers University Press, 1990.

Frantzen, Allen J. and John D. Niles. *Anglo-Saxonism and the Construction of Social Identity*. Edited by Allen J. Frantzen. Gainesville: University Press of Florida, 1997.

Frart, Roland. *A Parallel of the Ancient Architecture with the Modern*. London: Printed by T.W. for J. Walthoe, 1733.

Frazer, James. *The Golden Bough: A Study in Comparative Religion*. New York: Macmillan, 1894.

Freeman, Edward Augustus. *A History of Architecture*. London: J. Masters, 1849.

Friebe, Wolfgang. *Buildings of the World Exhibitions*. Leipzig, East Germany: Edition Leipzig, 1985.

Frye, Northrop. *Anatomy of Criticism: Four Essays*. Princeton: Princeton University Press, 1957.

Fulford, Tim, and Peter J. Kitson. *Romanticism and Colonialism: Writing and Empire, 1780–1830*. Edited by Tim Fulford. Cambridge: Cambridge University Press, 1998.

Ganim, John M. *Style and Consciousness in Middle English Narrative*. Princeton: Princeton University Press, 1983.

———. *Chaucerian Theatricality*. Princeton: Princeton University Press, 1990.

———. "The Literary Uses of the New History." In *The Idea of Medieval Literature New Essays on Chaucer and Medieval Culture in Honor of Donald R. Howard*, edited by James M. Dean, 209–26. New York: University of Delaware Press; Associated University Presses, 1992.

———. "The Myth of Medieval Romance." In *Medievalism and the Modernist Temper*. Edited by R. Howard Bloch and Stephen G. Nichols. 148–67. Baltimore: Johns Hopkins University Press, 1996.

Geary, Patrick J. *The Myth of Nations: The Medieval Origins of Europe*. Princeton: Princeton University Press, 2002.

Geertz, Clifford. *The Interpretation of Cultures: Selected Essays*. New York: Basic Books, 1973.

Geertz, Clifford. *Local Knowledge: Further Essays in Interpretive Anthropology*. New York: Basic Books, 1983.

Geoffrey of Monmouth. *The Historia Regum Britanniæ of Geoffrey of Monmouth*. Edited by Acton Griscom. London: Longmans, Green and Co., 1929.

———. *The History of the Kings of Britain*. The Penguin Classics. Baltimore: Penguin Books, 1966.

Germann, Georg. *Gothic Revival in Europe and Britain: Sources, Influences, and Ideas*. Cambridge: MIT Press, 1973.

Gillispie, Charles Coulston. *Monuments of Egypt the Napoleonic Edition: The Complete Archaeological Plates from la Description de l'Egypte*. Edited by Charles Coulston. Gillispie. Princeton, NJ: Princeton Architectural Press in association with the Architectural League of New York, the J. Paul Getty Trust, 1987.

Ginzburg, Carlo. *The Cheese and the Worms: The Cosmos of a Sixteenth-Century Miller*. Baltimore: Johns Hopkins University Press, 1980.

Ginzburg, Carlo. *Clues, Myths, and the Historical Method*. Baltimore: Johns Hopkins University Press, 1989.

Girouard, Mark. *The Return to Camelot: Chivalry and the English Gentleman*. New Haven: Yale University Press, 1981.

Glencross, Michael. *Reconstructing Camelot: French Romantic Medievalism and the Arthurian Tradition*. Arthurian Studies. Cambridge: D.S. Brewer, 1995.

Goldstein, R. James. *The Matter of Scotland: Historical Narrative in Medieval Scotland*. Regents Studies in Medieval Culture. Lincoln: University of Nebraska Press, 1993.

Gordon, Alexander. *Itinerarium Septentrionale or, A Journey Thro' Most of the Counties of Scotland, and Those in the North of England*. London: Printed for the author and sold by G. Strahan etc., 1726.

Gossman, Lionel. *Medievalism and the Ideologies of the Enlightenment: The World and Work of LaCurne de Sainte-Palaye*. Baltimore: Johns Hopkins Press, 1968.

Greenhalgh, Paul. *Ephemeral Vistas: The Expositions Universelles, Great Exhibitions, and World's Fairs, 1851–1939*. Manchester: Manchester University Press, 1988.

Gurevich, Aron. *Categories of Medieval Culture*. London: Routledge & Kegan Paul, 1985.

———. *Medieval Popular Culture: Problems of Belief and Perception*. Cambridge Studies in Oral and Literate Culture. Cambridge: Cambridge University Press, 1988.

———. *Historical Anthropology of the Middle Ages*. Edited by Jana Howlett. Chicago: University of Chicago Press, 1992.

Haddad, Emily A. *Orientalist Poetics: The Islamic Middle East in Nineteenth-Century English and French Poetry*. Aldershot: Ashgate, 2001.

Halfpenny, William and John Halfpenny. *Chinese and Gothic Architecture Properly Ornamented*. New York: B. Blom, 1968.

Hamy, Ernest T. *Études Ethnographiques et Archéologiques sur l'Exposition Coloniale et Indienne de Londres*. Paris: E. Leroux, 1887.

Hanning, Robert W. *The Vision of History in Early Britain from Gildas to Geoffrey of Monmouth*. New York: Columbia University Press, 1966.

Hardison, O.B. *Christian Rite and Christian Drama in the Middle Ages: Essays in the Origin and Early History of Modern Drama*. Baltimore: Johns Hopkins Press, 1965.

Harrison, Antony H. *Swinburne's Medievalism: A Study in Victorian Love Poetry*. Baton Rouge: Louisiana State University Press, 1988.

Hartley, L.P. *The Go-Between*. London: H. Hamilton, 1953.

Heffernan, Carol Falvo. *The Orient in Chaucer and Medieval Romance*. Studies in Medieval Romance. Woodbridge: D.S. Brewer, 2003.

Heine, Heinrich. *De l'Allemagne*. Paris: Presses d'aujourd'hui, 1979.

———. *The Romantic School and Other Essays*. Edited by Jost Hermand. The German Library. New York: Continuum, 1985.

———. *Religion and Philosophy in Germany: A Fragment*. London: Trübner & Co., 1882.

———. *Sämtliche Werke*. Edited by Hans Kaufmann. München: Kindler Verlag, 1964.

———. *History of Religion and Philosophy in Germany*. Edited by Paul Lawrence Rose. James Cook University of North Queensland Historical Publications. Townsville, Qld.: Dept. of History, James Cook University of North Queensland, 1982.

Heng, Geraldine. *Empire of Magic: Medieval Romance and the Politics of Cultural Fantasy*. New York: Columbia University Press, 2003.

Henson, Eithne. *The Fictions of Romantick Chivalry: Samuel Johnson and Romance*. Rutherford: Fairleigh Dickinson University Press; Associated University Presses, 1992.

Higden, Ranulf. *Polychronicon Ranulphi Higden Monachi Cestrensis Together with the English Translations of John Trevisa and of an Unknown Writer of the Fifteenth Century*.

Edited by John Trevisa. Rerum Britannicarum Medii Aevi Scriptores. London: Longman, 1865.

Hill, Christopher. *Puritans and Revolutionaries: Essays in Seventeenth-Century History Presented to Christopher Hill.* Edited by D.H. Pennington. Oxford: Clarendon Press, 1982.

Hobsbawm, E.J. and T.O. Ranger. *The Invention of Tradition.* Edited by E.J. Hobsbawm. Cambridge: Cambridge University Press, 1983.

Hodgen, Margaret Trabue. *Early Anthropology in the Sixteenth and Seventeenth Centuries.* Philadelphia: University of Pennsylvania Press, 1964.

Hoffenberg, Peter H. *An Empire on Display: English, Indian, and Australian Exhibitions from the Crystal Palace to the Great War.* Berkeley: University of California Press, 2001.

Holinshed, Raphael. *Holinshed's Chronicles—England, Scotland, and Ireland with a New Introd. by Vernon F. Snow.* New York: AMS Press, 1976.

Holsinger, Bruce. "Medieval Studies, Postcolonial Studies, and the Genealogies of Critique," *Speculum* 77 (2002): 1195–227.

Horace. *Satires, Epistles, and Ars Poetica with an English Translation.* Loeb Classical Library. Cambridge: Harvard University Press, 1932.

Horn, Georg. *De Originibus Americanis Libri Quatuor.* HagæComitis: Sumptibus Adriani Vlacq, 1652.

Howe, Irving. *A World More Attractive: A View of Modern Literature and Politics.* New York: Horizon Press, 1963.

Howe, Nicholas. *Migration and Mythmaking in Anglo-Saxon England.* New Haven: Yale University Press, 1989.

Huddesford, William, Thomas Warton, Thomas Hearne, Anthony à Wood, and Pre-1801 Imprint Collection (Library of Congress). *The Lives of Those Eminent Antiquaries John Leland, Thomas Hearne, and Anthony à Wood with an Authentick Account of Their Respective Writings and Publications, from Original Papers.* Edited by William Huddesford. Oxford: J. and J. Fletcher, etc., 1772.

Huet, Marie Hélène. *Monstrous Imagination.* Cambridge: Harvard University Press, 1993.

Huet, Pierre-Daniel. *A Treatise of Romances and Their Original.* London: Printed by R. Battersby for S. Heyrick, 1672.

Hugo, Victor. *Les Orientales.* Collection Poésie. Paris: Gallimard, 1964.

———. *Œvres Poétiques.* Bibliothèque de la Pléiade. Paris: Gallimard, 1964.

Hunter, Michael. *John Aubrey and the Realm of Learning.* New York: Science History Publications, 1975.

Hurd, Richard. *Hurd's Letters on Chivalry and Romance, with The Third Elizabethan Dialogue.* New York: AMS Press, 1976.

Husbands, John. *A Miscellany of Poems by Several Hands.* Oxford: Printed by Leon. Lichfield, 1731.

Hübsch, Heinrich. *In What Style Should We Build?: The German Debate on Architectural Style.* Translated by Wolfgang. Herrmann. Santa Monica, CA: Getty Center for the History of Art and the Humanities, 1992.

Inden, Ronald B. *Imagining India.* Oxford: Basil Blackwell, 1990.

Ingham, Patricia Clare, and Michelle R. Warren. *Postcolonial Moves: Medieval Through Modern*. Edited by Patricia Clare Ingham. New York: Palgrave Macmillan, 2003.

John Dagenais and Margaret Greer. "Decolonizing the Middle Ages: Introduction." *Journal of Medieval and Early Modern Studies* 30, no. 3 (2000): 431–48.

Johnson, Lesley. "Return to Albion." In *Arthurian Literature XIII*, 19–40. Woodbridge: D.S. Brewer, 1981.

Johnston, Arthur. *Enchanted Ground: The Study of Medieval Romance in the Eighteenth Century*. London: Athlone Press, 1964.

Jones, Owen. *The Alhambra Court in the Crystal Palace*. Guides and Handbooks, Crystal Palace. Lond., 1854.

———. *The Grammar of Ornament*. London: Day and Son, 1856.

———. *Lectures on Architecture and the Decorative Arts* [S.1.]: Printed for private circulation, 1863.

———. *The Complete "Chinese Ornament": 100 Plates*. Dover Pictorial Archive Series. New York: Dover, 1990.

Jones, William. *Poems, Consisting Chiefly of Translations from the Asiatick Languages To Which Are Added Two Essays*. Oxford: Clarendon Press, 1772.

———. *The Works of Sir William Jones. In Six Volumes*. Edited by Anne Marie Jones. London: Printed for G.G. and J. Robinson and R.H. Evans (successor to Mr. Edwards), 1799.

———. *The Letters of Sir William Jones*. Edited by Garland Hampton Cannon. Oxford: Clarendon Press, 1970.

———. *Discourses Delivered at the Asiatick Society, 1785–1792*. Edited by Roy Hanis and Koren Thomson. British Linguistics in the Eighteenth Century. London: Routledge, Thoemmes Press, 1993.

———. *Sir William Jones: A Reader*. Edited by Satya S. Pachori. Delhi and Oxford: Oxford University Press, 1993.

Jordanes. *Iordanis Romana et Getica*. Monumenta Germaniae Historica Inde Ab Anno Christi Quingentesimo Usque Ad Annum Millesimum et Quingentesimum. Berlin: Weidman, 1882.

———. *The Gothic History of Jordanes in English Version*. Cambridge: Speculum Historiale; Barnes & Noble, 1966.

Kalidasa. *Sacontalá, or, The Fatal Ring, Tr. [by Sir W. Jones]*. Translated by William Jones. Calcutta, 1789.

Kayser, Wolfgang. *The Grotesque in Art and Literature*. Bloomington: Indiana University Press, 1963.

Keller, Barbara G. *The Middle Ages Reconsidered: Attitudes in France from the Eighteenth Century Through the Romantic Movement*. New York: P. Lang, 1994.

Kendrick, T.D. *The Druids: A Study in Keltic Prehistory*. London: Methuen, 1927.

———. *British Antiquity*. London: Methuen, 1950.

Ker, W.P. *Epic and Romance*. London: Macmillan, 1897.

Kinchin, Perilla, Juliet Kinchin, and Neil Baxter. *Glasgow's Great Exhibitions: 1888, 1901, 1911, 1938, 1988*. Wendlebury, Bicester, Oxon: White Cockade, 1988.

Kliger, Samuel. "The 'Goths' in England: An Introduction to the Gothic Vogue in Eighteenth-Century Aesthetic Discussion." *Modern Philology* 43 (1945): 107–17.

Kliger, Samuel. *The Goths in England: A Study in Seventeenth and Eighteenth Century Thought*. New York: Octagon Books, 1972.

Koff, Leonard Michael and Brenda Deen Schildgen. *The Decameron and the Canterbury Tales: New Essays on an Old Question*. Eds. Leonard Michael Koff. Madison: Fairleigh Dickinson University Press, 2000.

Kontje, Todd Curtis. *German Orientalisms*. Ann Arbor: University of Michigan Press, 2004.

Kuklick, Henrika. *The Savage Within: The Social History of British Anthropology, 1885–1945*. Cambridge: Cambridge University Press, 1991.

Lane, Edward William. *An Account of the Manners and Customs of the Modern Egyptians*. London: C. Knight and Co., 1837.

La Peyrère, Isaac de. *Præadamitæ Sive Exercitatio Super Versibus Duodecimo, Decimotertio, & Decimoquarto, Capitis Quinti EpistolæD. Pauli Ad Romanos. Quibus Inducuntur Primi Homines Ante Adamum Conditi*. Amsterdam: Louis & Daniel Elzevier, 1655.

La Peyrère, Isaac de. *Men Before Adam. Or, A Discourse Upon the Twelfth, Thirteenth, and Fourteenth Verses of the Fifth Chapter of the Epistle of the Apostle Paul to the Romans. [Followed by] A Theological Systeme Upon That Presupposition, That Men Were Before Adam*. London, 1656.

Lasater, Alice E. *Spain to England: A Comparative Study of Arabic, European, and English Literature of the Middle Ages*. Jackson: University Press of Mississippi, 1974.

Lawrence, T.E. *Seven Pillars of Wisdom a Triumph*. London: J. Cape, 1935.

Lean, David. *Lawrence of Arabia*. Criterion Collection. United States: Columbia Pictures The Voyager Company, 1989.

Leask, Nigel. *British Romantic Writers and the East Anxieties of Empire*. Cambridge Studies in Romanticism. Cambridge: Cambridge University Press, 1992.

Lefkowitz, Mary R. ed. *Black Athena Revisited*. R. Chapel Hill: University of North Carolina Press, 1996.

Leigh, Charles. *The Natural History of Lancashire, Cheshire, and the Peak, in Derbyshire with an Account of the British, Phoenician, Armenian, Gr. and Rom. Antiquities in Those Parts*. Oxford: Printed for the Author, etc., 1700.

Levine, Joseph M. *Humanism and History: Origins of Modern English Historiography*. Ithaca: Cornell University Press, 1987.

Lewis, C.S. "De Descriptione Temporum." In *They Asked for a Paper: Papers and Addresses*. London: G. Bles, 1962.

———. "The Anthropological Approach." In *English and Medieval Studies Presented to J.R.R. Tolkien*, Norman Davis, 219–30. London: Allen, 1962.

List, Robert N. *Merlin's Secret: The African and Near Eastern Presence in the Ancient British Isles*. Lanham, Md.: University Press of America, 1999.

Littleton, C. Scott and Linda A. Malcor. *From Scythia to Camelot: A Radical Reassessment of the Legends of King Arthur, the Knights of the Round Table, and the Holy Grail*. Garland Reference Library of the Humanities. New York: Garland, 1994.

Loomis, Roger Sherman. *Celtic Myth and Arthurian Romance*. New York: Columbia University Press, 1927.

Loomis, Roger Sherman, ed. *Arthurian Literature in the Middle Ages: A Collaborative History*. Oxford: Clarendon Press, 1959.

Lopez, Donald S. *Curators of the Buddha: The Study of Buddhism Under Colonialism*. Edited by Donald S. Lopez. Chicago: University of Chicago Press, 1995.

Lowe, Lisa. *Critical Terrains: French and British Orientalisms*. Ithaca: Cornell University Press, 1991.

Mabire, Jean-Christophe. *L'Exposition Universelle de 1900*. Paris, France: Harmattan, 2000.

MacDougall, Hugh A. *Racial Myth in English History: Trojans, Teutons, and Anglo-Saxons*. Hanover: University Press of New England, 1982.

MacKenzie, John M. *Orientalism: History, Theory, and the Arts*. New York: St. Martin's Press, 1995.

Mack, John E. *A Prince of Our Disorder: The Life of T.E. Lawrence*. Boston: Little, Brown, 1976.

Maine, Henry Sumner. *Village Communities in the East and West* London: J. Murray, 1890.

Makdisi, Saree. *Romantic Imperialism: Universal Empire and the Culture of Modernity*. Cambridge Studies in Romanticism. Cambridge: Cambridge University Press, 1998.

Manasseh ben Israel. *The Hope of Israel*. Edited by Henry. Méchoulan. Translated by Henry. Méchoulan. Oxford: Published for the Littman Library by Oxford University Press, 1987.

Mancoff, Debra N. *The Arthurian Revival in Victorian Art*. Garland Reference Library of the Humanities. New York: Garland, 1990.

Mancoff, Debra N. *The Arthurian Revival: Essays on Form, Tradition, and Transformation*. Edited by Debra N. Mancoff. Garland Reference Library of the Humanities. New York: Garland Pub., 1992.

Mandell, Richard D. *Paris 1900: The Great World's Fair*. Toronto: University of Toronto Press, 1967.

Matthews, David. *The Making of Middle English, 1765–1910*. Medieval Cultures. Minneapolis: University of Minnesota Press, 1999.

Matthews, William. "The Egyptians in Scotland: The Political History of a Myth." *Viator* 1 (1970): 289–306.

McKisack, May. *Medieval History in the Tudor Age*. Oxford: Clarendon Press, 1971.

Menocal, Maria Rosa. *Shards of Love: Exile and the Origins of the Lyric*. Durham: Duke University Press, 1994.

———. *The Literature of Al-Andalus*. Edited by Maria Rosa. Menocal. Cambridge History of Arabic Literature. New York: Cambridge University Press, 2000.

Menocal, Maria Rosa. *The Ornament of the World: How Muslims, Jews, and Christians Created a Culture of Tolerance in Medieval Spain*. Boston: Little, Brown, 2002.

Menocal, Maria Rosa. *The Arabic Role in Medieval Literary History: A Forgotten Heritage*. Philadelphia: University of Pennsylvania Press, 2003.

Metcalf, George J. "The Indo-European Hypothesis in the Sixteenth and Seventeenth Centuries." In *Studies in the History of Linguistics: Traditions and Paradigms*, Dell Hymes, 233–57. Bloomington: Indiana University Press, 1974.

Metlitzki, Dorothee. *The Matter of Araby in Medieval England*. New Haven: Yale University Press, 1977.

Metzger, David. *Medievalism and the Academy II: Cultural Studies*. Edited by David Metzger. Studies in Medievalism. Cambridge: D.S. Brewer, 2000.

Mileur, Jean-Pierre. *The Critical Romance: The Critic as Reader, Writer, Hero*. Madison: University of Wisconsin Press, 1990.

Milton, John. *Complete Prose Works*. New Haven: Yale University Press, 1953.

Mitchell, Jerome. *Scott, Chaucer, and Medieval Romance: A Study in Sir Walter Scott's Indebtedness to the Literature of the Middle Ages*. Lexington: University Press of Kentucky, 1987.

Mitchell, Timothy. *Colonising Egypt*. Berkeley: University of California Press, 1988.

Mitter, Partha. *Much Maligned Monsters: History of European Reactions to Indian Art*. Oxford: Clarendon Press, 1977.

Molière. *Œvres de Molière*. Edited by Eugène André Despois and Paul Mesnard. Paris: Hachette et cie., 1873.

Morowitz, Laura and Elizabeth Emery. *Consuming the Past the Medieval Revival in Fin-de-Siècle France*. Aldershot: Ashgate, 2003.

Morton, P.A. *Hybrid Modernities: Architecture and Representation at the 1931 Colonial Exposition, Paris*. Cambridge: MIT Press, 2000.

Moser, Stephanie. *Ancestral Images: The Iconography of Human Origins*. Ithaca: Cornell University Press, 1998.

Mulryan, John. *Milton and the Middle Ages*. Edited by John Mulryan. Lewisburg: Bucknell University Press; Associated University Presses, 1982.

Néret, Gilles. *Description de l'Egypte*. Köln: Benedikt Taschen, 1994.

Nicholas, Constance. *Milton's Medieval British Readings*. Urbana, 1951.

Oergel, Maike. *The Return of King Arthur and the Nibelungen: National Myth in Nineteenth-Century English and German Literature*. European Cultures. New York: Walter de Gruyter, 1998.

Official Descriptive and Illustrated Catalogue of the Great Exhibition of the Works of Industry of All Nations, 1851. London: Spicer Brothers, 1851.

Ogilby, John. *America: Being the Latest, and Most Accurate Description of the New World*. London: Printed by the Author, 1671.

Olender, Maurice. *The Languages of Paradise: Aryans and Semites, a Match Made in Heaven*. New York: Other Press, 2002.

Parry, Graham. *The Trophies of Time: English Antiquarians of the Seventeenth Century*. Oxford: Oxford University Press, 1995.

Patterson, Lee. *Negotiating the Past: the Historical Understanding of Medieval Literature*. Madison: University of Wisconsin Press, 1987.

Patterson, Lee. *Literary Practice and Social Change in Britain, 1380–1530*. Edited by Lee Patterson. The New Historicism. Berkeley: University of California Press, 1990.

———. *Chaucer and the Subject of History*. Madison: University of Wisconsin Press, 1991.

Percy, Thomas. *Reliques of Ancient English Poetry*. London: L.A. Lewis, 1839.

Perry, Graham. *The Trophies of Time: English Antiquarians of the Seventeenth Century*. Oxford: Oxford University Press, 1995.

Picavet, François Joseph. *Les Idéologues: Essai sur l'Histoire Des Idées*. Paris: F. Alcan, 1891.

Piggott, Stuart. *William Stukeley: An Eighteenth-Century Antiquary*. Oxford: Clarendon Press, 1950.

Piggott, Stuart. *William Camden and the Britannia*. London, 1953.

————. *Celts, Saxons, and the Early Antiquaries*. Edinburgh: Edinburgh University Press, 1967.

————. *The Druids*. New York: Praeger, 1968.

————. *Ruins in a Landscape: Essays in Antiquarianism*. Edinburgh: Edinburgh University Press, 1976.

————. *Antiquity Depicted: Aspects of Archaeological Illustration*. Walter Neurath Memorial Lectures. New York: Thames and Hudson, 1978.

Piggott, Stuart. *Ancient Britons and the Antiquarian Imagination: Ideas from the Renaissance to the Regency*. London: Thames and Hudson, 1989.

Plum, Werner. *World Exhibitions in the Nineteenth Century, Pageants of Social and Cultural Change*. Bonn-Bad Godesberg: Friedrich-Ebert-Stiftung, 1977.

Pugin, A.W.N. *Contrasts or, A Parallel Between the Noble Edifices of the Middle Ages, and Corresponding Buildings of the Present Day, Shewing the Present Decay of Taste. Accompanied by Appropriate Text*. London: C. Dolman, 1841.

————. *The True Principles of Pointed or Christian Architecture*. London: J. Weale, 1841.

Quatremère de Quincy. *Dictionnaire Historique d'Architecture*. Paris: Librairie d'Adrien le Clere, 1832.

————. *The True, the Fictive, and the Real: The Historical Dictionary of Architecture of Quatremere de Quincy*. Translated by Samir Younés. London: A. Papadakis, 1999.

Quinet, Edger, *Le génie des religions*. Páris: Pagnerre, 1857.

Raleigh, Walter. *The History of the World*. Edited by C.A. Patrides. London: Macmillan, 1971.

Richards, Jeffrey, ed. *Imperialism and Juvenile Literature*. Manchester: Manchester University Press, 1989.

Ritson, Joseph. *Ancient Engleish Metrical Romanceës*. London: W. Bulmer and Company, for G. and W. Nicol, 1802.

Robson-Scott, W.D. *The Literary Background of the Gothic Revival in Germany: A Chapter in the History of Taste*. Oxford: Clarendon Press, 1965.

Rossi, Paolo. *The Dark Abyss of Time: The History of the Earth & the History of Nations from Hooke to Vico*. Chicago: University of Chicago Press, 1984.

Rougemont, Denis de. *Love in the Western World*. New York: Harcourt, Brace and Company, 1940.

Rowlands, Henry. *Mona Antiqua Restaurata*. Dublin: Printed by Aaron Rhames, for Robert Owen, 1723.

Ruskin, John. *The Works of John Ruskin*. Edited by Edward Tyas Cook. London: G. Allen, 1903.

————. *The Opening of the Crystal Palace Considered in Some of Its Relations to the Prospects of Art*. New York: J.B. Alden, 1973.

Rydell, Robert W. *All the World's a Fair: Visions of Empire at American International Expositions, 1876–1916*. Chicago: University of Chicago Press, 1984.

————. *The Books of the Fairs: Materials About World's Fairs, 1834–1916, in the Smithsonian Institution Libraries*. Chicago: American Library Association, 1992.

Rydell, Robert W., Nancy E. Gwinn, Smithsonian Institution, and James Burkhart Gilbert. *Fair Representations: World's Fairs and the Modern World*. Edited by Robert

2246

BIBLIOGRAPHY

W. Rydell. European Contributions to American Studies. Amsterdam: VU University Press, 1994.

Sahlins, Marshall David. *Islands of History*. Chicago: University of Chicago Press, 1985.

Said, Edward W. *Orientalism*. New York: Pantheon Books, 1978.

———. *The World, the Text, and the Critic*. Cambridge: Harvard University Press, 1983.

Sammes, Aylett. *Britannia Antiqua Illustrata or, The Antiquities of Ancient Britain, Derived from the Phœicians*. London: Printed by T. Roycroft, for the author, 1676.

Scherb, Victor I. "Assimilating Giants: The Appropriations of Gog and Magog in Medieval and Early Modern England." *Journal of Medieval and Early Modern Studies* 32, no. 1 (Winter 2002): 59–84.

Schildgen, Brenda Deen. *Pagans, Tartars, Moslems, and Jews in Chaucer's Canterbury Tales*. Gainesville: University Press of Florida, 2001.

———. *Dante and the Orient*. Illinois Medieval Studies. Urbana: University of Illinois Press, 2002.

Schlegel, Friedrich Von. *On the Language and Wisdom of the Indians*. London: Henry G. Bohn, 1849.

Schwab, Raymond. *Oriental Renaissance: Europe's Rediscovery of India and the East, 1680–1880*. New York: Columbia University Press, 1984.

Selden, John. *De Dis Syris Syntagmata II*. Lipsiae: Impensis J. Brendeli, 1662.

Selden, John and William Dugdale. *A Brief Discourse Touching the Office of Lord Chancellor of England*. Translated by William Dugdale. London: Printed for Thomas Lee, 1677.

Selden, John and W.A. Hauser. *The Fabulous Gods Denounced in the Bible*. Philadelphia: J.B. Lippincott & Co., 1880.

Sheringham, Robert. *De Anglorum Gentis*. Cantabrigiæ: Excudebat J. Hayes, impensis E. Story, 1670.

Shklar, Judith N. and Stanley Hoffmann. *Political Thought and Political Thinkers*. Edited by Stanley Hoffmann. Chicago: University of Chicago Press, 1998.

Simmons, Clare A. *Reversing the Conquest: History and Myth in Nineteenth-Century British Literature*. New Brunswick: Rutgers University Press, 1990.

———. *Medievalism and the Quest for the "Real" Middle Ages*. Edited by Clare A. Simmons. London, Portland, OR: F. Cass, 2001.

Simons, John. *From Medieval to Medievalism*. Edited by John Simons. Basingstoke: Macmillan, 1992.

Simpson, Roger. *Camelot Regained: The Arthurian Revival and Tennyson, 1800–1849*. Arthurian Studies. Cambridge: D.S. Brewer, 1990.

Smiles, Sam. *The Image of Antiquity: Ancient Britain and the Romantic Imagination*. New Haven: Published for the Paul Mellon Centre for Studies in British Art by Yale University Press, 1994.

Smith, Andrew and William Hughes. *Empire and the Gothic: The Politics of Genre*. Edited by Andrew Smith. New York: Palgrave, 2003.

Smith, Anthony D. *The Ethnic Origins of Nations*. Oxford: B. Blackwell, 1987.

———. *Myths and Memories of the Nation*. New York: Oxford University Press, 1999.

Smith, R.J. *The Gothic Bequest: Medieval Institutions in British Thought, 1688–1863*. Cambridge: Cambridge University Press, 1987.

Snorri Sturluson. *The Prose Edda*. Translated by Arthur Brodeur. New York: The American-Scandinavian Foundation, 1916.

———. *Heimskringla: The Norse King Sagas*. Translated by Samuel Laing. London: J.M. Dent and E.P. Dutton, 1930.

Soo, Lydia M. *Wren's 'Tracts' on Architecture and Other Writings*. Cambridge: Cambridge University Press, 1998.

Sparling, Tobin Andrews and Laura C. Roe. *The Great Exhibition: A Question of Taste*. New Haven: Yale Center for British Art, 1982.

Speirs, John. *Medieval English Poetry: The Non-Chaucerian Tradition*. London: Faber and Faber, 1957.

Steeves, Harrison R. *Learned Societies and English Literary Scholarship in Great Britain and the United States*. New York: Columbia University Press, 1913.

Stocking, George W. *Victorian Anthropology*. New York: Free Press, 1987.

———. *After Tylor: British Social Anthropology, 1888–1951*. Madison: University of Wisconsin Press, 1995.

Stoianovich, Traian. *French Historical Method: The Annales Paradigm*. Ithaca: Cornell University Press, 1976.

Stow, John and Edmund Howes. *The Annales, or, Generall Chronicle of England*. Londini: Impensis Thomae Adams, 1615.

Strabo. *Strabonis Revm Geographicarvm Libri XVII*. Lutetiæ Parisiorum: Typis regüs, 1620.

Stukeley, William. *Abury, a Temple of the British Druids, with Some Others, Described. Wherein is a More Particular Account of the First and Patriarchal Religion; and of the Peopling the British Islands*. Illustrated by William Stukeley. London: Printed for the author and sold by W. Innys, R. Manby, B. Dod, J. Brindley, and the booksellers in London, 1743.

———. *Stonehenge, a Temple Restor'd to the British Druids; Abury, a Temple of the British Druids*. Myth & Romanticism. New York: Garland Pub., 1984.

Taine, Hippolyte. *History of English Literature*. New York: H. Holt and Company, 1886.

Thomas, David Wayne. " 'Replicas and Originality: Picturing Agency in Daniel Gabriel Rossetti and Victorian Manchester.' " *Victorian Studies* 43, no. 1 (2000): 67–102.

Thorowgood, Thomas. *Ievves in America, or, Probabilities That the Americans Are of That Race*. London: Printed by W[illiam]. H[unt]. for Tho. Slater, and are be to [sic] sold at his shop at the signe of the Angel in Duck lane, 1650.

Trautmann, Thomas R. *Aryans and British India*. Berkeley: University of California Press, 1997.

Turhan, Filiz. *The Other Empire: British Romantic Writings About the Ottoman Empire*. Literary Criticism and Cultural Theory. New York: Routledge, 2003.

Twyne, John. *De Rebvs Albionicis, Britannicis Atqve Anglicis, Commentariorum Libri Duo. . .* Edited by Thomas Twyne. Londini: Excudebat E. Bollifantus, pro R. Watkins, 1590.

Ussher, James. *Britannicarum Ecclesiarvm Antiqvitates*. Dublinii: Ex officinâ typographicâ Societatis bibliopolarum, 1639.

Ussher, James. *The Annals of the World. Deduced from the Origin of Time*. London: Printed by E. Tyler 1658.

Utz, Richard J. *Chaucer and the Discourse of German Philology: A History of Reception and an Annotated Bibliography of Studies, 1793–1948*. Making the Middle Ages. Turnhout: Brepols, 2002.

Utz, Richard J., T.A. Shippey, and Leslie J. Workman. *Medievalism in the Modern World Essays in Honour of Leslie J. Workman*. Edited by Richard J. Utz. Making the Middle Ages. Turnhout: Brepols, 1998.

Vallancey, Charles. *An Essay on the Antiquity of the Irish Language*. Dublin: Printed by and for S. Powell, 1772.

Vasari, Giorgio. *Le Opere di Giorgio Vasari*. Firenze: Sansoni, 1973.

Verduin, Kathleen. *Medievalism in North America*. Edited by Kathleen. Verduin. Studies in Medievalism. Cambridge: D.S. Brewer, 1994.

Vergil, Polydore. *Polydore Vergil's English History*. Edited by Henry Ellis. London: J.B. Nichols, 1846.

———. *Historia Anglica, 1555*. Menston: Scolar Press, 1972.

Verstegan, Richard. *A Restitution of Decayed Intelligence*. English Recusant Literature, 1558–1640. Ilkley [Eng.]: Scolar Press, 1976.

Waddell, L.A. *The Phoenician Origin of Britons, Scots & Anglo-Saxons Discovered by Phoenician & Sumerian Inscription in Britain, by Pre-Roman Briton Coins & a Mass of New History*. London: Williams and Norgate, 1924.

Ward, Patricia A. *The Medievalism of Victor Hugo*. Pennsylvania State University Studies. University Park: Pennsylvania State University Press, 1975.

Warren, Michelle R. *History on the Edge: Excalibur and the Borders of Britain, 1100–1300*. Medieval Cultures. Minneapolis: University of Minnesota Press, 2000.

Warton, Thomas. *Observations on the Fairy Queen of Spenser*. London: R. and J. Dodsley, 1762.

———. *Essays on Gothic Architecture*. Illustrated by Thomas Warton. London: Printed by S. Gosnell for J. Taylor, 1800.

———. *The History of English Poetry*. Edited by Richard Price. London: Printed for T. Tegg, 1824.

Weever, John. *Ancient Funerall Monuments*. The English Experience, Its Record in Early Printed Books Published in Facsimile. Amsterdam: Theatrum Orbis Terrarum, 1979.

Weir, David. *Brahma in the West: William Blake and the Oriental Renaissance*. Albany, NY: State University of New York Press, 2003.

Weisl, Angela Jane. *The Persistence of Medievalism: Narrative Adventures in Contemporary Culture*. New Middle Ages. New York: Palgrave, 2003.

Wellek, René. *The Rise of English Literary History*. Chapel Hill: University of North Carolina Press, 1941.

———. *A History of Modern Criticism: 1750–1950*. New Haven: Yale University Press, 1955.

Widukind. *Rerum Gestarum Saxonicarum Libri Tres*. Monumenta Germaniae Historica. Hannover: Hahnsche Buchhandlung, 1989.

Wittig, Susan. *Stylistic and Narrative Structures in the Middle English Romances*. Austin: University of Texas Press, 1978.

Workman, Leslie J. *Medievalism in England*. Edited by Leslie J. Workman. Studies in Medievalism. Cambridge: D.S. Brewer, 1992.

———. *Medievalism in Europe*. Edited by Leslie J. Workman. Studies in Medievalism. Cambridge: D.S. Brewer, 1994.

Workman, Leslie J., and Kathleen Verduin. *Medievalism in England II*. Edited by Leslie J. Workman. Studies in Medievalism. Cambridge: D.S. Brewer, 1996.

Workman, Leslie J., Kathleen. Verduin, and David Metzger. *Medievalism and the Academy*. Edited by Leslie J. Workman. Studies in Medievalism. Cambridge: D.S. Brewer, 1999.

Yeager, Robert F., Charlotte C. Morse, and V.A. Kolve. *Speaking Images: Essays in Honor of V.A. Kolve*. Asheville, NC: Pegasus Press, 2001.

Zettl, Ewald. *An Anonymous Short English Metrical Chronicle*. Edited by Ewald Zettl. Early English Text Society (Series). London: Pub. for the Early English Text Society by H. Milford, Oxford University Press, 1935.

INDEX